P9-DDC-634

BRAIDED LIVES

AN ANTHOLOGY OF MULTICULTURAL AMERICAN WRITING

MINNESOTA HUMANITIES COMMISSION
MINNESOTA COUNCIL OF TEACHERS OF ENGLISH

ABOUT THE COVER: Artist Amy Cordova draws on her dreams, memories of her childhood, and a mixture of cultural traditions in the oil pastel entitled *All My Relations*. Her Hispanic and Native American heritage is an important influence in her painting. Amy lives in St. Paul, dividing her time between her family and her studio windows that look out on the Capitol.

Braided Lives was funded by the Minnesota Humanities Commission in cooperation with the National Endowment for the Humanities and the Minnesota State Legislature, with generous assistance from The Hitachi Foundation and the U S WEST Foundation.

Project Director: Jenny Keyser
Project Consultant: Chris Watkins
Cover Illustration: Amy Cordova
Cover Design: Earl Gutnik
Text Design and Typesetting: Peregrine Publications
Printing: Viking Press Inc.

TABLE OF CONTENTS

ACKNOWLEDGMENTS

THIS BOOK would not have been possible without the work of many people – the writers who shared their talent and hard work; the publishers, many of them small presses, who first brought these works to our attention; the teachers and scholars who loved the things they read enough to want to make sure others had a chance to read them, too. Our thanks to all of them. The members of the editorial and advisory boards are listed below, and a list of the contributors and the sources from which the works were drawn appears on page 285.

Editorial Board
Deborah Appleman, Carleton College, Northfield
Patricia Carlson, Detroit Lakes High School
Paul Goodnature, Albert Lea High School
Mike Oiseth, Richfield High School
Cheryll Ostrom, Osseo High School
Margaret Reed, South High School, Minneapolis
Gretchen Schade, Rushford-Peterson High School
Nancy Storm, Rosemount High School
Jean Vinton, Wayzata High School
DeBorah Zackery, Kellogg Junior High School, Rochester

Advisory Board

Ron Barron, President, Minnesota Council of Teachers of English
Juanita Garciagodoy, Department of Spanish, Macalester College
Diane Glancy, Department of English, Macalester College
Paul Gruchow, Chair, Minnesota Humanities Commission
Ramona Jones, South High School, Minneapolis
Musa Moore-Foster, Higher Education Consortium for Urban
    Affairs
David Mura, Department of English, St. Olaf College
Guillermo Rojas, Chair, Chicano Studies Department, University
    of Minnesota
Charles Sugnet, Department of English, University of Minnesota

INTRODUCTION

PEOPLE BECOME avid readers when they find personal meaning in literature. We read with conviction, commitment, and motivation those works that reflect our own experiences or histories or speak to us in ways that are real and true. The stories and poems in this volume attest to the surprise and wonder of finding these connections between literature and life. As the storyteller in James Baldwin's "Sonny's Blues" discovers, "For while the tale of how we suffer and how we are delighted and how we may triumph is never new, it always must be heard."

Braided Lives amplifies over forty different voices, bringing their distinctive sounds and stories to high school readers. It is the result of a collaboration between the Minnesota Council of Teachers of English and the Minnesota Humanities Commission. Both organizations share a mission of promoting the study of literature as part of the humanities and of contributing to quality education for all Minnesotans. Both also agree that the multiplicity of American views, beliefs, and histories is a story that always must be heard.

The kind of anthology that Minnesota teachers wanted for their students did not exist. So teachers had to invent it. We dreamed of a strikingly beautiful collection of stories and poems that would reveal the abundance and diversity of American writing. We wanted it to include eloquent works that for one reason or another are often missing from classroom anthologies. And we wanted teachers, writers, and scholars who care about these works to introduce them to students.

In the summer of 1990, an editorial board was formed to create this anthology. This diverse group of English teachers from all corners of Minnesota chose to focus on four distinctive strands of American literature—Native American, African American, Hispanic American, and Asian American. We read widely and eagerly, and were moved and inspired.

With the help of scholars and writers from the four traditions, we selected—from the hundreds of works we read—the outstanding writings that appear in this collection. With a limited number of pages, a wealth of material, and the passionate opinions of teachers, agreement on only forty selections was nearly impossible. We hope our efforts will lead other readers to collect their favorites.

We chose works that felt alive, that were representative of the stunning literary quality we found, and that would be meaningful to students. Readers will encounter well-known works and more recent writings; female and male writers and characters; unity and conflict within families and communities; and a healthy pluralism that insists on tolerance and respect but does not gloss over profound differences among people.

We are confident that these poems and short stories, and the original essays that introduce them, will inspire lively discussions in classrooms throughout Minnesota. We hope the writings will raise questions and provide openings for further reading, writing, and conversation. But most of all, we hope *Braided Lives* will challenge and delight, and be a reminder that reading is an invitation to life.

Deborah Appleman
Margaret Reed
Cochairs, Editorial Board

NATIVE AMERICAN SELECTIONS

THE FIRE DRAGON
AND SWEAT

AN INTRODUCTORY ESSAY

WHAT CAN be said of the Native American? A diverse collection of those-who-were-here-when-the-others-came. Seemingly fragmented and broken. Some now mixed with other races. Those-who-lost-in-the-19th-century-battle-for-land. Actually it was disease that conquered the Indian. Smallpox. Cholera. Measles. And the loss of buffalo, which resulted in starvation. The white man killed off millions of buffalo in a ten-year period.

So what's left of those-who-walk-in-two-worlds? Those-who-walk-on-the-outside? What do you do anyway when two cultures meet head-on?

A little native blood probably runs everywhere.

What of the heart that beats in this literature? The words that close the teepee-flap, the wigwam, wickiup, and longhouse door to life as it was on the plains and woodlands and southwest desert? Until 1890 anyway. And open the reservation four-wall, the woodshed, the urban apartment?

In the old days, literature was the oral tradition and the teepee-lining painted with exploits of the individual and the tribe. Even the name of the person, the clothing and marks of body-paint, told a story. Now literature is poems and stories that record the action and characters and themes of Native American life.

Stories of resilience, defiance, power, vision, toughness, pain, loss, anger, sarcasm, a humiliation built on welfare, a humor built on irony.

There is awareness of nature and the spirit world. Respect of elders. Families. Children running everywhere. Tell-me-who-your-relatives-are-and-I-will-tell-you-who-you-are.

A way of life that involves sharing and relationships. Stories in which time is not always linear, but circular, and not so hurried and defined as white-time.

There is a paradox: isolation yet community. A fierce sense of privacy, yet the love of dress and show. A caring for Mother Earth and the warning against pollution, yet a littered campground after pow-wow. There is also the importance of family, yet fathers and mothers who can't live together and share responsibilities.

The Indian faced extermination or acculturation. They are those-who-stood-in-the-way-when-others-came-to-take-the-land. Those-who-would-never-belong. Those-who-are-aliens-on-their-own-land. Who run from the police and social workers. Who know hopelessness and poverty, alcoholism and purposelessness.

The worst is visible on inner-city streets and dusty reservation roads. The best is visible in ceremonial costume on pow-wow grounds. In those-who-live-both-in-their-own-culture-and-in-this-world-that-is.

I remember seeing an Indian lawyer in her braids and geometric-design Pendleton wool jacket. Way to go, I thought. She was in a Minneapolis courtroom defending other Indians in trouble for drunkenness and disorderliness. There are many others who work and run businesses while keeping the tradition of spiritual beliefs and ceremonies that make people strong.

They survive the trouble with this world. Settings of not-enough-rain or too-much-snow. Like the mixture of "Christian holy water and thunderclouds," in Leslie Silko's "The Man to Send Rain Clouds." They have legs that walk between the noise of traffic and the silence of the prairie.

I like to see Indians at pow-wows in lawn chairs eating snowcones. Indians concerned with tribal elections, bingo, bowling leagues, veterans' reunions, and doing what most Americans do. Driving vans. Playing basketball. Teens maybe thinking of going to college, but afraid to leave the family group. Adults worried about economic stability.

It's the new electronic Indian tuned into video and tv.

Still about the business of assimilation or holding out for tradition only. Sometimes uncomfortable with one another.

There's not one "Indian-ness" after all, but hundreds of tribes differing in language, government, custom, and belief. Sometimes I see another Indian and feel self-conscious. We're supposed to be one, yet we have little in common. Often I don't know what to say.

Sometimes there are even disagreements within groups about how to live.

It seems, overall, the new war cry is to "use your mind to beat the distance," as the young runner says in Barry Milliken's story. The new warriors are those who face their lives in homes and offices and school gymnasiums and ceremonial grounds with courage and endurance and imagination.

It takes both magic and sweat. The fire dragon of Roberta Hill Whiteman's story and the hard work of Barry Milliken's "Run." I can dream and imagine the good road ahead, but I also need the discipline to set goals and strive to achieve them. Vision and work. The sense of being a real person in this world-that-is.

Diane Glancy
St. Paul, Minnesota

LOUISE ERDRICH

Louise Erdrich's first novel, Love Medicine, *won the National Book Award. She says: "My father used to give me a nickel for every story I wrote and my mother wove strips of construction paper together and stapled them into book covers. So at an early age I felt myself to be a published author earning substantial royalties." Born in Little Falls, Minnesota, she now lives in New Hampshire. Her tribal affiliation is Turtle Mountain Chippewa.*

AMERICAN HORSE

THE WOMAN SLEEPING on the cot in the woodshed was Albertine American Horse. The name was left over from her mother's short marriage. The boy was the son of the man she had loved and let go. Buddy was on the cot too, sitting on the edge because he'd been awake three hours watching out for his mother and besides, she took up the whole cot. Her feet hung over the edge, limp and brown as two trout. Her long arms reached out and slapped at things she saw in her dreams.

Buddy had been knocked awake out of hiding in a washing machine while herds of policemen with dogs searched through a large building with many tiny rooms. When the arm came down, Buddy screamed because it had a blue cuff and sharp silver buttons. "Tss," his mother mumbled, half awake, "wasn't nothing." But Buddy sat up after her breathing went deep again, and he watched.

There was something coming and he knew it.

It was coming from very far off but he had a picture of it in his mind. It was a large thing made of metal with many barbed hooks, points, and drag chains on it, something like a giant potato peeler that rolled out of the sky, scraping clouds down with it and jabbing or crushing everything that lay in its path on the ground.

Buddy watched his mother. If he woke her up, she would know

what to do about the thing, but he thought he'd wait until he saw it for sure before he shook her. She was pretty, sleeping, and he liked knowing he could look at her as long and close up as he wanted. He took a strand of her hair and held it in his hands as if it was the rein to a delicate beast. She was strong enough and could pull him along like the horse their name was.

Buddy had his mother's and his grandmother's name because his father had been a big mistake.

"They're all mistakes, even your father. But *you* are the best thing that ever happened to me."

That was what she said when he asked.

Even Kadie, the boyfriend crippled from being in a car wreck, was not as good a thing that had happened to his mother as Buddy was. "He was a medium-sized mistake," she said. "He's hurt and I shouldn't even say that, but it's the truth." At the moment, Buddy knew that being the best thing in his mother's life, he was also the reason they were hiding from the cops.

He wanted to touch the satin roses sewed on her pink tee-shirt, but he knew he shouldn't do that even in her sleep. If she woke up and found him touching the roses, she would say, "Quit that, Buddy." Sometimes she told him to stop hugging her like a gorilla. She never said that in the mean voice she used when he oppressed her, but when she said that he loosened up anyway.

There were times he felt like hugging her so hard and in such a special way that she would say to him, "Let's get married." There were also times he closed his eyes and wished that she would die, only a few times, but still it haunted him that his wish might come true. He and Uncle Lawrence would be left alone. Buddy wasn't worried, though, about his mother getting married to somebody else. She had said to her friend, Madonna, "All men suck," when she thought Buddy wasn't listening. He had made an uncertain sound, and when they heard him they took him in their arms.

"Except for you, Buddy," his mother said. "All except for you and maybe Uncle Lawrence, although he's pushing it."

"The cops suck the worst though," Buddy whispered to his mother's sleeping face, "because they're after us." He felt tired again, slumped down, and put his legs beneath the blanket. He closed his eyes and got the feeling that the cot was lifting up beneath him, that it was arching its canvas back and then traveling, traveling very fast and in the wrong direction for when he looked up he saw the three of them were advancing to meet the great metal thing with hooks and barbs and all sorts of sharp equipment to catch their bodies and draw their blood. He heard its insides as it rushed toward them, purring softly like a powerful motor and then they were right in its shadow. He pulled the reins as hard as he could and the beast reared, lifting him. His mother clapped her hand across his mouth.

"Okay," she said. "Lay low. They're outside and they're gonna hunt."

She touched his shoulder and Buddy leaned over with her to look through a crack in the boards.

They were out there all right, Albertine saw them. Two officers and that social worker woman. Vicki Koob. There had been no whistle, no dream, no voice to warn her that they were coming. There was only the crunching sound of cinders in the yard, the engine purring, the dust sifting off their car in a fine light brownish cloud and settling around them.

The three people came to a halt in their husk of metal—the car emblazoned with the North Dakota State Highway Patrol emblem which is the glowing profile of the Sioux policeman, Red Tomahawk, the one who killed Sitting Bull. Albertine gave Buddy the blanket and told him that he might have to wrap it around him and hide underneath the cot.

"We're gonna wait and see what they do." She took him in her lap and hunched her arms around him. "Don't you worry," she whispered against his ear. "Lawrence knows how to fool them."

Buddy didn't want to look at the car and the people. He felt his mother's heart beating beneath his ear so fast it seemed to push the satin roses in and out. He put his face to them carefully and breathed the deep, soft powdery woman smell of her. That smell was also in her little face cream bottles, in her brushes, and around the washbowl after she used it. The satin felt so unbearably smooth against his cheek that he had to press closer. She didn't push him away, like he expected, but hugged him still tighter, until he felt as close as he had ever been to back inside her again where she said he came from. Within the smells of her things, her soft skin and the satin of her roses, he closed his eyes then, and took his breaths softly and quickly with her heart.

They were out there, but they didn't dare get out of the car yet because of Lawrence's big, ragged dogs. Three of these dogs had loped up the dirt driveway with the car. They were rangy, alert, and bounced up and down on their cushioned paws like wolves. They didn't waste their energy barking, but positioned themselves quietly, one at either car door and the third in front of the bellied-out screen door to Uncle Lawrence's house. It was six in the morning but the wind was up already, blowing dust, ruffling their short moth-eaten coats. The big brown one on Vicki Koob's side had unusual black and white markings, stripes almost, like a hyena and he grinned at her, tongue out and teeth showing.

"Shoo!" Miss Koob opened her door with a quick jerk.

The brown dog sidestepped the door and jumped before her, tip-toeing. Its dirty white muzzle curled and its eyes crossed suddenly as if it was zeroing its cross-hair sights in on the exact place it would bite her. She ducked back and slammed the door.

"It's mean," she told Officer Brackett. He was printing out some type of form. The other officer, Harmony, a slow man, had not yet reacted to the car's halt. He had been sitting quietly in the back seat, but now he rolled down his window and with no change in expression unsnapped his holster and drew his pistol out and pointed it at the dog on his side. The dog smacked down on its belly, wiggled under the car and was out and around the back of the house before Harmony drew his gun back. The other dogs vanished with him. From wherever they had disappeared to they began to yap and howl, and the door to the low shoebox style house fell open.

"Heya, what's going on?"

Uncle Lawrence put his head out the door and opened wide the one eye he had in working order. The eye bulged impossibly wider in outrage when he saw the police car. But the eyes of the two officers and Miss Vicki Koob were wide open too because they had never seen Uncle Lawrence in his sleeping get up or, indeed, witnessed anything like it. For his ribs, which were cracked from a bad fall and still mending, Uncle Lawrence wore a thick white corset laced up the front with a striped sneakers lace. His glass eye and his set of dentures were still out for the night so his face puckered here and there, around its absences and scars, like a damaged but fierce little cake. Although he had a few gray streaks now, Uncle Lawrence's hair was still thick, and because he wore a special contraption of elastic straps around his head every night, two oiled waves always crested on either side of his middle part. All of this would have been sufficient to astonish, even without the most striking part of his outfit—the smoking jacket. It was made of black satin and hung open around his corset, dragging a tasseled belt. Gold thread dragons struggled up the lapels and blasted their furry red breath around his neck. As Lawrence walked down the steps, he put his arms up in surrender and the gold tassels in the inner seams of his sleeves dropped into view.

"My heavens, what a sight." Vicki Koob was impressed.

"A character," apologized Officer Harmony.

As a tribal police officer who could be counted on to help out the State Patrol, Harmony thought he always had to explain about Indians or get twice as tough to show he did not favor them. He was slow-moving and shy but two jumps ahead of other people all the same, and now, as he watched Uncle Lawrence's splendid approach, he gazed speculatively at the torn and bulging pocket of the smoking jacket. Harmony had been inside Uncle Lawrence's house before and knew that above his draped orange-crate shelf of war medals a blue-black German luger was hung carefully in a net of flat-headed nails and fishing line. Thinking of this deadly exhibition, he got out of the car and shambled toward Lawrence with a dreamy little smile of welcome on his face. But when he searched Lawrence, he found that the bulging pocket held only the lonesome looking dentures from Lawrence's empty jaw. They were still dripping denture polish.

"I had been cleaning them when you arrived," Uncle Lawrence explained with acid dignity.

He took the toothbrush from his other pocket and aimed it like a rifle.

"Quit that, you old idiot." Harmony tossed the toothbrush away. "For once you ain't done nothing. We came for your nephew."

Lawrence looked at Harmony with a faint air of puzzlement.

"Ma Frere, listen," threatened Harmony amiably, "those two white people in the car came to get him for the welfare. They got papers on your nephew that give them the right to take him."

"Papers?" Uncle Lawrence puffed out his deeply pitted cheeks. "Let me see them papers."

The two of them walked over to Vicki's side of the car and she pulled a copy of the court order from her purse. Lawrence put his teeth back in and adjusted them with busy workings of his jaw.

"Just a minute," he reached into his breast pocket as he bent close to Miss Vicki Koob. "I can't read these without I have in my eye."

He took the eye from his breast pocket delicately, and as he popped it into his face the social worker's mouth fell open in a consternated O.

"What is this," she cried in a little voice.

Uncle Lawrence looked at her mildly. The white glass of the eye was cold as lard. The black iris was strangely charged and menacing.

"He's nuts," Brackett huffed along the side of Vicki's neck. "Never mind him."

Vicki's hair had sweated down her nape in tiny corkscrews and some of the hairs were so long and dangly now that they disappeared into the zippered back of her dress. Brackett noticed this as he spoke into her ear. His face grew red and the backs of his hands prickled. He slid under the steering wheel and got out of the car. He walked around the hood to stand with Leo Harmony.

"We could take you in too," said Brackett roughly. Lawrence eyed the officers in what was taken as defiance. "If you don't cooperate, we'll get out the handcuffs," they warned.

One of Lawrence's arms was stiff and would not move until he'd rubbed it with witch hazel in the morning. His other arm worked fine though, and he stuck it out in front of Brackett.

"Get them handcuffs," he urged them. "Put me in a welfare home."

Brackett snapped one side of the handcuffs on Lawrence's good arm and the other to the handle of the police car.

"That's to hold you," he said. "We're wasting our time. Harmony, you search that little shed over by the tall grass and Miss Koob and myself will search the house."

"My rights is violated!" Lawrence shrieked suddenly. They ignored him. He tugged at the handcuff and thought of the good heavy file he kept in his tool box and the German luger oiled and ready but never loaded, because of Buddy, over his shelf. He should have used it on these bad ones, even Harmony in his big-time white man job. He wouldn't last long in that job anyway before somebody gave him what for.

"It's a damn scheme," said Uncle Lawrence, rattling his chains against the car. He looked over at the shed and thought maybe Albertine and Buddy had sneaked away before the car pulled into the yard. But he sagged, seeing Albertine move like a shadow within the boards. "Oh, it's all a damn scheme," he muttered again.

"I want to find that boy and salvage him," Vicki Koob explained to Officer Brackett as they walked into the house. "Look at his family life – the old man crazy as a bedbug, the mother intoxicated somewhere."

Brackett nodded, energetic, eager. He was a short, hopeful redhead who failed consistently to win the hearts of women. Vicki Koob intrigued him. Now, as he watched, she pulled a tiny pen out of an ornamental clip on her blouse. It was attached to a retractable line that would suck the pen back, like a child eating one strand of spaghetti. Something about the pen on its line excited Brackett to the point of discomfort. His hand shook as he opened the screen door and stepped in, beckoning Miss Koob to follow.

They could see the house was empty at first glance. It was only one rectangular room with whitewashed walls and a little gas stove in the middle. They had already come through the cooking lean-to with the other stove and washstand and rusty old refrigerator. That refrigerator had nothing in it but some wrinkled potatoes and a package of turkey necks. Vicki Koob noted that in her perfect-bound notebook. The beds along the walls of the big room were covered with quilts that Albertine's mother, Sophie, had made from bits of old wool coats and pants that the Sisters sold in bundles at the mission. There was no one hiding beneath the beds. No one was under the little aluminum dinette table covered with a green oilcloth, or the soft brown wood chairs tucked up to it. One wall of the big room was filled with neatly stacked crates of things – old tools and springs and small half-dismantled appliances. Five or six television sets were stacked against the wall. Their control panels spewed colored wires and at least one was cracked all the way across. Only the topmost set, with coathanger antenna angled sensitively to catch the bounding signals around Little Shell, looked like it could possibly work.

Not one thing escaped Vicki Koob's trained and cataloguing gaze. She made note of the cupboard that held only commodity flour and coffee. The unsanitary tin oil drum beneath the kitchen window, full of empty surplus pork cans and beer bottles, caught her eye as did Uncle Lawrence's physical and mental deteriorations. She quickly described these "benchmarks of alcoholic dependency within the extended family of Woodrow (Buddy) American Horse" as she walked around the room with the little notebook open, pushed against her belly to steady it. Although Vicki had been there before,

Albertine's presence had always made it difficult for her to take notes.

"Twice the maximum allowable space between door and threshold," she wrote now. "Probably no insulation. 2-3 inch cracks in walls inadequately sealed with whitewash mud." She made a mental note but could see no point in describing Lawrence's stuffed reclining chair that only reclined, the shadeless lamp with its plastic orchid in the bubble glass base, or the three dimensional picture of Jesus that Lawrence had once demonstrated to her. When plugged in, lights rolled behind the water the Lord stood on so that he seemed to be strolling although he never actually went forward, of course, but only pushed the glowing waves behind him forever like a poor tame rat in a treadmill.

Brackett cleared his throat with a nervous rasp and touched Vicki's shoulder.

"What are you writing?"

She moved away and continued to scribble as if thoroughly absorbed in her work. "Officer Brackett displays an undue amount of interest in my person," she wrote. "Perhaps?"

He snatched playfully at the book, but she hugged it to her chest and moved off smiling. More curls had fallen, wetted to the base of her neck. Looking out the window, she sighed long and loud.

"All night on brush rollers for this. What a joke."

Brackett shoved his hands in his pockets. His mouth opened slightly, then shut with a small throttled cluck.

When Albertine saw Harmony ambling across the yard with his big brown thumbs in his belt, his placid smile, and his tiny black eyes moving back and forth, she put Buddy under the cot. Harmony stopped at the shed and stood quietly. He spread his arms wide to show her he hadn't drawn his big police gun.

"Ma Cousin," he said in the Michif dialect that people used if they were relatives or sometimes if they needed gas or a couple of dollars, "why don't you come out here and stop this foolishness?"

"I ain't your cousin," Albertine said. Anger boiled up in her suddenly. "I ain't related to no pigs."

She bit her lip and watched him through the cracks, circling, a big tan punching dummy with his boots full of sand so he never stayed down once he fell. He was empty inside, all stale air. But he knew how to get to her so much better than a white cop could. And now he was circling because he wasn't sure she didn't have a weapon, maybe a knife or the German luger that was the only thing that her father, Albert American Horse, had left his wife and daughter besides his name. Harmony knew that Albertine was a tall strong woman who took two big men to subdue when she didn't want to go in the drunk tank. She had hard hips, broad shoulders, and stood tall like her Sioux father, the American Horse who was killed threshing in Belle Prairie.

"I feel bad to have to do this," Harmony said to Albertine. "But for godsakes, let's nobody get hurt. Come on out with the boy why don't you. I know you got him in there."

Albertine did not give herself away this time. She let him wonder. Slowly and quietly she pulled her belt through its loops and wrapped it around and around her hand until only the big oval buckle with turquoise chunks shaped into a butterfly stuck out over her knuckles. Harmony was talking but she wasn't listening to what he said. She was listening to the pitch of his voice, the tone of it that would tighten or tremble at a certain moment when he decided to rush the shed. He kept talking slowly and reasonably, flexing the dialect from time to time, even mentioning her father.

"He was a damn good man. I don't care what they say, Albertine, I knew him."

Albertine looked at the stone butterfly that spread its wings across her fist. The wings looked light and cool, not heavy. It almost looked like it was ready to fly. Harmony wanted to get to Albertine through her father but she would not think about American Horse. She concentrated on the sky-blue stone.

Yet the shape of the stone, the color, betrayed her.

She saw her father suddenly, bending at the grill of their old grey car. She was small then. The memory came from so long ago it seemed like a dream—narrowly focused, snapshot clear. He was bending by the grill in the sun. It was hot summer. Wings of sweat, dark blue, spread across the back of his work shirt. He always wore soft blue shirts, the color of shade cloudier than this stone. His stiff hair had grown out of its short haircut and flopped over his forehead. When he stood up and turned away from the car, Albertine saw that he had a butterfly.

"It's dead," he told her. "Broke its wings and died on the grill."

She must have been five, maybe six, wearing one of the boy's tee-shirts Mama bleached in hilex-water. American Horse took the butterfly, a black and yellow one, and rubbed it on Albertine's collarbone and chest and arms until the color and the powder of it were blended into her skin.

"For grace," he said.

And Albertine had felt a strange lightening in her arms, in her chest, when he did this and said, "For grace." The way he said it, grace meant everything the butterfly was. The sharp delicate wings. The way it floated over grass. The way its wings seemed to breathe fanning in the sun. The wisdom of the way it blended into flowers or changed into a leaf. In herself she felt the same kind of possibilities and closed her eyes almost in shock or pain she felt so light and powerful at that moment.

Then her father had caught her and thrown her high into the air. She could not remember landing in his arms or landing at all. She only remembered the sun filling her eyes and the world tipping crazily behind her, out of sight.

"He was a damn good man," Harmony said again.

Albertine heard his starched uniform gathering before his boots hit the ground. Once, twice, three times. It took him four solid jumps to get right where she wanted him. She kicked the plank door open when he reached for the handle and the corner caught him on the jaw. He faltered, and Albertine hit him flat on the chin with the butterfly. She hit him so hard the shock of it went up her arm like a string pulled taut. Her fist opened, numb, and she let the belt unloop before she closed her hand on the tip end of it and sent the stone butterfly swooping out in a wide circle around her as if it was on the end of a leash. Harmony reeled backward as she walked toward him swinging the belt. She expected him to fall but he just stumbled. And then he took the gun from his hip.

Albertine let the belt go limp. She and Harmony stood within feet of each other, breathing. Each heard the human sound of air going in and out of the other person's lungs. Each read the face of the other as if deciphering letters carved into softly eroding veins of stone. Albertine saw the pattern of tiny arteries that age, drink, and hard living had blown to the surface of the man's face. She saw the spoked wheels of his iris and the arteries like tangled threads that sewed him up. She saw the living net of springs and tissue that held him together, and trapped him. She saw the random, intimate plan of his person.

She took a quick shallow breath and her face went strange and tight. She saw the black veins in the wings of the butterfly, roads burnt into a map, and then she was located somewhere in the net of veins and sinew that was the tragic complexity of the world so she did not see Officer Brackett and Vicki Koob rushing toward her, but felt them instead like flies caught in the same web, rocking it.

"Albertine!" Vicki Koob had stopped in the grass. Her voice was shrill and tight. "It's better this way, Albertine. We're going to help you."

Albertine straightened, threw her shoulders back. Her father's hand was on her chest and shoulders lightening her wonderfully. Then on wings of her father's hands, on dead butterfly wings, Albertine lifted into the air and flew toward the others. The light powerful feeling swept her up the way she had floated higher, seeing the grass below. It was her father throwing her up into the air and out of danger. Her arms opened for bullets but no bullets came. Harmony did not shoot. Instead, he raised his fist and brought it down hard on her head.

Albertine did not fall immediately, but stood in his arms a moment. Perhaps she gazed still farther back behind the covering of his face. Perhaps she was completely stunned and did not think as she sagged and fell. Her face rolled forward and hair covered her features, so it was impossible for Harmony to see with just what particular expression she gazed into the headsplitting wheel of light, or blackness, that overcame her.

Harmony turned the vehicle onto the gravel road that led back to town. He had convinced the other two that Albertine was more trouble than she was worth, and so they left her behind, and Lawrence too. He stood swearing in his cinder driveway as the car rolled out of sight. Buddy sat between the social worker and Officer Brackett. Vicki tried to hold Buddy fast and keep her arm down at the same time, for the words she'd screamed at Albertine had broken the seal of antiperspirant beneath her arms. She was sweating now as though she'd stored an ocean up inside of her. Sweat rolled down her back in a shallow river and pooled at her waist and between her breasts. A thin sheen of water came out on her forearms, her face. Vicki gave an irritated moan but Brackett seemed not to take notice, or take offense at least. Air-conditioned breezes were sweeping over the seat anyway, and very soon they would be comfortable. She smiled at Brackett over Buddy's head. The man grinned back. Buddy stirred. Vicki remembered the emergency chocolate bar she kept in her purse, fished it out, and offered it to Buddy. He did not react, so she closed his fingers over the package and peeled the paper off one end.

The car accelerated. Buddy felt the road and wheels pummeling each other and the rush of the heavy motor purring in high gear. Buddy knew that what he'd seen in his mind that morning, the thing coming out of the sky with barbs and chains, had hooked him. Somehow he was caught and held in the sour tin smell of the pale woman's armpit. Somehow he was pinned between their pounds of breathless flesh. He looked at the chocolate in his hand. He was squeezing the bar so hard that a thin brown trickle had melted down his arm. Automatically, he put the bar in his mouth.

As he bit down he saw his mother very clearly, just as she had been when she carried him from the shed. She was stretched flat on the ground, on her stomach, and her arms were curled around her head as if in sleep. One leg was drawn up and it looked for all the world like she was running full tilt into the ground, as though she had been trying to pass into the earth, to bury herself, but at the last moment something had stopped her.

There was no blood on Albertine, but Buddy tasted blood now at the sight of her, for he bit down hard and cut his own lip. He ate the chocolate, every bit of it, tasting his mother's blood. And when he had the chocolate down inside him and all licked off his hands, he opened his mouth to say thank you to the woman, as his mother had taught him. But instead of a thank you coming out he was astonished to hear a great rattling scream, and then another, rip out of him like pieces of his own body and whirl onto the sharp things all around him.

LINDA HOGAN

Linda Hogan, born in 1947 in Oklahoma, now lives and works in Colorado. She received her master's degree from the University of Colorado, gives poetry workshops, taught at the University of Minnesota, and writes plays, poems, and stories. Her most recent novel, Mean Spirit, *describes what happens when "the cursed blessing of oil" is discovered under Osage Indian land in the 1920s. Her tribal affiliation is Chickasaw.*

MAKING DO

ROBERTA JAMES became one of the silent people in Seeker County when her daughter, Harriet, died at six years of age.

Harriet died of what they used to call consumption.

After the funeral, Grandmother Addie went to stay with Roberta in her grief, as she had done over the years with her children and grandchildren. Addie, in fact, had stayed with Roberta during the time of her pregnancy with Harriet, back when the fifteen-year-old girl wore her boyfriend's black satin jacket that had a map of Korea on the back. And she'd visited further back than that, back to the days when Roberta wore white full skirts and white blouses and the sun came in the door, and she lay there in that hot sun like it was ironed flat against the floor, and she felt good with clean hair and skin and singing a little song to herself. There were oak trees outside. She was waiting. Roberta was waiting there for something that would take her away. But the farthest she got was just outside her skin, that black jacket against her with its map of Korea.

Addie never told Roberta a word of what she knew about divided countries and people who wear them on their backs, but later Roberta knew that her grandmother had seen way down the road what was coming, and warned her in little ways. When she brushed Roberta's dark hair, she told her, "You were born to a different life, Bobbie."

After the funeral, Roberta's mother offered comfort in her own way.

"Life goes on," Neva said, but she herself had long belonged to that society of quiet Indian women in Seeker, although no one would have guessed this of the woman who wore Peach Promise lipstick, smiled generously, and kissed the bathroom mirror, leaving a message for Roberta that said, "See you in the a.m. Love."

Grandma Addie tended Angela, Roberta's younger daughter. She fed the baby Angela spoonfuls of meal, honey, and milk and held her day and night while Roberta went about the routines of her life. The chores healed her a little; perking coffee and cleaning her mother's lipstick off the mirror. She swept away traces of Harriet with the splintered broom, picking up threads from the girl's dress, black hair from her head, wiping away her footprints.

Occasionally Neva stopped in, clasped her daughter's thin cold hands between her warm ones, and offered advice. "That's why you ought to get married," she said. She wrapped Roberta's shoulders in a large gray sweater. "Then you'd have some man to help when things are down and out. Like Ted here. Well, anyway, Honey," she said at eye level to Roberta, "you sure drew a good card when Harriet was born. Didn't she, Ted?"

"Sure sugar, an ace."

But when Roberta wasn't looking, Neva shook her head slowly and looked down at the floor, and thought their lives were all hopeless.

Roberta didn't get married like her mother suggested. She did take some comfort on those long nights by loving Tom Wilkins. Each night she put pieces of cedar inside his Red Wing boots, to keep him close, and neatly placed them beneath her bed. She knew how to care for herself with this man, keeping him close in almost the same space Harriet had abandoned. She wept slightly at night after he held her and he said, "There now. There now," and patted her on the back.

He brought her favorite Windmill cookies with him from town and he sang late at night so that the ghost of Harriet could move on more easily, like he eventually moved on when Roberta stopped placing cedar in his boots.

"Why didn't that Wilkins boy come back?" Grandma asked. "Choctaw, wasn't he?"

Roberta shrugged as if she hadn't left his boots empty of cedar. "He was prettier than me." She pushed her straggly hair back from her face to show Grandma what she meant.

A month later, Roberta was relieved when the company summoned Tom Wilkins to Louisiana to work on a new oil field and she didn't have to run into him at the store any longer.

Roberta's next child, a son she named Wilkins after the father, died at birth, strangled on his own cord. Roberta had already worn a dark shawl throughout this pregnancy. She looked at his small roughbox and said, "He died of life and I know how that can happen."

She held on to her grandmother's hand.

Grandma Addie and Neva talked about Roberta. "A woman can only hold so much hurt," Grandma said.

"And don't think I don't know it," said Neva.

Roberta surfaced from her withdrawal a half year later, in the spring of 1974, when Angela looked at her like a little grandmother and said, "Mother, I know it is hard, but it's time for me to leave you," and immediately became feverish. Roberta bathed her with alcohol and made blessing-root tea, which she dropped into little Angela's rose-petal mouth with an eye dropper. She prayed fervently to God or Jesus, she had never really understood which was which, and to all the stones and trees and gods of the sky and inner earth that she knew well, and to the animal spirits, and she carried her little Angel to the hospital in the middle of praying, to that house made of brick and window and cinders where dying bodies were kept alive, carried the girl with soft child skin in a small quilt decorated with girls in poke bonnets, and thought how funny it was to wrap a dying child in such sweetness as those red-cheeked girls in the calico bonnets. She blamed herself for ignoring Angela in her own time of grief. Four days later Angela died, wearing a little corn necklace Roberta made, a wristlet of glass beads, and covered with that quilt.

"She even told Roberta she was about to die," Neva told Ted. "Just like an old woman, huh, Bert?"

Roberta went on with her silence through this third death, telling herself over and over what had happened, for the truth was so bad she could not believe it. The inner voice of the throat spoke and repeated the words of loss and Roberta listened hard. "My Angel. My Harriet. All my life gone and broken while I am so young. I'm too young for all this loss."

She dreamed of her backbone and even that was broken in pieces. She dreamed of her house in four pieces. She was broken like the country of Korea or the land of the tribe.

They were all broken, Roberta's thin-skinned father broken by the war. He and Neva raised two boys whose parents had "gone off" as they say of those who come under the control of genie spirits from whiskey bottles, and those boys were certainly broken. And Neva herself had once been a keeper of the gates; she was broken.

In earlier days she read people by their faces and bodies. She was a keeper of gates, opening and closing ways for people to pass through life. "This one has been eating too much grain," she'd say, or "That one was born too rich for her own good and is spoiled. That one is broken in the will to live by this and that." She was a keeper of the family gates as well. She closed doors on those she disliked, if they were dishonest, say, or mean, or small. There was no room for smallness in her life, but she opened the doors wide for those who moved her slightly, in any way, with stirrings of love or pity. She had lusty respect for belligerence, political rebellion, and for vandalism against automobiles or businesses or bosses, and those vandals were among those permitted inside her walls.

And now she was broken, by her own losses and her loneliness.

Roberta cried against Addie's old warm shoulder and Grandma Addie stayed on, moving in all her things, cartons of canning jars, a blue-painted porcelain horse, her dark dresses and aprons, pictures of her grandchildren and great-grandchildren, rose-scented candles of the virgin of Guadalupe, even though she was never a Catholic, and the antlers of the deer.

Roberta ignored her cousins from the churches of the brethren of this and that when they came to comfort her in their ways, telling her that all things were meant to be and that the Lord gives and takes.

Uncle James was older and so he said nothing, and she sat with him, those silent ones together.

Roberta's mother left messages on the bathroom mirror. "There is a time for everything in heaven."

With Grandma there to watch over Neva and the house, Roberta decided one day to pack her dishes, blankets, and clothes into the old Chevy she had bought from Ted, and she drove away from the little square tombstones named Angela, Wilkins, and Harriet, though it nearly broke her heart to leave them. She drove away from all those trying to comfort her with what comforted them. The sorrow in her was like a well too deep for young ground; the sides caved in with anger, but Roberta planned still to return for Grandma

Addie. She stopped once, in the flat, neutral land of Goodland, Kansas, and telephoned back.

"You sure you don't want to come with me? It's kind of pretty out this way, Grandma," she lied. She smelled truck exhaust from the phone booth and she watched the long, red-faced boys walking past, those young men who had eaten so much cattle they began to look like them.

"Just go and get settled. I'll be out to visit as soon as you get the first load of laundry hung on the line."

Roberta felt her grandma smile. She hung up the phone and headed back to the overloaded, dusty white car.

She headed for Denver, but wound up just west of there, in a mountain town called The Tropics. Its name was like a politician's vocabulary, a lie. In truth, The Tropics was arid. It was a mine town, uranium most recently. Dust devils whirled sand off the mountains. Even after the heaviest of rains, the water seeped back into the ground, between stones, and the earth was parched again. Still, *Tropics* conjured up visions of tall grasses in outlying savannas, dark rivers, mists, and deep green forests of ferns and trees and water-filled vines. Sometimes it seemed like they were there.

Roberta told herself it was God's acres, that it was fate she had missed the Denver turn-offs from the freeway, that here she could forgive and forget her losses and get on with living. She rented a cabin, got a part-time job working down at the Tropics Grocery where she sold single items to customers who didn't want to travel to town. She sold a bag of flour to one, a can of dog food to another, candy to schoolchildren in the afternoon. She sold boxed doughnuts and cigarettes to work crews in the mornings and 3.2 beer to the same crews after five. She dusted and stacked the buckling shelves, and she had time to whittle little birds, as her Uncle James had done. She whittled them and thought of them as toys for the spirits of her children and put them in the windows so the kids would be sure and see them. "This one's for Harriet," she'd tell no one in particular.

When she didn't work she spent her time in bed, completely still and staring straight at the ceiling. They used to say if a person is motionless, their soul will run away from the body, and Roberta counted on that. They say that once a soul decides to leave, it can't be recalled. Roberta lay in that room with its blue walls and blue-flowered blanket. She lay there with her hair pulled back from her round forehead. She held the sunbonnet quilt in her hands and didn't move.

To her disappointment, she remained alive. Every night she prayed to die and join her kids, but every morning she was still living, breathing. Some mornings she pulled at her flesh just to be certain, she was so amazed and despairing to be still alive.

Her soul refused to leave. It had a mind of its own. So Roberta got up and began a restless walking. There were nights in The Tropics that she haunted the dirt roads like a large-shouldered, thin-hipped ghost, like a tough girl with her shoulders held high to protect her broken heart. Roberta Diane James with her dark hair that had been worn thin from the hours she spent lying down trying to send her soul away. Roberta, with her eyes the color of dark river water after a storm when the gold stirs up in it. The left eye still held the trace of a wink in it, despite the thinness of skin stretched over her forehead, the smell of Ivory soap on her as she tried over and over to wash the grief from her flesh.

2

When I first heard how bad things were going for Roberta, I thought about going home, but I heard my other voices tell me it wasn't time. "There is a season for all things," Mom used to say, and I knew Mom would be telling Roberta just that, in her own words, and that Roberta would be fuming inside as I had done with Mom's fifty-cent sayings.

I knew this much: Roberta would need to hold on to her grief and her pain.

Us Chickasaws have lost so much we hold on to everything. Even our muscles hold on to their aches. We love our lovers long after they are gone, better than when they were present.

When we were girls, Roberta and I saved the tops of Coke bottle-caps and covered them with purple cloth like grapes. We made clusters of grapes sitting out there on the porch, or on tire swings in the heat, and we sewed the grapes together. We made do. We drank tea from pickle jars. We used potato water to starch our clothes. We even used our skinny dark legs as paper for tic-tac-toe. Now the girls turn bleach containers into hats, cutting them in fours and crocheting them together.

Our Aunt Bell is famous for holding on and making do. There's a nail in her kitchen for plastic six-pack rings, a box for old jars, a shelf or box for everything, including all the black and white shoes she's worn out as a grown woman. Don't think those boxes or nails mean she's neat, either. She's not. She has hundreds of dusty salt and pepper shakers people gave her, and stacks of old magazines and papers, years of yellowed history all contained in her crowded rooms, and I love her for it, for holding on that way. I have spent hours of my younger life looking at those shakers and reading those papers. Her own children tell her it is a miracle the viruses of science aren't growing to maturity in there.

We save ourselves from loss in whatever ways we can, collecting things, going out to Danceland, getting drunk, reading westerns or finding new loves, but the other side of all this salvation is that we deny the truth. When some man from town steals our land, we say, "Oh, he wouldn't do that. Jimmy Slade is a good old boy. I knew his folks. I used to work for the Slades during the Depression." Never mind that the Slades were not the hungry ones back then.

Some of us southern Indians used to have ranches and cattle. They were all lost piece by piece, or sold to pay for taxes on some land that was also lost. Now and then someone comes around and tells us we should develop our land like we once did. Or they tell us just to go out in the world. We nod and smile at them.

Now and then some of us young people make a tidal wave in the ocean of our history, an anxiety attack in the heart monitor of our race. We get angry and scream out. We get in the news. We strip ourselves bare in the colleges that recruited us as their minority quota and we run out into the snowstorm naked and we get talked about for years as the crazy Indian that did this or that, the one that drove to the gas station and went on straight to Canada, the girl who took out the garbage and never turned and went back. We made do.

I knew some people from up north. You could always tell they were from up north because my friend's daughter had a walleye with a hook tattooed on her forearm. Once we went to a pow-wow together and some of the women of the People wore jingle dresses, with what looked like bells. "What are those?" I asked my friend.

They were snuff can lids. Those women of the forests and woodlands, so much making do just like us, like when we use silver salt cans in our dances instead of turtle-shell rattles. We make music of those saltshakers, though now and then some outsider decides we have no culture because we use store-bought shakers and they are not traditional at all.

I defy them. Salt is the substance of our blood, sweat, our secretions, our semen. It is the ocean of ourselves.

Once I saw a railroad engineer's hat in a museum. It was fully beaded. I thought it was a new style like the beaded tennis shoes or the new beaded truckers' hats. But it was made in the late 1800s when the Lakota were forbidden to make traditional items. The mothers took to beading whatever was available, hats of the engineers of death. They covered colony cotton with their art.

We make art out of our loss.

That's why when I heard Roberta was in Colorado and was carving wooden birds, I figured it made sense. Besides, we come from a long line of whittlers and table carvers, people who work with wood, including the Mexican great-grandfather who made santos and a wooden mask that was banned by the priests. Its presence got him excommunicated.

Uncle James carves chains out of trees. We laugh and say it sounds like something *they* would do.

Roberta was carving wooden birds, crows, mourning doves, and even a scissortail or two. She sent some of the birds back home to have Aunt Bell put them on the graves of her little ones.

I think she was trying to carve the souls of her children into the birds. She was making do.

BARRY MILLIKEN

Barry Milliken lives, writes, and works as a free-lance artist in Canada. He was born on the Kettle Point Reserve on Lake Huron in 1944 and now lives in Dutton, Ontario. His tribal affiliation is Ojibway.

RUN

"UHNEE-PEESH MAH?" my mother asks. She has been watching me since I came downstairs, and, now that I have eaten, she knows that I'm going.

"Up the road," I say. That is all I tell her because that is all I know. She doesn't say anything for a minute, just stands by the noisy old wash machine looking grumpy and feeding wet clothes into the wringer. Her hair is tied by a rubber band at the back, but many strands are loose and hang like little droopy antennas beside her face. I see many lines that weren't there before my father died. In her eyes there is sadness that makes me mad when I see it, just like everything seems to do lately. I know what she is going to say next, and I turn away as she does.

"When you gonna be back?"

For a minute I stand like that, with my back to her, feeling suddenly like I want to cry. But I am fifteen, so I will not.

"Peter?"

A loud bump, and then my sister's laughing comes from above me. The mad feeling gets worse. I shrug my shoulders.

"Are you going to Budge's?"

I shrug again and hear her sigh; I know that some of the sadness in her eyes is because of me.

36

"If you're going to Budge's, I want you to take something to her."

Finally, I turn halfway around and nod.

She goes to the cupboard, and, from the edge of my vision, I see her reach up to the top shelf. My sister's baby starts to cry in her high chair. My mother comes to me and holds out her hand. Without looking up, I take the thing and shove it into my back pocket.

"Don't forget," she says. I turn and go, feeling her eyes on me. As I reach the front door, I think I hear her say my name, but, when I turn, she has gone into the kitchen and I hear the high chair bang as she lifts the baby from it.

Out on the porch, I can see, without looking, the mess of beer bottles and cigarette butts around me on the floor. After the washing, and after the baby is cleaned up, my mother will come like a servant woman and clean up this mess my sister and her friends made last night. Her and Tucker.

Above me, the clouds look like blankets, dark and light, a big unmade bed.

In front of the house is Tuck's car, which sits exactly as he left it yesterday about four o'clock. That's when he and my sister's friends arrived. All around it the ground is bare and oily, littered with tools, flattened old cigarette packages, beer bottles from other days and yesterday. The trunk and one door are open. On a table beside the car there is part of a carburetor and beside this Sacha, our cat, is sprawled. As I come down the porch steps, she gets up yawning and stretching. A car comes along the road and stops in a big cloud of dust. It backs up, then comes up our laneway with the wheels spinning, throwing dirt and stones behind it and sending Sacha running. I recognize who it is before the car comes to a stop about three feet from Tuck's. They are two of his friends, Manny and Sly. One look and I know they have been drinking all night. Manny's eyes are only half open, as he tilts his head out the window.

"Hey Pee-pee," he says and leans his head back on the seat. His mouth is twisted into a half-smile, and he looks about ready to pass out.

"C'mere."

When I go up beside the car, he lifts his arm and lets it rest along the top of the door. In his hand is a half-full bottle of beer.

"Wanna drink?"

I say no and stare at a tattoo he has put on his arm himself, the shape of a star with letters at the points. With his head still back, he squints up at me.

"Where's Tuck?"

I look toward the lake and shrug my shoulders.

"Sleeping, I guess," I say.

He repeats the word "sleeping" so softly I can hardly hear it. His eyes close, and, for a minute, I think he is gone. But, then, in a voice louder and harder, he says:

"Don't you know?"

His eyes half open and fix on me. There is white stuff around the corners of his mouth.

"Nope," I say, and bend forward, letting a gob of spit fall to the ground beside the car. For a minute again his eyes close and he says nothing, then when I glance down I see a little smile has come to his face.

"Hey Pee-pee, I hear you're a fast runner."

His smile gets bigger. "'Nother fug'n Longboat, I hear."

I shrug and say nothing. Sly laughs from his side of the car, and Manny rolls his head to look at him.

"'Nother fug'n Longboat," he says again.

They laugh harder. I turn and walk away and see the black shape of my dog back along the tree-line. He stops and looks up when I whistle and comes toward me as I start to trot along the path leading south from home. Manny calls out something, and Sly's laughing reaches me like high, strange barking, pushing me faster. Boog comes jumping through the high grass and reaches the road the same time as me. There is dust and pieces of dry grass on his black fur. Once free of the grass, he leaps high beside me, then runs ahead. He will stop and sniff around a tree or pole until I pass, then run on again. He was a present from my father for my tenth birthday. Now he's the best friend I have.

At first, as I run, the road feels hard; I hear my feet on the gravel which lies along both sides. There are bumps in the middle where I never go except to cross, and now I find the smooth part which lies just beside the gravel. My feet under me go faster; the air hits harder, cleaning me, crashing away the sound behind me.

Because it is Sunday morning, there is no one around and no cars in sight. The lake on my right doesn't sparkle the way it does when the sun is out, but it doesn't matter. I fall into a good pace, and

I know that soon nothing will matter. The ground lies out flat and straight, my feet flash under me, and I am filled with something that washes everything else away. It is a power that makes me know that when I run I am strong, and there is nobody who is better. That's the way it has been since the first time the strangeness happened nearly two years ago when I had just turned fourteen.

People were just starting to notice how fast and far I could run, although I hadn't yet raced against Simon Cloud, who was known to be the fastest runner on the reserve.

An older boy bet me that I couldn't run from his place, out to the highway and back, in less than an hour. I told him I had no money to bet, but I knew, too, that I hesitated because I wasn't sure I could do it. The distance he talked about was four and a half miles each way. I had never gone more than six miles without a rest, and never against a clock. I also knew that my mother wouldn't want me getting into something like that. Nine miles without a rest. It scared me all right. But the more I thought about it, the more I wanted to try it.

Carman Fisher was there, and, rather than see a good bet go down the drain, he covered the other boy's money, then told me that if I could do it, I'd get ten dollars.

It was very hot that day, and fifteen minutes after I started I was wishing that I had put it off till evening. But I found a pace that I knew I could keep until at least the halfway point, and, although it seemed like an hour before I reached the highway, someone yelled as I started back that twenty-four minutes were gone.

I had done better than I thought, but now as I ran the sun seemed like a torch that hung too close above me, the road stonier than I ever remembered it. I knew that it was because I was afraid. Please God, I said inside, don't let me fail and shame myself. Don't let it happen that they laugh at me.

But, as I ran, my arms and legs went away from me and became only things I saw faintly, at the edges of my vision. My breath became a useless noise that flew in and out of my open mouth. Sweat flew from me and into my eyes, until I had to close them. Please, I said again. Then ahead of me the road blurred and a brightness flashed that seemed to go into me like a shock, and suddenly, not as much in vision, but in feeling as strong as the flash of light had been, my father was there, around me, in me. The tiredness was gone, the road and the air helped me again. But more than that was the joy I felt that my father had come back to me.

All I knew about Carman Fisher before I made that run was that he was about three years older than me, he had a car, and he worked at the lumberyard in town. After that day, he'd honk his horn if he passed me on the road, or sometimes he'd stop and talk a little.

One day he asked if I'd like to go for a ride. I felt important and honoured to be considered a friend by someone who was working and had his own car. We went to the beach where he met some people he knew—older kids, like him. When they offered him a beer, he said, "I hope you got one for my buddy here. We're gonna be watchin' him in the Olympics one day." Everybody laughed, but Carman looked at me and winked as if to say, "You'll show 'em."

The beer made me feel good, almost like when I run.

After that I didn't see him for a long time, then I heard he had found a job in the city and was living there.

It was around then that the trouble at home started. When my father died, he took something that had made everything good for our family. After he was gone, we couldn't seem to talk, but instead, as if like dogs, we each took our sorrow to a different part of the house, not willing to share it.

My sister quit school and started going with Tuck, who is a good-for-nothing drunk. The next thing I knew, he was living with us and sharing my sister's bed every night. She had a child one year after my father died. The boy is a symbol of the shame she has brought to our family. He cries and messes, and it is my mother who sees to him, and cooks the meals, and cleans up.

"We need the money Glenda gives me," she says. "You want us to live on welfare?"

I want to tell her that it wouldn't be any worse to have that shame than it is to have the shame of living the way we are. At least then she'd be able to tell them to get out. But of course I don't say it, because I know she wouldn't do it. That's the real shame. She has let it happen. She has betrayed my father. And that's why I have to go. Now, as I run, I have decided. I will do what has been in the back of my mind to do for a long time. It's a good day for running and I have a good start. Almost fifty miles to the city, almost two marathons.

Something I remember, too, makes me more excited. A while ago I saw Carman when he was back for a weekend, and, though

I didn't write it down, I remember his address because he joked about it.

"Just think of thirteen turtles walking down the road," he said. That was it, 13 Turtlewalk Road.

Now that I have decided to go, I want to save all the time and distance I can. Two miles along the lake road, I turn east following a creek that winds through the bush. Though the path is rocky in parts and I have to watch my step, most of it is smooth and wide.

Boog runs past me and disappears into the bush up ahead. Seeing him makes me sad, because I know how hard it's going to be to leave him behind. I tried to think of some way I could take him with me, but I know that he would never be happy in the city. Then I remember Aunt Budge once saying that if she had a dog she would want it to be like Boog. He'll be happy there, because he likes her, too.

Out of the bush and onto a dirt road that takes me to her place, I notice that something isn't right. My wind? My stride?

Before I can think any more about it, I am there, and as I go up the lane, I see that her car is gone. Boog circles the house, barking loudly. Although I want to see her before I go, I'm relieved that she's gone to church. I know it would be hard not to let her talk me out of it. This way is sneaky, but at least I'll be gone.

Her back door is padlocked, so I look in the shed for what I need. Because there are no windows, I leave the door open and Boog comes in to sniff around. I find a piece of cardboard, but there is no rope. After watching him for a minute, I know what I have to do, although it's not what I wanted. He comes like a black ghost out of the darkness when I call. Already, as I bend to say goodbye, my throat is tight, my eyes full of tears. I say no words, but circle his neck with my arms. As if starting to know what is happening, he whimpers. I tell him to stay, then go to the door. When I turn to close it, he takes a step toward me, confused. Quickly I close and hook it, then stand for a minute listening. He knows I'm still here and waits quietly to see what game we're playing. For the first time since deciding to go, I am unsure, and for a while longer I stand. Am I really doing this—locking Boog up in a shed so I can run away? It seems wrong. But then I think about home, and it's enough to get me moving again. I dig in my pockets for the pencil stub I keep and come across what my mother gave me for Aunt Budge. It's a photograph of my parents that must have been taken just before my father died, one that I haven't seen before. They stand beside my father's car, my father looking at the camera, my mother looking at him. Aunt Budge probably took the picture. It looks as if she has just called to my father, because the camera has caught him with a look that he hardly ever had—serious, maybe even sad. My mother, too, is caught with a faint smile and a brightness in her eyes, her hand in mid-air, just above my father's arm. Suddenly, I can't look any longer. I stand, jamming the picture back into my pocket and start to print a message on the cardboard. My hand shakes, the pencil barely shows up, but it will do. Boog whimpers in the shed, then barks.

Aunt Budge, left because I have to. Can't take home any longer. Boog is yours now, I'll be with a friend—don't worry. Love, Peter.

I fold it and wedge it in beside the door handle, then, after glancing again toward the shed, I trot back down the laneway to the road, hearing Boog bark and rattle the door as he jumps against it.

The highway is good to run on, like the track at school, my feet barely seem to touch it as I go. But after a while, I start to have the feeling again that something is wrong. I have only come about four miles, and my breathing already is too hard and quick. Another mile. I concentrate on what Mr. Quinto, my track coach, teaches me: *Use your mind to beat the distance. Distract yourself from the tiredness.* I see myself in the last miles before the city, still strong and sure in my stride, still with the power. I try to bring it back, to feel it come into me now, but it won't. There is only the pain of going on. Six miles, but it feels like sixty. I go on until the highway becomes a haze. I see the photograph again: my father looking straight at me; the great love in my mother's eyes as she looks at him. Great love where there is only sadness now. My body burns; my feet pound as I make them go.

N. SCOTT MOMADAY

N. Scott Momaday was born in 1934 in Lawton, Oklahoma. His autobiography tells of growing up on a number of reservations in the Southwest, traveling with his parents who worked for the Indian service. He won the Pulitzer Prize in 1969 with the publication of House Made of Dawn, *and has taught at the University of Arizona and Stanford University. His tribal affiliation is Kiowa.*

from
HOUSE MADE OF DAWN

H E HAD SEEN a strange thing, an eagle overhead with its talons closed upon a snake. It was an awful, holy sight, full of magic and meaning.

The Eagle Watchers Society was the sixth to go into the kiva at the summer and autumn rain retreats. It was an important society, and it stood apart from the others in a certain way. This difference—this superiority—had come about a long time ago. Before the middle of the last century, there was received into the population of the town a small group of immigrants from the Tanoan city of Bahkyula, a distance of seventy or eighty miles to the east. These immigrants were a wretched people, for they had experienced great suffering. Their land bordered upon the Southern Plains, and for many years they had been an easy mark for marauding bands of buffalo hunters and thieves. They had endured every kind of persecution until one day they could stand no more and their spirit broke. They gave themselves up to despair and were then at the mercy of the first alien wind. But it was not a human enemy that overcame them at last; it was a plague. They were struck down by so deadly a disease that when the epidemic abated, there were fewer than twenty survivors in all. And this remainder, too, should surely have perished among the ruins of Bahkyula had it not been for these *patrones*, these distant relatives who took them in at the certain risk of their own lives and the lives of their children and grandchildren. It is said that the cacique himself went out to welcome and escort the visitors in. The people of the town must have looked narrowly at those stricken souls who walked slowly toward them, wild in their eyes with grief and desperation. The Bahkyush immigrants brought with them little more than the clothes on their backs, but even in this moment of deep hurt and humiliation they thought of themselves as a people. They carried four things that should serve thereafter to signal who they were: a sacred flute; the bull and horse masks of Pecos; and the little wooden statue of their patroness María de los Angeles, whom they called Porcingula. Now, after the intervening years and generations, the ancient blood of this forgotten tribe still ran in the veins of men.

The Eagle Watchers Society was the principal ceremonial organization of the Bahkyush. Its chief, Patiestewa, and all its members were direct descendants of those old men and women who had made that journey along the edge of oblivion. There was a look about these men, even now. It was as if, conscious of having come so close to extinction, they had got a keener sense of humility than their benefactors, and paradoxically a greater sense of pride. Both attributes could be seen in such a man as old Patiestewa. He was hard, and he appeared to have seen more of life than had other men. In their uttermost peril long ago, the Bahkyush had been fashioned into seers and soothsayers. They had acquired a tragic sense, which gave to them as a race so much dignity and bearing. They were medicine men; they were rainmakers and eagle hunters.

He was not thinking of the eagles. He had been walking since daybreak down from the mountain where that year he had broken a horse for the rancher John Raymond. By the middle of the morning he was on the rim of the Valle Grande, a great volcanic crater that lay high up on the western slope of the range. It was the right eye of the earth, held open to the sun. Of all places that he knew, this valley alone could reflect the great spatial majesty of the sky. It was scooped out of the dark peaks like the well of a great, gathering storm, deep umber and blue and smoke-colored. The view across the diameter was magnificent; it was an unbelievably great expanse. As many times as he had been there in the past, each new sight of it always brought him up short, and he had to catch his breath. Just there, it seemed, a strange and brillant light lay upon the world, and all the objects in the landscape were washed clean and set away in the distance. In the morning sunlight the Valle Grande was dappled with the shadows of clouds and vibrant with rolling winter grass. The clouds were always there, huge, sharply described, and shining in the pure air. But the great feature of the valley was its size. It was almost too great for the eye to hold, strangely beautiful and full of distance. Such vastness makes for illusion, a kind of illusion that comprehends reality, and where it exists there is always wonder and exhilaration. He looked at the facets of a boulder that lay balanced on the edge of the land, and the first thing beyond, the vague misty field out of which it stood, was the floor of the valley itself, pale and blue-green, miles away. He shifted the focus of his gaze, and he could just make out the clusters of dots that were cattle grazing along the river in the faraway plain.

Then he saw the eagles across the distance, two of them, riding low in the depths and rising diagonally toward him. He did not know what they were at first, and he stood watching them, their far, silent flight erratic and wild in the bright morning. They rose and swung across the skyline, veering close at last, and he knelt down behind the rock, dumb with pleasure and excitement, holding on to them with his eyes.

They were golden eagles, a male and a female, in their mating flight. They were cavorting, spinning and spiraling on the cold, clear columns of air, and they were beautiful. They swooped and hovered, leaning on the air, and swung close together, feinting and screaming with delight. The female was full-grown, and the span of her broad wings was greater than any man's height. There was a fine flourish to her motion; she was deceptively, incredibly fast, and her pivots and wheels were wide and full-blown. But her great weight was streamlined and perfectly controlled. She carried a rattlesnake; it hung shining from her feet, limp and curving out in the trail of her flight. Suddenly her wings and tail fanned, catching full on the wind, and for an instant she was still, widespread and spectral in the blue, while her mate flared past and away, turning around in the distance to look for her. Then she began to beat upward at an angle from the rim until she was small in the sky, and she let go of the snake. It fell slowly, writhing and rolling, floating out like a bit of silver thread against the wide backdrop of the land. She held still above, buoyed up on the cold current, her crop and hackles gleaming like copper in the sun. The male swerved and sailed. He was younger than she and a little more than half as large. He was quicker, tighter in his moves. He let the carrion drift by; then suddenly he gathered himself and stooped, sliding down in a blur of motion to the strike. He hit the snake in the head, with not the slightest deflection of his course or speed, cracking its long body like a whip. Then he rolled and swung upward in a great pendulum arc, riding out his momentum. At the top of his glide he let go of the snake in turn, but the female did not go for it. Instead she soared out over the plain, nearly out of sight, like a mote receding into the haze of the far mountain. The male followed, and Abel watched them go, straining to see, saw them veer once, dip and disappear.

Now there was the business of the society. It was getting on toward the end of November, and the eagle hunters were getting ready to set forth to the mountains. He brooded for a time, full of a strange longing; then one day he went to old Patiestewa and told him of what he had seen. "I think you had better let me go," he said. The old chief closed his eyes and thought about it for a long time. Then he answered: "Yes, I had better let you go."

The next day the Bahkyush eagle watchers started out on foot, he among them, northward through the canyon and into the high timber beyond. They were gone for days, holding up here and there at the holy places where they must pray and make their offerings. Early in the morning they came out of the trees on the edge of the Valle Grande. The land fell and reached away in the early light as far as the eye could see, the hills folding together and the gray grass rolling in the plain, and they began the descent. At midmorning they came to the lower meadows in the basin. It was clear and cold, and the air was thin and sharp like a shard of glass. They needed bait, and they circled out and apart, forming a ring. When the circle was formed, they converged slowly toward the center, clapping and calling out in a high, flat voice that carried only a little way. And as they closed, rabbits began to jump up from the grass and bound. They got away at first, many of them, while the men were still a distance apart, but gradually the ring grew small and the rabbits crept to the center and hid away in the brush. Now and then one of them tried to break away, and the nearest man threw his stick after it. These weapons were small curved clubs, and they were thrown with deadly accuracy by the eagle hunters, so that when the ring was of a certain size and the men only a few feet apart, very few of the animals got away.

He bent close to the ground, his arm cocked and shaking with tension. A great jack-rabbit buck bounded from the grass, straight past him. It struck the ground beyond and sprang again, nearly thirty feet through the air. He spun around and hurled the stick. It struck the jack rabbit a glancing blow just as it bounded again, and the animal slumped in the air and fell heavily to the ground.

The clapping and calling had stopped. He could feel his heart beating and the sweat growing cold on his skin. There was something like remorse or disappointment now that the rabbits were still and strewn about on the ground. He picked one of the dead animals from the brush—it was warm and soft, its eyes shining like porcelain, full of the luster of death—then the great buck, which was not dead but only stunned and frozen with fear. He felt the warm living weight of it in his hands; it was brittle with life, taut with hard, sinewy strength.

When he had bound the bait together and placed it in the sack, he gathered bunches of tall grass and cut a number of evergreen boughs from a thicket in the plain; these he tied in a bundle and carried in a sling on his back. He went to the river and washed his head in order to purify himself. When all was ready, he waved to the others and started off alone to the cliffs. When he came to the first plateau, he rested and looked out across the valley. The sun was high, and all around there was a pale, dry uniformity of light, a winter glare on the clouds and peaks. He could see a crow circling low in the distance. Higher on the land, where a great slab of white rock protruded from the mountain, he saw the eagle-hunt house; he headed for it. The house was a small tower of stone, built around a pit, hollow and open at the top. Near it was a shrine, a stone shelf in which there was a slight depression. There he placed a prayer offering. He got into the house, and with boughs he made a latticework of beams across the top and covered it with grass. When it was finished, there was a small opening at the center. Through it he raised the rabbits and laid them down on the boughs. He could see here and there through the screen, but his line of vision was vertical, or nearly so, and his quarry would come from the sun. He began to sing, now and then calling out, low in his throat.

The eagles soared southward, high above the Valle Grande. They were almost too high to be seen. From their vantage point the land below reached away on either side to the long, crooked tributaries of the range; down the great open corridor to the south were the wooded slopes and the canyon, the desert and the far end of the earth bending on the sky. They caught sight of the rabbits and were deflected. They veered and banked, lowering themselves into the crater, gathering speed. By the time he knew of their presence, they were low and coming fast on either side of the pit, swooping with blinding speed. The male caught hold of the air and fell off, touching upon the face of the cliff in order to flush the rabbits, while the female hurtled in to take her prey on the run. Nothing happened; the rabbits did not move. She overshot the trap and screamed. She was enraged and she hurled herself around in the air. She swung back with a great clamor of her wings and fell with fury on the bait. He saw her in the instant she struck. Her foot flashed out and one of her talons laid the jack rabbit open the length of its body. It stiffened and jerked, and her other foot took hold of its skull and crushed it. In that split second, when the center of her weight touched down upon the trap, he reached for her. His hands closed upon her legs and he drew her down with all his strength. For one instant only did she recoil, splashing her great wings down upon the beams and boughs—and she very nearly broke from his grasp; but then she was down in the darkness of the well, hooded, and she was still.

At dusk he met with the other hunters in the plain. San Juanito, too, had got an eagle, but it was an aged male and poor by comparison. They gathered around the old eagle and spoke to it, bidding it return with their good will and sorrow to the eagles of the crags. They fixed a prayer plume to its leg and let it go. He watched it back away and stoop, flaring its wings on the ground, glowering, full of fear and suspicion. Then it took leave of the ground and beat upward, clattering through the still shadows of the valley. It gathered speed, driving higher and higher until it reached the shafts of reddish-gold final light that lay like bars across the crater. The light caught it up and set a dark blaze upon it. It leveled off and sailed. Then it was gone from sight, but he looked after it for a time. He could see it still in the mind's eye and hear in his memory the awful whisper of its flight on the wind. It filled him with longing. He felt the great weight of the bird which he held in the sack. The dusk was fading quickly into night, and the others could not see that his eyes were filled with tears.

That night, while the others ate by the fire, he stole away to look at the great bird. He drew the sack open; the bird shivered, he thought, and drew itself up. Bound and helpless, his eagle seemed drab and shapeless in the moonlight, too large and ungainly for flight. The sight of it filled him with shame and disgust. He took hold of its throat in the darkness and cut off its breath.

LESLIE MARMON SILKO

*Leslie Marmon Silko was born in Albuquerque, New Mexico in 1948
and grew up on the Laguna Pueblo Reservation, of which she says: "What
I know is Laguna. This place I am from is everything I am as a writer
and human being." Her first novel,* Ceremony, *was published in 1977,
and* Storyteller, *a collection of poems and stories, was published in 1981.*

THE MAN TO SEND
RAIN CLOUDS

ONE

THEY FOUND HIM under a big cottonwood tree. His Levi jacket
and pants were faded light-blue so that he had been easy to
find. The big cottonwood tree stood apart from a small grove of
winterbare cottonwoods which grew in the wide, sandy arroyo. He
had been dead for a day or more, and the sheep had wandered and
scattered up and down the arroyo. Leon and his brother-in-law,
Ken, gathered the sheep and left them in the pen at the sheep camp
before they returned to the cottonwood tree. Leon waited under
the tree while Ken drove the truck through the deep sand to the
edge of the arroyo. He squinted up at the sun and unzipped his
jacket—it sure was hot for this time of year. But high and northwest
the blue mountains were still deep in snow. Ken came sliding down
the low, crumbling bank about fifty yards down, and he was bringing the red blanket.

Before they wrapped the old man, Leon took a piece of string
out of his pocket and tied a small gray feather in the old man's long
white hair. Ken gave him the paint. Across the brown wrinkled
forehead he drew a streak of white and along the high cheekbones

49

he drew a strip of blue paint. He paused and watched Ken throw pinches of corn meal and pollen into the wind that fluttered the small gray feather. Then Leon painted with yellow under the old man's broad nose, and finally, when he had painted green across the chin, he smiled.

"Send us rain clouds, Grandfather." They laid the bundle in the back of the pickup and covered it with a heavy tarp before they started back to the pueblo.

They turned off the highway onto the sandy pueblo road. Not long after they passed the store and post office they saw Father Paul's car coming toward them. When he recognized their faces he slowed his car and waved for them to stop. The young priest rolled down the car window.

"Did you find old Teofilo?" he asked loudly.

Leon stopped the truck. "Good morning, Father. We were just out to the sheep camp. Everything is O.K. now."

"Thank God for that. Teofilo is a very old man. You really shouldn't allow him to stay at the sheep camp alone."

"No, he won't do that any more now."

"Well, I'm glad you understand. I hope I'll be seeing you at Mass this week—we missed you last Sunday. See if you can get old Teofilo to come with you." The priest smiled and waved at them as they drove away.

TWO

Louise and Teresa were waiting. The table was set for lunch, and the coffee was boiling on the black iron stove. Leon looked at Louise and then at Teresa.

"We found him under a cottonwood tree in the big arroyo near sheep camp. I guess he sat down to rest in the shade and never got up again." Leon walked toward the old man's bed. The red plaid shawl had been shaken and spread carefully over the bed, and a new brown flannel shirt and pair of stiff new Levis were arranged neatly beside the pillow. Louise held the screen door open while Leon and Ken carried in the red blanket. He looked small and shriveled, and after they dressed him in the new shirt and pants he seemed more shrunken.

It was noontime now because the church bells rang the Angelus. They ate the beans with hot bread, and nobody said anything until after Teresa poured the coffee.

Ken stood up and put on his jacket. "I'll see about the gravediggers. Only the top layer of soil is frozen. I think it can be ready before dark."

Leon nodded his head and finished his coffee. After Ken had been gone for awhile, the neighbors and clanspeople came quietly to embrace Teofilo's family and to leave food on the table because the gravediggers would come to eat when they were finished.

THREE

The sky in the west was full of pale-yellow light. Louise stood outside with her hands in the pockets of Leon's green army jacket that was too big for her. The funeral was over, and the old men had taken their candles and medicine bags and were gone. She waited until the body was laid into the pickup before she said anything to Leon. She touched his arm, and he noticed that her hands were still dusty from the corn meal that she had sprinkled around the old man. When she spoke, Leon could not hear her.

"What did you say? I didn't hear you."

"I said that I had been thinking about something."

"About what?"

"About the priest sprinkling holy water for Grandpa. So he won't be thirsty."

Leon stared at the new moccasins that Teofilo had made for the ceremonial dances in the summer. They were nearly hidden by the red blanket. It was getting colder, and the wind pushed gray dust down the narrow pueblo road. The sun was approaching the long mesa where it disappeared during the winter. Louise stood there shivering and watching his face. Then he zipped up his jacket and opened the truck door. "I'll see if he's there."

FOUR

Ken stopped the pickup at the church, and Leon got out; and then Ken drove down the hill to the graveyard where people were waiting. Leon knocked at the old carved door with its symbols of the Lamb. While he waited he looked up at the twin bells from the king of Spain with the last sunlight pouring around them in their tower.

The priest opened the door and smiled when he saw who it was. "Come in! What brings you here this evening?"

The priest walked toward the kitchen, and Leon stood with his cap in his hand, playing with the earflaps and examining the living room—the brown sofa, the green armchair, and the brass lamp that hung down from the ceiling by links of chain. The priest dragged a chair out of the kitchen and offered it to Leon.

"No thank you, Father. I only came to ask you if you would bring your holy water to the graveyard."

The priest turned away from Leon and looked out the window at the patio full of shadows and the dining-room windows of the nuns' cloister across the patio. The curtains were heavy, and the light from within faintly penetrated; it was impossible to see the nuns inside eating supper. "Why didn't you tell me he was dead? I could have brought the Last Rites anyway."

Leon smiled. "It wasn't necessary, Father."

The priest stared down at his scuffed brown loafers and the worn hem of his cassock. "For a Christian burial it was necessary."

His voice was distant, and Leon thought that his blue eyes looked tired.

"It's O.K. Father, we just want him to have plenty of water."

The priest sank down into the green chair and picked up a glossy missionary magazine. He turned the colored pages full of lepers and pagans without looking at them.

"You know I can't do that, Leon. There should have been the Last Rites and a funeral Mass at the very least."

Leon put on his green cap and pulled the flaps down over his ears. "It's getting late, Father. I've got to go."

When Leon opened the door Father Paul stood up and said, "Wait." He left the room and came back wearing a long brown overcoat. He followed Leon out the door and across the dim churchyard to the adobe steps in front of the church. They both stooped to fit through the low adobe entrance. And when they started down the hill to the graveyard only half of the sun was visible above the mesa.

The priest approached the grave slowly, wondering how they had managed to dig into the frozen ground; and then he remembered that this was New Mexico, and saw the pile of cold loose sand beside the hole. The people stood close to each other with little clouds of steam puffing from their faces. The priest looked at them and saw a pile of jackets, gloves, and scarves in the yellow, dry tumble-weeds that grew in the graveyard. He looked at the red blanket, not sure that Teofilo was so small, wondering if it wasn't some perverse Indian trick—something they did in March to ensure a good harvest—wondering if maybe old Teofilo was actually at sheep camp corraling the sheep for the night. But there he was, facing into a cold dry wind and squinting at the last sunlight, ready to bury a red wool blanket while the faces of his parishioners were in shadow with the last warmth of the sun on their backs.

His fingers were stiff, and it took him a long time to twist the lid off the holy water. Drops of water fell on the red blanket and soaked into dark icy spots. He sprinkled the grave and the water disappeared almost before it touched the dim, cold sand; it reminded him of something—he tried to remember what it was, because he thought if he could remember he might understand this. He sprinkled more water; he shook the container until it was empty, and the water fell through the light from sundown like August rain that fell while the sun was still shining, almost evaporating before it touched the wilted squash flowers.

The wind pulled at the priest's brown Franciscan robe and swirled away the corn meal and pollen that had been sprinkled on the blanket. They lowered the bundle into the ground, and they didn't bother to untie the stiff pieces of new rope that were tied around the ends of the blanket. The sun was gone, and over on the highway the eastbound lane was full of headlights. The priest walked away slowly. Leon watched him climb the hill, and when he had disappeared within the tall, thick walls, Leon turned to look up at the high blue mountains in the deep snow that reflected a faint red light from the west. He felt good because it was finished, and he was happy about the sprinkling of the holy water; now the old man could send them big thunderclouds for sure.

ROBERTA HILL WHITEMAN

Roberta Hill Whiteman lives in St. Paul, Minnesota. Her first book of poems, Star Quilt, *was published in 1984. She says, "It is the artisan's responsibility to sing clear so that we can walk across the earth, in a place fit for flowers." Her tribal affiliation is Oneida.*

FIRE DRAGON, FALL NEAR ME AGAIN

"YOU'RE NEVER gonna find it, Allen." The older boy sneered, stretching his long jean-clad legs over the rumpled blanket on Allen's bed. Allen threw tee shirts and underwear to one side of the banged-up maple drawer while the mirror attached to the top shivered. As he grubbed around, slamming the top drawer and yanking open another, the sun buried itself in a summer cloud. Lyle watched his brother's anxious rummaging, then rolled on his back to stare with cool conviction at the ceiling. Every now and then, Allen saw his brother's face in the mirror gleaming with a well-balanced beauty: two prominent eyes emphasized by a wide sweep of cheek, the long nose and slightly up-turned mouth, reflecting a mild, but permanent jeer. The younger boy, a scrawny seven-year-old, reached under a second pile of jeans and grabbed a nub of granite.

"I found you at last," he cried, stroking the bumpy black and white rock. He hopped past his brother to the window ledge and set it down, waiting for sunlight to catch hold and make it glitter.

"That's not gonna help," Lyle said, sliding over to the window for a peek. "You think rocks are alive? Listen, mental, another comet isn't gonna fall just because you set up a rock tower. All those tales Grandpa told you are superstitions. Not little, but super. You think something's gonna happen just for you? Comets and meteors burn up. Fizst. Little cinders no bigger'n an ant. You hear me? Fizst. Fizst." With each sound, Lyle popped open both fists into Allen's weasel face. Allen knew what was next—a slam on the arm. Scooping up the rock, he plunked it in his pocket, ran down the dark hall past Lyle's bedroom and into the living room.

Following him, Lyle caught up before he reached the couch and gripped one thin arm above the elbow until the strands of muscle shifted under his pressure.

"Gimme it, fool," said Lyle.

"No. Leave me alone," shouted Allen, squirming to reach the couch. From the living room, both boys heard their mother washing dishes around the corner.

"Lyle," she called out. "You want me to call Uncle Junior again?" The dishes clanged against the sink.

"This one time I'll forget it," Lyle said as his brother swung beneath him and thudded on the floor. "I don't want to hear anymore about Fire Dragons and old stories. Some of my friends think you're too weird to be my brother."

Without a glance behind him, Lyle walked down the narrow hallway past the kitchen and out the back door. Allen got up and sat at the table. He watched his mother washing dishes and looking out the window over the sink. A small woman with large waves in her greying hair, she cared for him and Lyle, who had already gotten a head taller than she was. Last year Uncle Martin, her youngest brother, had gone to jail for a long time, they said. After that, they all moved back to Oneida. Then last winter, Dad went to Chicago to look for work. It seemed so long since he had written them. His mother slammed a pan into the drying rack and Allen said a prayer, hoping his dad would come back soon.

"Ya know what, Mom? I'm gonna get something really great, something Grandpa Emory said to get for all the people."

His mother glanced back at him past the corner cupboards. "I doubt if you understand how senile Grandpa was before he died. He would have come to stay with us now, but he was eighty-six and very hard to talk to."

"I'm gonna do it like he said, and get a Fire Dragon to come save the people," Allen said, walking past her to the back door.

"Honey," answered his mother, "the only thing that's gonna save the people is hard work. Did you clean your room?" But Allen was out the door and running through the trees with the nub of granite in his pocket.

"*Onʌ ya*," he whispered as he trudged through the trees behind the house. "Help me. I carried you from the quarry and I'm taking you to the ridge to join the others. I don't know if this will work because Green Bay is so close." He remembered how Grandpa Emory shook his head when he spoke of *kanata· ke*, as he called it in Indian. Allen needed a few plants, the right stones, and the right August night. A white stone guided the people through long periods of war, so they called themselves *One yote a· a gah*, People of the Standing Stone.

He could hear Grandpa Emory's soft lisp as the words, English and Indian, wafted on the summer wind. Allen could see the stone moving, turtle-like, through the hardwoods. Those woods weren't like they are now, Grandpa had said. Now people see three or four stubby trees and call it woods. Then the woods crowded millions of lives around the people. The stone gleamed in the middle and told the people how all the lives were related. As he walked he tried to remember the names of the plants. Bloodroot grew deep along the creek; its pale flowers snuggled in shadows and moisture. Everlasting rose up along ridges with a garland of small white flowers and stems soft as a winter sheet. What were their names? His mind swelled up with the answer. *Tewatnikwʌhtalyaks*. Now the other. He pulled out the granite and put it close to his ear, hoping to hear its soft, high-pitched voice. Maybe the lost words would come to him more easily after the Fire Dragon came.

Grateful the alarm didn't wake anyone else, Allen rose fully dressed and shoved a small mirror, a pouch of tobacco, and a rattle in his pockets. With leaves stirring above him, he loped past the playground, the community building, and elderly housing, out to the road. Moonlight rippled into each woods and along the meadows, where a startled lark cried out in dark weeds. Chirring crickets lightened his gait, while, warm and heavy with the scent of roses and mallow, the wind affirmed a cherished hunger in his lungs.

He climbed the hill and passed horses sleeping in the fields of their new white owner. What were horses and solid frame houses compared to the power of a Fire Dragon, a child of that everlasting being, *ladnʌʔalúdyéda*, He Who Bumps His Head? Ears mossy from the silence, Allen slowed for the first time to look up at sweeping bands of stars. Amazed and drained, he flapped feet downhill and felt a mystery close to insanity or love. He broke his stride in wistful pauses and rubbed the sack of tobacco with a sweaty thumb.

"I'm gonna do it like you said," he whispered to himself. "Get a charm to help my kind." He thought about the trouble such charms could cause, yet Grandpa had said we needed them as much today as ever, at least as much as cars, cash registers, and atom bombs.

Mosquitoes landed on his neck and forehead first. Teasing him in clusters, they were the remains, he told them, with long pauses between each phrase like his Grandpa, only the remains of a giant killer hacked to pieces long ago.

After he offered tobacco to the water, crossed the bridge, and began to climb the hill, something on the fringe of his senses made his neck tingle. A metallic scraping keened through the moist night air. A grizzled white and brown dog hopped over the grass, coming his way. He heard it snort in the wind behind him, its chain jingling in the grass. It followed him steadily along the ditch.

Along the ridge, the lights of the reservation were scattered blobs of red, blue, and white, while to the northeast, the glow of Green Bay lit up a few clouds and dissolved the stars. Allen loved the moonlit night, the soft colors of the trees, and the perfume of the roses. That August thirteenth, he lay in the grass and thought how Lyle had changed. It wasn't the distance of years. Secret hurts and resentments built slowly after Dad left. Lyle, whom he had once loved so fiercely and who had chased him, tickled him until he peed, now refused to share anything. Lyle had gotten lost somewhere inside the house while Dad had gotten lost somewhere in Chicago.

Not one star let go a chip of light. Perhaps he missed the meteors. He peered into the darkness toward the path in the oaks and saw the dog scratching itself twenty feet in front of him. Every now and then, its tail thrumped into the grass and its ears twisted back and forth as if to catch an echo of distant voices.

"Here boy, come on," Allen called hesitantly, wanting someone to meet with, other than the wide sky and shadowed earth. "Maybe you're a mad dog and that's why you won't come." The dog whined, wagged its fluffy tail, and skirted away. As it passed, Allen saw its intelligent eyes and heard its sniffing. Next he waded through thistles and Queen Anne's lace to reach his favorite tree, a massive burl oak growing in a meadow, gradually being overtaken by scrub.

If he were strong and believed the songs, Grandpa Emory said a Fire Dragon just might come. At first Allen thought "strong" meant physical strength, but leaning against the tree, he thought it might be closer to patience or hope. From his position, Allen saw the tower in the clearing to his right, yet in the moonlight, it often merged with grasses and changed places with red willow or hawthorn. It wasn't large. He walked toward it and sat down, rubbing the twelve stones piled in a rough pyramid with everlasting flowers sticking out around the bottom and wilted bloodroot petals, appearing like white luminescent paint, scattered across the top. He had counted on all those everlasting beings like the Fire Dragon for help. *Yowelu·tu*, the wind, the water and the rattle, the thick night and the star. He tried to remember the other plants and animals, but sorrow clutched his lungs and he felt the obstinate night wind run through the grasses nearby.

"Oh, Grandpa, I thought surely you were right, being so old." A great sob shook him and he curled around the tower, head down in the grass, drawing in his thin knees and letting the great wheel go spinning its way sunward.

A beetle darted out from under his rocks. Something landed—thwip—in the grass. A gold-green cinder went out. He sat up as fireflies dazzled the border between oak and meadow. Beginning high in the treetops, they blinked in fits and fell lower and lower among the brush and grass. He rose and tried to catch one, but they confused him. Appearing closer than he thought, then suddenly flashing above his hand, they taught him the meaning of space. He went to sit under the oak, turning his back on the tower. They can have the meadow, he thought, taking out the rattle and shaking it as he sang softly.

From the tree's shadow, he felt the edge of moonlight miss his face. Was it that dog's whine, or a tear in the moonlight that made him look up through the dark leaves? One meteor slipped from the dark, plunging into the lights near *kanata·ke*. Another meteor burst above him, careening fuller and faster toward his tree until it was snuffed out directly overhead.

He took out the mirror and focused it toward the tower behind him. He sucked in the air, hoping he wouldn't die from the Dragon's poisonous breath. He saw a zig-zag flash, like a will-o'-the-wisp, spurt along the ridge through the oaks. Fireflies? A small chameleon scampered over the rocks. From its throat, a rattling submerged the woods and brought down the stars' soft colors.

Singing like blackbirds at dawn, then again like wind in the oak, the Fire Dragon spoke to Allen's heart. It didn't look lizard-like anymore. Big as a dog with a snout, it lay on the earth, curved around the tower, its body streaming rainbows through the air. He wasn't certain how it spoke, but songs came from deep in his mind, songs he never knew before. It spoke of how it had known grandfathers before grandfathers way back in the beginning. It sang of the universe and of love. It taught him how to sense the future in the rocks. It sang of famine and disease, as it sank like lake water into the rocks of the tower to become his shadow and guide.

When he woke, his hand was thick with goose bumps. Toward the east, a trace of white tinged half the sky and the warm and brilliant stars hung suspended from webs in the deep blue. Hearing a dog's whine, Allen watched the flop-eared dog come bouncing toward him from the scrub. Frightened, he shoved his things in his pockets, straightened his numb legs, and hobbled to the tower. The dog peered through the grass as Allen sifted through the gravel remains of his tower until he found it—no larger than his palm and perfectly round—a small moon dropped earthward for him. He dropped it in his tobacco pouch and walked back up the dirt road through the trees, listening for that dog's ching, ching, ching along with the wind's familiar flutter in the grass. Meadowlarks sprang up singing in the early dawn, redwinged blackbirds called to him, "*kaskali'saks*," and every blade in meadow and field sparkled deep green, silvery with dew, as Allen headed home.

Allen spent two days caring for the rock. He straightened up his toy men, his collection of beat-up stuffed animals, and his cars. He made a cave for the rock out of a small cardboard box covered with tee shirts in his drawer. When he slept, he put it under his pillow. One afternoon he brought it down the hall, through the living room, circling through the dining room, the kitchen, and out the back door, explaining how he felt and how it was on earth.

He explained how he loved his bedroom, even if the window sill had teethmarks from a child who lived there before. He could jump on the green vinyl sofa in the living room because a spring had already shot through. The plastic-topped table had enough chairs for all of them when his Dad returned. Another day Allen left the rock in his drawer and spoke to it in his heart. He offered it his first bite of food and felt its presence like a small bellyache in his chest.

That bright afternoon he came into the living room as his mother shook out the towels and folded them. Careful not to sit on the broken spring, he said, "I did it, Mom. We've got a Fire Dragon to help us now."

"Allen," she answered, picking up another towel and snapping it in the air, "you're hanging onto something that's gone. I know Grandpa meant a great deal to you and with your father gone, I know it's hard. Now, go help your brother dig potatoes out back."

"But Ma, you don't understand. I saw a fire out of the sky colored like a rainbow."

His mother smiled and ruffled his hair. "Yes, Allen, I'm sure you did. Now go on," she said, giving him a light shove toward the back door.

He slammed the back door and walked down the path toward the garden on the opposite side of the house. Grasshoppers flipped out of his way as he stomped toward Lyle, whose hair stuck up as he jumped on the pitchfork and pulled up a plant. He scooped up four potatoes and tossed them into one of the boxes at the end of the row.

"It's about time, wiener dreamer," he said. "You only took four hours to clean your room. Grab the pitchfork or pull out the potatoes from the turned-over plants."

Allen flopped down in the dirt and plowed his hands through the clods.

"Over here, thimble brain," Lyle called, pointing to a plant. "Look in here. The potatoes are bigger 'n rocks and so fun to dig up. You might find some little guy in there."

"Lyle," Allen said, shoving the cool earth up to his elbows. "Lyle, you gonna run away if Dad comes back?"

"Prob'ly."

"Lyle, I did see it. The Fire Dragon." Allen leaned toward his brother as Lyle dropped down to dig out a few more potatoes. Allen heard Lyle's breathing and caught his cynical eyes.

"It was all blue and red and green. It floated into the white rock I got hid in my dresser." Allen waved his arms, showing how it could float. "It's got the future inside, just like those rocks you crack open for fossils. I know it'll guide us now."

"I pounded it to bits this morning, mental," Lyle said, more to the buried potato than to anyone else. Lyle glanced at his dwarf of a brother, as if getting ready to make a joke. "It didn't scream.

You gotta learn or other kids'll beat that shit outa you. This is America. Magic is for babies. Nothing happens just for you. Not for anyone else either."

"But Lyle," Allen started, making fists with his hands in the dirt.

Lyle continued, raising his voice. "See that dumb brown dog sniffing around the shed at Cornelius'? He's as close to a Fire Dragon as you're gonna get. Go talk to dogs. At least other kids'll think you're ok."

Allen wanted to shovel himself into the earth. He saw blood and faces flying apart from bombs. He heard a thunder in his ears he couldn't squelch as he threw potatoes, pebbles, dirt, stems, and leaves at Lyle. As he jerked off his shoes and hurled them with fury, he screamed, "We're doomed. Doomed. You don't care about anybody or anything."

Lyle covered his face as a large potato hit him above the temple. He tried to rise again, but a shoe struck his ear and he winced in pain, collapsing, his eyes narrowing into slits. As Allen saw Lyle's mouth begin to form words, Allen grabbed the pitchfork and smashed the handle against Lyle's mouth. The dog bounded toward the fighting boys. Blood dripped down Lyle's chin. He twisted and gouged at his back and buttocks, arching his back against an over-turned potato plant. Allen pounded him on the ribs and hips, shrieking, "No heart. No heart. We'll all die 'cause of you. You threw everything away. Lakes and trees, flowers and people. We're doomed forever."

Lyle writhed on his belly, softly gasping for Allen to take something out of his back pocket. The dog yipped and pranced around them both. Allen saw the bulge and dug out the white rock. With spit in the corners of his mouth, Lyle choked to regain his breath.

"Liar," Allen said bitterly. "The Fire Dragon told me his father's coming back here. A great comet who'll make everyone hungry. He'll change the wind's direction and the earth'll wrinkle up under everything like it's all on a rug." He sighed, lowering his voice as he continued. "The fields will burn because people like you don't care about anything. The Fire Dragon inside this rock is the great comet's child. He said he'd guide us through the awful time if only we'd take care, but how can I, Lyle?" Allen's narrow face darkened. "Grandpa knew, really he did." Allen brought the rock closer to Lyle so he could see it. The dog whined at them as it lay, watching at the end of the row, its chin down in the dirt.

Allen looked up at the great expanse above, the bright sun pulsing through the sky, and the shadows darkening under ash and beech trees. When the wind rose in a long purling blast, he saw a long sweep of green-yellow light curve beyond the garden, then roll, rising into blue green above him. Below him, his brother spit out his blood. It trickled down his forearm into the dirt. Between them both, nestled in Allen's palm, the round white rock sparkled with blue and green reflections from the sun, while Allen, still uncertain, tried to remember words that meant "forgive us" in his own lost tongue.

PAULA GUNN ALLEN

Paula Gunn Allen was born in 1939. She says: "When I read a poem, I look for several things: I want right away to know what it says. I want also to know what it feels. I want to know how it is. I want to know who its mother is: that is, what context it comes out of." Her own "context" includes Lebanese and Laguna ancestors, growing up in New Mexico, teaching at the University of California, writing poems, and editing books like Spider Woman's Granddaughters.

P O W W O W 7 9 , D U R A N G O

haven't been to one in almost three years
there's six drums and 200 dancers a few
booths piled with jewelry and powwow stuff
some pottery and oven bread
everyone gathers
stands for the grand entry
two flag songs
and the opening prayer by some guy
works for the BIA
who asks our father
to bless our cars
to heal our hearts
to let the music here tonight
make us better, cool
hurts and unease
in his son's name, amen.
my daughter arrives, stoned,
brown face ashy from the weed,
there's no toilet paper
in the ladies room she accuses me
there's never any toilet paper
in the *ladies* room at a powwow she glares
changes
calms
it's like being home after a long time

are you gonna dance I ask
here's my shawl
not dressed right she says
the new beaded ties I bought her swing
from her long dark braids
why not you have dark blue on I say
look.
we step inside the gym
eyes sweep the rubber floor
jackets, jeans, down-filled vests,
sweatshirts all dark blue.
have to look close to pick out
occasional brown or red on older folks
the dark brown faces rising on the bleachers
the dark hair on almost every head
ever see so many Indians
you're dressed right
we look at the bleachers
quiet like shadows
the people sit watching the floor below
where dancers circle the beating drums
exploding color in the light.

DIANE BURNS

Diane Burns is a poet and a painter. She is Anishinabe and Chemehuevi and lives in New York.

SURE YOU CAN ASK ME A PERSONAL QUESTION

How do you do?
    No, I am not Chinese.
No, not Spanish.
    No, I am American Indi—uh, Native American.
No, not from India.
    No, not Apache.
No, not Navajo.
    No, not Sioux.
No, we are not extinct.
    Yes, Indian.
Oh?
    So that's where you got those high cheekbones.
Your great grandmother, huh?
    An Indian Princess, huh?
Hair down to there?
    Let me guess. Cherokee?
Oh, so you've had an Indian friend?
    That close?
Oh, so you've had an Indian lover?
    That tight?
Oh, so you've had an Indian servant?
    That much?

Yeah, it was awful what you guys did to us.
    It's real decent of you to apologize.
No, I don't know where you can get peyote.
    No, I don't know where you can get Navajo rugs real cheap.
No, I didn't make this. I bought it at Bloomingdales.
    Thank you. I like your hair too.
I don't know if anyone knows whether or not Cher is really Indian.
    No, I didn't make it rain tonight.
Yeah. Uh-huh. Spirituality.
    Uh-huh. Yeah. Spirituality. Uh-huh. Mother
Earth. Yeah. Uh'huh. Uh-huh. Spirituality.
    No, I didn't major in archery.
Yeah, a lot of us drink too much.
    Some of us can't drink enough.
This ain't no stoic look.
    This is my face.

DIANE GLANCY

Diane Glancy was born in 1941 to an English-German mother and a part-Cherokee father. She now teaches at Macalester College in St. Paul, Minnesota, after living, writing, and working in Missouri and Oklahoma. "Out of my eight great-grandparents, only one was Cherokee. How can the influence of one be as strong as seven together?" she asks. "I am part heir to the Indian culture, and even that small part has leavened the whole lump," she answers.

WITHOUT TITLE

for my Father who lived without ceremony

It's hard you know without the buffalo,
the shaman, the arrow,
but my father went out each day to hunt
as though he had them.
He worked in the stockyards.
All his life he brought us meat.
No one marked his first kill,
no one sang his buffalo song.
Without a vision he had migrated to the city
and went to work in the packing house.
When he brought home his horns and hides
my mother said
get rid of them.
I remember the animal tracks of his car
out the drive in snow and mud,
the aerial on his old car waving
like a bow string.
I remember the silence of his lost power,
the red buffalo painted on his chest.
Oh, I couldn't see it
but it was there, and in the night I heard
his buffalo grunts like a snore.

MAURICE KENNY

Maurice Kenny lives in Brooklyn in the winter, but heads north to his Iroquois home in the summer for wild strawberries. He says: "The two-legged human beings are wont to forget the totality of the Creator's gift, and in their egotism seem to almost deplore the right to survival of other creations. For me it is of the utmost importance to touch earth, the earth where the berries grow, bleed into the soil renewing life."

THEY TELL ME I AM LOST

For Lance Henson

my feet are elms, roots in the earth
my heart is the hawk
my thought the arrow that rides
    the wind across the valley
my spirit eats with eagles on the mountain crag
    and clashes with the thunder
the grass is the breath of my flesh
    and the deer is the bone of my child
my toes dance on the drum
    in the light of the eyes of the old turtle

my chant is the wind
my chant is the muskrat
my chant is the seed
my chant is the tadpole
my chant is the grandfather

    and his many grandchildren
    sired in the frost of March
    and the summer noon of brown August
my chant is the field that turns with the sun

and feeds the mice
and the bear red berries and honey
my chant is the river
that quenches the thirst of the sun
my chant is the woman who bore me
and my blood and my flesh of tomorrow
my chant is the herb that heals
and the moon that moves the tide
and the wind that cleans the earth
of old bones singing in the morning dust
my chant is the rabbit, skunk, heron
my chant is the red willow, the clay
and the great pine that bulges the woods
and the axe that fells the birch
and the hand that breaks the corn from the
stalk
and waters the squash and catches stars
my chant is a blessing to the trout, beaver
and a blessing to the young pheasant
that warms my winter
my chant is the wolf in the dark
my chant is the crow flying against the sun
my chant is the sun
sleeping on the back of the grass
in marriage
my chant is the sun
while there is sun I cannot be lost
my chant is the quaking of the earth
angry and bold

although I hide in the thick forest
or the deep pool of the slow river
though I hide in a shack, a prison
though I hide in a word, a law
though I hide in a glass of beer
or high on steel girders over the city
or in the slums of that city
though I hide in a mallard feather
or the petals of the milkwort
or a story told by my father

though there are eyes that do not see me
    and ears that do not hear my drum
    or hands that do not feel my wind
    and tongues which do not taste my blood

I am the shadow on the field
    the rain on the rock
    the snow on the limb
    the footprint on the water
    the vetch on the grave
I am the sweat on the boy
    the smile on the woman
    the paint on the man

I am the singer of songs
    and the hunter of fox
I am the glare on the sun
    the frost on the fruit
    the notch on the cedar
I am the foot on the golden snake
I am the foot on the silver snake
I am the tongue of the wind
    and the nourishment of grubs
I am the claw and the hoof and the shell
I am the stalk and the bloom and the pollen
I am the boulder on the rim of the hill
I am the sun and the moon
    the light and the dark
I am the shadow on the field

I am the string, the bow and the arrow

MARY TALLMOUNTAIN

Mary TallMountain was born on the Yukon in 1918 and now lives in San Francisco, where she claims to be retired. She changed her name from Demonski to TallMountain because she loved the mountains. Her first book of poems, There is No Word for Goodbye, *won the Pushcart Prize in 1981. She is of mixed ancestry, Scots-Irish, Russian, and Athabaskan.*

GOOD GREASE

The hunters went out with guns
at dawn.
We had no meat in the village,
no food for the tribe and the dogs.
No caribou in the caches.

All day we waited.
At last!
As darkness hung at the river
we children saw them far away.
Yes! They were carrying caribou!
We jumped and shouted!

By the fires that night
we feasted.
The old ones clucked,
sucking and smacking,
sopping the juices with sourdough bread.
The grease would warm us
when hungry winter howled.

Grease was beautiful
oozing,
dripping and running down our chins,

brown hands shining with grease.
We talk of it
when we see each other
far from home.

Remember the marrow
sweet in the bones?
We grabbed for them like candy.
Good.
Gooooood.

Good grease.

INDIAN BLOOD

On the stage I stumbled,
my fur boot caught
on a slivered board.
Rustle of stealthy giggles.

Beendaaga' made of velvet
crusted with crystal beads
hung from brilliant tassels of wool,
wet with my sweat.

Children's faces stared.
I felt their flowing force.
Did I crouch like *goh*
in the curious quiet?

They butted to the stage,
darting questions; pointing.
        Do you live in an igloo?
        Hah! You eat blubber!

Hemmed in by ringlets of brass,
grass-pale eyes,
the fur of *daghooda-aak*
trembled.

Late in the night
I bit my hand until it was
pierced
with moons of dark
Indian blood.

Translations:
  beendaaga'   mittens
  goh   rabbit
  daghooda-aak caribou parka

LAURA TOHE

Laura Tohe was raised on the Navajo reservation in Arizona and New Mexico. She left home at fifteen to attend school in Albuquerque and later moved to Nebraska, but says: "I consider them only as places where I've lived and not my home. It is the way I feel about the reservation—the land, the people, and the culture—that makes it my home."

CAT OR STOMP

to all the former cats and stomps
of the Navajo Nation

The first few days back at the Indian School
     after summer vacation
you wore your new clothes wrangler tight jeans stitched on the side
and boots (if you were lucky enough to have a pair)
Tony Lama
Nacona
or Acme
a true stomp listened to country western music   Waylon and
   George Jones
dying cowboy music and all that stuff

you wore
go go boots and bell bottoms if you were a cat and danced to the
Rolling Stones
even if you wore tennis shoes it was clear which side you were on

Every year the smoking greyhound buses pulled up in front of the old
gymnasium bringing loads of students
fresh off the reservation dragging metal trunks, train cases and
cardboard boxes precariously tied with string
the word spread quickly
of some new kid from Chinle or Many Farms
"is he a cat or stomp?" someone would ask
"Stomp"
and those with appropriate clothing would get their chance to
dance with him that night

FURTHER READINGS

All references are to most recent editions of works cited.

Black Elk. *Black Elk Speaks*. John Neihardt, editor. Lincoln: University of Nebraska Press, 1988. Black Elk's vivid narrative, as told to John Neihardt, portrays Lakota world views and customs both before and after the tribe was forced onto reservations. Although we now know that Neihardt made considerable changes in the material Black Elk gave him, this book—first published in 1932—remains a classic memoir.

Louise Erdrich. *Love Medicine*. Troy, Missouri: Holt, Rinehart & Winston, 1984. In her depiction of three generations on a North Dakota reservation, Erdrich creates a panorama of North American Indian life in this century. The novel jumps back and forth in time from 1934 to 1984, and is shared among six characters who speak to us directly in first-person narration. This first novel was followed by two others, *The Beet Queen* (1986) and *Tracks* (1988). Erdrich's story, "American Horse," appears on page 16 of this volume.

Diane Glancy. *Offering: Poetry and Prose*. Duluth: Holy Cow! Press, 1988. Writing out of her Cherokee heritage, Diane Glancy's accomplished poems explore the prairie landscape, take us on a tour of the Carnegie Museum of Natural History, conjure up great-great-grandmother from the spirit world, and commemorate Sequoyah's invention of the Cherokee alphabet. A poem from her recent book, *Iron Woman*, appears on page 67 of this volume.

N. Scott Momaday. *House Made of Dawn*. New York: Harper & Row, 1989. An excerpt from this novel appears on page 43 of this volume. In addition to this 1969 Pulitzer Prize-winning novel, Momaday has written a collection of tales and lyric impressions, *The Way to Rainy Mountain* (1969); two volumes of poems; a family memoir of growing up in Oklahoma and New Mexico, *The Names* (1976); and numerous critical essays and reviews.

Simon J. Ortiz. *Fightin': New and Collected Stories*. Chicago: Thunder's Mouth Press, 1983. Simon Ortiz, raised in the Acoma Pueblo community, writes these short stories about ordinary people, white and Indian, and about "fightin'" for what is true and right.

Songs from this Earth on Turtle's Back: Contemporary American Indian Poetry. Joseph Bruchac, editor. Greenfield Center, New York: Greenfield Review Press, 1983. Taking its title from an Indian creation story, this comprehensive anthology includes fifty-two poets from more than thirty-five American Indian nations. Photographs and brief biographies of each poet are included. Bruchac, an Abenaki Indian, has edited a number of other anthologies of Native American writings, collected and retold tales of the Iroquois and Abenaki for readers of all ages, and is a published poet.

Spider Woman's Granddaughters: Traditional Tales and Contemporary Writing by Native American Women. Paula Gunn Allen, editor. Boston: Beacon Press, 1989. Cherokee legend says that Grandmother Spider brought the light of intelligence and experience to her people. This collection of stories brings to light the connections between traditional native tales and contemporary writing, between past and present ways of living. The book's editor, Paula Gunn Allen, provides an introductory essay and brief introductions to each of the stories. Allen is one of Spiderwoman's many granddaughters, an author of six books of poetry, a novel, and the critically acclaimed volume of essays, *The Sacred Hoop: Recovering the Feminine in American Indian Tradition*. Her poem, "Powwow 79, Durango," appears on page 63 of this volume.

That's What She Said: Contemporary Poetry and Fiction by Native American Women. Rayna Green, editor. Bloomington: Indiana University Press, 1984. In her introduction, Green writes that stories have always been told by native women: "In clay or reeds. In wool or cotton. In grass or paint or words to songs." The writers collected here are from many tribes and represent the diversity of American Indian women's experiences. The collection includes well-known writers such as Joy Harjo, Linda Hogan, and Wendy Rose, and less familiar writers, along with a glossary and a bibliography of works by and about Native American women writers.

The Third Woman: Minority Women Writers of the United States. Dexter Fischer, editor. Boston: Houghton Mifflin, 1980. This large, superb collection features fiction by women from Asian American, African American, Hispanic American, and Native American traditions. Stories by Paula Gunn Allen, Janet Campbell, and Leslie Silko are among those included.

Touchwood: A Collection of Ojibway Prose. Gerald Vizenor, editor. Minneapolis: New Rivers Press, 1987. In this collection, Ojibway poet and writer Gerald Vizenor includes historical selections by 19th-century writers such as William Warren and George Copway, as well as contemporary writers like Louise Erdrich and Jim Northrup. In his introduction, Vizenor writes that the Ojibway, or Anishinabe, as the tribal culture is called in the oral tradition, claim "more published writers than any other tribe on this continent."

Leslie Marmon Silko. *Ceremony.* New York: Penguin, 1986. This novel is about a mixed-blood Laguna man, Tayo, who returns from fighting in World War II to search for his identity. Through ceremonies, storytelling, and reunification with the land, Tayo finds his place in the life of the Laguna. The novel draws upon the Keresan and Navajo oral traditions, and conveys the distinct feeling that you are listening to a storyteller. Silko's *Storyteller,* appearing in 1981, collects short stories, poetry, reminiscences of her early life at Laguna Pueblo in New Mexico, and her experiences among Eskimo peoples in Alaska. One of her stories appears on page 49 of this volume.

James Welch. *Winter in the Blood.* New York: Penguin, 1986. The narrator of this novel wanders in the winter landscape of a Blackfoot reservation in Montana, and says of himself: "I was as distant from myself as a hawk from the moon." Sometimes hilarious and sometimes sad and dark, the novel is written in a straightforward and clear style and the characters are naturally and believably drawn. Two other important novels by Welch are *The Death of Jim Loney* (1979) and *Fool's Crow* (1986).

HISPANIC AMERICAN SELECTIONS

THE WAKE-UP CALL

AN INTRODUCTORY ESSAY

¿QUIÉN ME HABLA? Who's addressing me, you might ask yourself as you read these pages. Like you, I am a reader. I learned to read in Spanish as well as English, as I was born and raised in Mexico City by a mother from Minnesota and a father from Guadalajara, Mexico. Still, perhaps like you, it wasn't until recently that I began to read the works of—what shall we call them—Spanish-American, Caribbean-American, Mexican-American, Hispanic-American, Latino writers. The problem of how to refer to us is complicated by the fact that we are, in fact, a very heterogeneous group. We are not all immigrants. We are not all *chicanas* and *chicanos*, nor *puertorriqueños* nor *cubanas*. We do not all speak Spanish. The United States Census Bureau calls us Hispanic, but we often call ourselves Latinas and Latinos. Individually we may consider ourselves simply American.

So you are addressed here by a late riser who has opened her eyes to discover that she has missed the dawn of Latino literature and is welcomed by bright morning. I hear music and laughter. I hear games, fights, tears, dramas all in the accents, so to speak, of these American writers of Hispanic heritage. I can see, now that I am up, that there is much to witness and discover, much to read.

Consider me your wake-up call. I call those of you who are new to this tradition to wake up, jump out of your bed of familiar readings, leap out the door, and make a dash for the native guides who are already striding powerfully on their literary paths. Catch up to them, one after the other, fall into step with each one, and listen. No, they are not exactly like you if you are of Asian, Native American, African, or European heritage.

Be curious at first about her polysyllabic or bilingual name, his brown velvet skin, her space-black eyes and hair. Be drawn and enchanted by the accent, the idioms, the rhythm, the *palabra*, the word you had not heard. But please, strong traveler of narrative roads, walk long enough with these guides so that their exoticism melts away like the stars at dawn. As you forget to remark on their superficial differences, you will see that you are listening to a storyteller or a poet who can reveal what you might not have imagined on your own, but what you can now see and hear and know with her or him.

Be aware, adventurous reader, that the writers who are calling us here to accompany them are just a handful of the many Spanish-, Caribbean-, and Mexican-Americans who are writing and have written out of and about their traditions—constructing, criticizing, and commenting on that tradition with each line. They are as different as ten of you and your friends are, and as similar.

One characteristic several of these writers share is bilingualism. A number of them were raised as I was, speaking both English and Spanish, and sometimes specific dialects such as the ones Gloria Anzaldúa lists in "How to Tame a Wild Tongue." Spanish words slip into their speech or writing so naturally that they don't want to translate them into English. Their Spanish is an intimate part of their identity, and they want us to see it as clearly as we would see the color of their skin.

Another characteristic that distinguishes these writers is their history. Those who are not recent immigrants belong to families of the oldest settlers of what we now call the United States. A dozen states were settled by Spaniards. These settlers spoke Spanish and lived the culture of Spain for 200 years, until they were integrated bureaucratically, linguistically, and culturally into the established culture of this country.

The writers included in this section know their history as well as they know their childhood. It is not a history composed only of facts and statistics, but of stories. The Mexican-Americans, for example, know the legend of how their ancestors, the Aztecs, left their native Aztlán, which might have been what is now New Mexico. Their god Huitzilopochtli told them to travel south until they saw an eagle devouring a snake. There they were to settle, in time creating México-Tenochtitlan, a city that was larger, cleaner, more beautiful, with bigger buildings, more people, and better waterworks than the cities from which the Spanish conquerors came in their search for wealth and power.

Writers like Gloria Anzaldúa are very conscious of the fact that their Native American ancestors lost their languages to the language of the conquering Spaniards, and, in turn, that some of their Spanish-speaking ancestors lost their languages to the ruling English speech of the United States. They will invite you to discover what it means to speak a forbidden language. They will invite you to feel the sense of loss in the generations in which monolingualism became the rule.

A feature of Spanish culture derived from Spain's Muslim influence is the sharp distinction in the roles ascribed to women and men, to girls and boys. You will recognize this in Helena María Viramontes' short story, "Growing." In the most traditional Spanish and Hispanic communities, women are feared because of our ability to conceive children. We are said to be ruled by our instinct to reproduce, and so must be controlled, hidden, and restrained by chaperones and rules. At the same time, women are considered to be the source of honor or dishonor for our families, and that honor has much to do with abstention from sexual activity, which might even be extended to include conversation with male strangers.

Some of these selections offer examples of traditional ways of life that have disappeared from the more Americanized Latina communities. You will read about *curanderas*, women (men can also be *curanderos*) who practice forms of health care based on herbs and diet and common sense. In "The Iguana Killers" by Alberto Alvaro Ríos and the poems, "The Phone Booth at the Corner" by Juan Delgado and "Ciprianita" by Juanita M. Sánchez, characters and speakers accustomed to a simple existence encounter and sometimes rebel against unfamiliar technology and customs.

Finally, a tragic feature shown in some of these writings is the violence that poverty, racism, and ethnocentrism inflict on the lives of people. Don't recoil from the sorrow in these pages. It is part of this world in which you live, in which you were born and raised and which, if you allow yourselves to be courageously open and free of prejudice and indifference, you can help change in your lifetime.

Those of us who have chosen these stories and poems hope they will offer you new perspectives on American life. It is a gentle introduction because the writing is clear and strong and beautiful. It is a powerful introduction because the storytellers are revealing details of what is vitally important to them. So, awake and arise. Read with attention, with vigor and goodwill, matching the steps of the Latinas and Latinos who offer now to guide you.

Juanita Garciagodoy
Minneapolis, Minnesota

RUDOLFO A. ANAYA

Rudolfo A. Anaya, born in 1937, grew up speaking Spanish and now teaches English at the University of New Mexico. His first novel, Bless Me, Ultima, *is part of the trilogy completed by* Heart of Aztlán *and* Tortuga. *"In New Mexico," he says, "everyone tells stories, it is a creative process."*

from
BLESS ME, ULTIMA

My mother did not like the people of the llano. To her they were worthless drunkards, wanderers. She did not understand their tragedy, their search for the freedom that was now forever gone. My mother had lived in the llano many years when she married my father, but the valley and the river were too ingrained in her for her to change. She made only two lasting friends in Las Pasturas, Ultima, for whom she would lay down her life, and Narciso, whose drinking she tolerated because he had helped her when her twins were born.

It was late in the summer and we were all seated around the kitchen table making our plans to go to El Puerto for the harvest when my mother with strange premonition remembered Narciso. "He is a fool, and he is a drunkard, but he did help me in my hour of need—"

"Ah yes, that Narciso is a gentleman," my father winked and teased her.

"Bah," my mother scoffed, and went on. "That man didn't sleep for three days, rushing around getting things for Ultima and me, and he never touched the bottle."

"Where was Papá?" Deborah asked.

85

"Who knows. The railroad took him to places he never told me about," my mother answered angrily.

"I had to work," my father said simply, "I had to support your family—"

"Anyway," my mother changed the subject, "it has been a good summer at El Puerto. The harvest will be good, and it will be good to see my papá, and Lucas—" She turned and looked thankfully at Ultima.

"This calls for a drink of thanksgiving," my father smiled. He too wanted to preserve the good spirits and humor that were with us that night. He was standing when Narciso burst through the kitchen door. He came in without knocking and we all jumped from our seats. One minute the kitchen was soft and quiet and the next it was filled with the huge figure of Narciso. He was the biggest man I had ever seen. He wore a huge mustache and his hair flowed like a lion's mane. His eyes were wild and red as he stood over us, gasping and panting for breath; saliva dripped from his mouth. He looked like a huge, wounded monster. Deborah and Theresa screamed and ran behind my mother.

"Narciso!" my father exclaimed, "what is the matter?"

"Teh-Teh-norio!" Narciso gasped. He pointed at Ultima and ran and kneeled at her feet. He took her hand and kissed it.

"Narciso," Ultima smiled. She took his hand and made him stand.

"¿Qué pasa?" my father repeated.

"He is drunk!" my mother exclaimed anxiously. She clutched Deborah and Theresa.

"No! No!" Narciso insisted, "Tenorio!" he gasped and pointed to the kitchen door. "Grande, you must hide!" he pleaded with Ultima.

"You don't make sense," my father said. He took Narciso by the shoulders. "Sit down, catch your breath—María, send the children to bed."

My mother pushed us past Narciso, who sank into my father's chair. I didn't know what was happening, nobody seemed to know, but I was not about to miss the action simply because I was a child. My mother's first concern was to rush the frightened Deborah and Theresa up the stairs to their room. I held back and slipped into the darkness beneath the stairs. I huddled down and watched with anticipation the drama that unfolded as Narciso regained his composure and related his story.

"Grande must hide!" he insisted. "We must waste no time! Even now they come!"

"Why must I hide, Narciso?" Ultima asked calmly.

"Who is coming?" my mother added as she returned to the kitchen. She had not missed me and I was glad for it.

Narciso roared. "Oh my God!"

At that moment I heard Ultima's owl hoot a danger cry outside. There was someone out there. I looked at Ultima and saw her smile vanish. She held her head high, as if sniffing the wind, and the strength I had seen when she dealt with Tenorio at the bar filled her face. She, too, had heard the owl.

"We know nothing," my father said, "now make sense, hombre!"

"Today Tenorio's daughter, nay, his witch died. The small evil one died at El Puerto today—"

"What has that to do with us?" my father asked.

"¡Ay Dios!" Narciso cried and wrung his hands, "living on this cursed hill, away from town, you hear nothing! Tenorio has blamed la Grande for his daughter's death!" He pointed to Ultima.

"¡Ave María Purísima!" my mother cried. She went to Ultima and put her arms around her. "That is impossible."

"You must take her away, hide her until this evil story is ended—"

Again I heard the owl cry, and I heard Ultima whisper, "It is too late—"

"Bah!" my father almost laughed, "Tenorio spreads rumors like an old woman. The next time I see him I will pull his dog-beard and make him wish he had never been born."

"It is not rumor," Narciso pleaded, "he has gathered his cronies around him at the bar, he has filled them with whiskey all day, and he has convinced them to burn a witch! They come on a witchhunt!"

"¡Ay!" my mother choked a sob and crossed her forehead.

I held my breath at what I heard. I could not believe that anyone could ever think that Ultima was a witch! She did only good. Again the owl cried. I turned and stared into the darkness, but I could see nothing. Still I felt something or someone lurking in the shadows, else why should the owl cry?

"Who told you this wild story," my father demanded.

"Jesús Silva has come from El Puerto. I spoke to him just minutes ago and came running to warn you! You know his word is gold!" Narciso answered. My father nodded in agreement.

"¡Gabriel! What are we to do?" my mother cried.

"What proof does Tenorio have?" my father asked.

"Proof!" Narciso roared. He was now nearly out of his mind with the deliberateness of my father. "He does not need proof, hombre! He has filled the men with whiskey; he has spread his poisonous vengeance into them!"

"We must flee!" my mother cried.

"No," Ultima cut in. She looked at my father and measured him carefully with her intent gaze. "A man does not flee from the truth," she said.

"Ay, Grande," Narciso moaned, "I am only thinking of your welfare. One does not talk about the truth to men drunk with whiskey and the smell of a lynching—"

"If he has no proof, then we need not be concerned with the stories a wolf spreads," my father said.

"All right!" Narciso jumped up, "if it is proof you insist on before you hide la Grande, I will tell you what Jesús told me! Tenorio has told the men who would listen to him that he found la Grande's stringed bag, you know the kind the curanderas wear around their neck, under the bed of his dead daughter!"

"It cannot be!" I jumped up and shouted. I rushed to my father. "It could not be Ultima's, because I have it!" I tore open my shirt and showed them the stringed scapular. And at the same time we heard the loud report of a shot and running men carrying burning torches surrounded our house.

"It is them! It is too late!" Narciso moaned and slumped back into the chair. I saw my father look at his rifle on the shelf, then dismissing it he walked calmly to the door. I followed closely behind him.

"¡Gabriel Márez!" an evil voice called from beyond the dancing light of the torches. My father stepped outside and I followed him. He was aware of me, but he did not send me back. He was on his land and as such would not be shamed in front of his son.

At first we could see only the flaring light of the piñón torches. Then our eyes grew accustomed to the dark and we could see the dark outlines of men, and their red, sweating faces by the light of their torches. Some of the men had drawn charcoal crosses on their foreheads. I trembled. I was afraid, but I vowed I would not let them take Ultima. I waited for my father to speak.

"¿Quién es?" my father asked. He spread his feet as if ready to fight.

"We have no quarrel with you, Márez!" the evil voice called out. "We only want the witch!"

My father's voice was tense with anger now. "Who speaks?" he asked loudly. There was no answer.

"Come, come!" my father repeated, almost shouting. "You know me! You call me by name, you walk upon my land! I want to know who speaks!"

The men glanced nervously at each other. Two of them drew close to each other and whispered secretly. A third came from around the house and joined them. They had thought taking Ultima would be easy, but now they realized that my father would let no man invade his home.

"Our business here tonight is not with you, Márez," the voice of Tenorio squeaked in the dark. I recognized the voice from the bar at El Puerto.

"You walk on my land! That is my business!" my father shouted.

"We do not want to quarrel with you, Márez; it is the old witch we want. Give her to us and we will take her away. There will be no trouble. Besides, she is of no relation to you, and she stands accused of witchcraft—"

"Who accuses her?" my father asked sternly. He was forcing the men to identify themselves, and so the false courage the whiskey and the darkness had lent them was slipping away. In order to hold the men together Tenorio was forced to speak up.

"It is I, Tenorio Trementina, who accuses her!" he shouted and jumped forward so that I could plainly see his ugly face. "¡La mujer que no ha pecado es bruja, le juro a Dios!"

He did not have a chance to finish his accusation because my father reached out and grabbed him by the collar. Tenorio was not a small man, but with one hand my father jerked him off his feet and pulled the cringing figure forward.

"You are a cabrón," he said, almost calmly, into Tenorio's evil, frightened face. "You are a whoring old woman!" With his left hand he grabbed at the tuft of hair that grew on Tenorio's chin and yanked it hard. Tenorio screamed in pain and rage. Then my father extended his arm and Tenorio went flying. He landed screaming in the dust, and then scrambling to his feet he ran to find refuge behind two of his coyotes.

"Wait, Márez!" one of the men shouted and jumped between my father and Tenorio. "We did not come to fight you! There is no man here that does not hold you in respect. But witchcraft is a serious accusation, you know that. We do not like this any better than you do, but the charge must be cleared up! This morning Tenorio's daughter died. He has proof that it is Ultima's curse that killed her—"

The rest of the men nodded and moved forward. Their faces were sullen. They all held hastily made crosses of green juniper and piñón branches. The light of the torches danced off crosses of pins and needles they had pinned on their coats and shirts. One man had even run needles through the skin of his lower lip so that no curse might enter him. Blood trickled down his lip and dropped from his chin.

"Is that you, Blas Montaño?" my father asked of the man who had just spoken.

"Sí," the man answered and bowed his head.

"Give us the witch!" Tenorio shouted from behind the safety of his men. He was raging with insult, but he would not approach my father.

"There is no witch here!" my father anwered and crouched as if to await their attack.

"Tenorio has proof!" another man shouted.

"¡Chinga tu madre!" my father retorted. They were going to have to fight him to take Ultima, but there were too many for him! I thought of running for the rifle.

"Give us the bruja!" Tenorio shouted. He urged the men foward and they answered as a chorus, "Give us the witch! Give us the witch!" The man with the crossed needles on his lip waved his juniper cross towards the house. The others waved their torches back and forth as they slowly approached my father.

"Give us the witch! Give us the witch!" they chanted and moved foward, but my father held his ground. The hissing of the torches frightened me but I took courage from my father. They were almost upon us when they suddenly stopped. The screen door banged and Narciso stepped forward. Instead of a bumbling drunkard there now stood in the path of the mob a giant man. He held my father's rifle casually in his hands, as he surveyed the mob.

"¿Qué pasa aquí?" his booming voice broke the tense silence. "Why are farmers out playing vigilantes when they should be home, sitting before a warm fire, playing cards, counting the rich harvest, eh? I know you men, I know you, Blas Montaño, Manuelito, and you Cruz Sedillo—and I know you are not men who need the cover of darkness to hide your deeds!"

The men glanced at each other. The man they considered the town drunk had shamed them by pointing out the lowliness of their deed. One man took a drink from a bottle he held and tried to pass it on, but no one would take it. They were silent.

"You shame your good names by following this jodido Tenorio!" Narciso continued.

"Aieeeee!" Tenorio groaned with rage and hate, but there was nothing he dared to do.

"This cabrón has lost a daughter today, and for that El Puerto can sleep easier now that her evil-doing is gone to hell with her!"

"Animal!" Tenorio spit out.

"I may well be a beast," Narciso laughed, "but I am not a fool!"

"We are not fools!" Blas shouted back. "We came on an errand that is a law by custom. This man has proof that the curandera Ultima is a witch, and if it is her curse that caused a death then she must be punished!" The men around him nodded in agreement. I was mortally afraid that Narciso, like my father, would anger the mob and we would be overrun. Then I knew they would take Ultima and kill her.

Narciso's throat rumbled with laughter. "I do not question your right to charge someone with witchcraft, it is so in custom. But you are fools, fools for drinking the devil's whiskey!" and he pointed at Tenorio, "and fools for following him across the countryside in the middle of the night—"

"You have insulted me, and for that you will pay!" Tenorio shouted and waved his fist, "and now he calls you fools!" He turned to the men. "Enough of this talking. We came to take the witch! Let it be done!"

"¡Sí!" the men nodded in agreement.

"Wait!" Narciso stopped them. "Yes, I called you fools, but not to insult you. Listen my friends, you have already violated this man's land—you have come and created much bad blood when you could have done this simply. You have the right to charge someone with witchcraft, and to discover the truth of that charge there is a very simple test!" He reached forward and pulled the needles from the man's lip. "Are these needles holy?" he asked the man.

"Sí," the man answered, "blessed just last Sunday by the priest." He wiped the blood on his lip.

"I call you fools because you all know the test for a bruja, and yet you did not think to use it. It is simple. Take the holy needles and pin them to the door. Put them in so they are crossed—and in the name of God!" he roared, "you all know that a witch cannot walk through a door so marked by the sign of Christ!"

"¡Ay sí!" the men exclaimed. It was true.

"It is a true test," the man called Cruz Sedillo spoke. He took the needles from Narciso. "It is legal in our customs. I have seen it work."

"But we must all abide by the trial," Narciso said. He looked at my father. For the first time my father turned and looked at the kitchen door. In the light were the two huddled figures of my mother and Ultima. Then he glanced at Narciso. He placed his faith in his old friend.

"I will abide by the test," he said simply. I crossed my forehead. I had no doubt that Ultima could walk by the way of the holy cross. Now everyone turned and looked at Tenorio, for it was he who had accused Ultima.

"I will abide," he muttered. He had no other choice.

"I will place the needles," Cruz Sedillo said. He walked to the door and stuck the two needles in the form of a cross at the top of the door frame. Then he turned and spoke to the men. "It is true that no person of evil, no bruja, can walk through a door guarded by the sign of the holy cross. In my own lifetime I have seen a woman so judged, because her body burned with pain at the sight of the cross. So if Ultima cannot step through the threshold, then our work tonight has just begun. But if she crosses the threshold, then she can never again be accused of witchcraft— we call God as our witness," he finished and stepped back. All the men made the sign of the cross and murmured a prayer.

We all turned and looked at the door. The fire from the torches was dying, and in fact some of the men had already dropped their smoldering torches to the ground. We could see Ultima plainly as she walked to the door.

"Who is it that accuses me?" she asked from behind the screen door. Her voice was very clear and powerful.

"Tenorio Trementina accuses you of being a witch!" Tenorio answered in a savage, hate-filled voice. He had stepped forward to shout his accusation, and as he did I heard Ultima's owl shriek in the dark. There was a rustling and whirling of wings above us, and all the men ducked and held their hands up to protect themselves from the attack. But the owl sought only one man, and it found him. It hurled itself on Tenorio, and the sharp talons gouged out one eye from the face of the evil man.

"Aieeeeeeeee!" he screamed in pain. "I am blinded! I am blinded!" In the dying light I saw blood spurt from the dark pit and bloody pulp that had once been an eye.

"¡Madre de Dios!" the men cried. They cringed in fear around the screaming, cursing Tenorio. They trembled and looked into the dark sky for the owl, but it was gone.

"¡Mira!" one of the them cried. He pointed and they turned to see Ultima. She had walked through the door!

"It is proven!" Narciso cried.

Ultima took a step towards the men and they fell back. They could not understand why the owl had attacked Tenorio, they could not understand the power of Ultima. But she had walked through the door, and so the power of la curandera was good.

"It is proven," Cruz Sedillo said, "the woman is free of the accusation." He turned and walked to the hill where they had left their trucks and several of the men hurried after him. Two stayed to help Tenorio.

"Your evil bird has blinded me!" he cried. "For that I curse you! I will see you dead! And you, Narciso, I swear to kill you!" The men pulled him away. They disappeared out of the dim light of the sputtering torches and into the darkness.

"¡Grande!" It was my mother who now burst through the door. She put her arms around Ultima and led her back into the house.

"Ay, what a night," my father shrugged as he looked after the men who had slunk away. Up on the hill we heard their trucks start, then leave. "Someday I may have to kill that man," he said to himself.

"He needs killing," Narciso agreed.

"How can I thank you, old friend," my father said turning to Narciso.

"I owe la Grande my life," Narciso said, "and I owe you many favors, Márez. What are thanks among friends."

My father nodded. "Come, I need a drink—" They walked into the house. I followed, but paused at the door. A faint glitter caught my eye. I bent down and picked up the two needles that had been stuck to the top of the door frame. Whether someone had broken the cross they made, or whether they had fallen, I would never know.

GLORIA ANZALDÚA

Gloria Anzaldúa writes about both the physical and psychological borders between cultures. She describes herself as a Tejana Chicana, growing up in Texas near the Mexican border. She says in her introduction to This Bridge Called My Back: *"Books saved my sanity, knowledge opened the locked places in me and taught me first how to survive and then how to soar."*

HOW TO TAME A WILD TONGUE

"WE'RE GOING to have to control your tongue," the dentist says, pulling out all the metal from my mouth. Silver bits plop and tinkle into the basin. My mouth is a motherlode. The dentist is cleaning out my roots. I get a whiff of the stench when I gasp. "I can't cap that tooth yet, you're still draining," he says.

"We're going to have to do something about your tongue," I hear the anger rising in his voice. My tongue keeps pushing out the wads of cotton, pushing back the drills, the long thin needles. "I've never seen anything as strong or as stubborn," he says. And I think, how do you tame a wild tongue, train it to be quiet, how do you bridle and saddle it? How do you make it lie down?

> "Who is to say that robbing a people of
> its language is less violent than war?"
> —Ray Gwyn Smith

I remember being caught speaking Spanish at recess—that was good for three licks on the knuckles with a sharp ruler. I remember being sent to the corner of the classroom for "talking back" to the Anglo teacher when all I was trying to do was tell her how to pronounce my name. "If you want to be American, speak

'American.' If you don't like it, go back to Mexico where you belong."

"I want you to speak English. *Pa' hallar buen trabajo tienes que saber hablar el inglés bien. Qué vale toda tu educación si todavía hablas inglés con un* 'accent,'" my mother would say, mortified that I spoke English like a Mexican. At Pan American University, I, and all Chicano students were required to take two speech classes. Their purpose: to get rid of our accents.

Attacks on one's form of expression with the intent to censor are a violation of the First Amendment. *El Anglo con cara de inocente nos arrancó la lengua.* Wild tongues can't be tamed, they can only be cut out.

OVERCOMING THE TRADITION OF SILENCE

> *Ahogadas, escupimos el oscuro.*
> *Peleando con nuestra propia sombra*
> *el silencio nos sepulta.*

En boca cerrada no entran moscas. "Flies don't enter a closed mouth" is a saying I kept hearing when I was a child. *Ser habladora* was to be a gossip and a liar, to talk too much. *Muchachitas bien criadas,* well-bred girls don't answer back. *Es una falta de respeto* to talk back to one's mother or father. I remember one of the sins I'd recite to the priest in the confession box the few times I went to confession: talking back to my mother, *hablar pa' 'tras, repelar. Hocicona, repelona, chismosa,* having a big mouth, questioning, carrying tales are all signs of being *mal criada.* In my culture they are all words that are derogatory if applied to women—I've never heard them applied to men.

The first time I heard two women, a Puerto Rican and a Cuban, say the word "*nosotras*," I was shocked. I had not known the word existed. Chicanas use *nosotros* whether we're male or female. We are robbed of our female being by the masculine plural. Language is a male discourse.

> And our tongues have become
> dry   the wilderness has
> dried out our tongues   and
> we have forgotten speech.
> —Irena Klepfisz

Even our own people, other Spanish speakers *nos quieren poner candados en la boca.* They would hold us back with their bag of *reglas de academia.*

OYÉ COMO LADRA: EL LENGUAJE DE LA FRONTERA

Quien tiene boca se equivoca.
— Mexican saying

"*Pocho*, cultural traitor, you're speaking the oppressor's language by speaking English, you're ruining the Spanish language," I have been accused by various Latinos and Latinas. Chicano Spanish is considered by the purist and by most Latinos deficient, a mutilation of Spanish.

But Chicano Spanish is a border tongue which developed naturally. Change, *evolución, enriquecimiento de palabras neuvas por invención o adopción* have created variants of Chicano Spanish, *un nuevo lenguaje. Un lenguaje que corresponde a un modo de vivir.* Chicano Spanish is not incorrect, it is a living language.

For a people who are neither Spanish nor live in a country in which Spanish is the first language; for a people who live in a country in which English is the reigning tongue but who are not Anglo; for a people who cannot entirely identify with either standard (formal, Castillian) Spanish nor standard English, what recourse is left to them but to create their own language? A language which they can connect their identity to, one capable of communicating the realities and values true to themselves—a language with terms that are neither *español ni inglés*, but both. We speak a patois, a forked tongue, a variation of two languages.

Chicano Spanish sprang out of the Chicanos' need to identify ourselves as a distinct people. We needed a language with which we could communicate with ourselves, a secret language. For some of us, language is a homeland closer than the Southwest—for many Chicanos today live in the Midwest and the East. And because we are a complex, heterogeneous people, we speak many languages. Some of the languages we speak are:

1. Standard English
2. Working class and slang English
3. Standard Spanish
4. Standard Mexican Spanish
5. North Mexican Spanish dialect
6. Chicano Spanish (Texas, New Mexico, Arizona and California have regional variations)
7. Tex-Mex
8. *Pachuco* (called *caló*)

My "home" tongues are the languages I speak with my sister and brothers, with my friends. They are the last five listed, with 6 and 7 being closest to my heart. From school, the media and job situations, I've picked up standard and working class English. From Mamagrande Locha and from reading Spanish and Mexican literature, I've picked up Standard Spanish and Standard Mexican Spanish. From *los recién llegados*, Mexican immigrants, and *braceros*, I learned the North Mexican dialect. With Mexicans I'll try to speak either Standard Mexican Spanish or the North Mexican dialect. From my parents and Chicanos living in the Valley, I picked up Chicano Texas Spanish, and I speak it with my mom, younger brother (who married a Mexican and who rarely mixes Spanish with English), aunts and older relatives.

With Chicanas from *Nuevo México* or *Arizona* I will speak Chicano Spanish a little, but often they don't understand what I'm saying. With most California Chicanas I speak entirely in English (unless I forget). When I first moved to San Francisco, I'd rattle off something in Spanish, unintentionally embarrassing them. Often it is only with another Chicana *tejana* that I can talk freely.

Words distorted by English are known as anglicisms or *pochismos*. The *pocho* is an anglicized Mexican or American of Mexican origin who speaks Spanish with an accent characteristic of North Americans and who distorts and reconstructs the language according to the influence of English. Tex-Mex, or Spanglish, comes most naturally to me. I may switch back and forth from English to Spanish in the same sentence or in the same word. With my sister and my brother Nune and with Chicano *tejano* contemporaries I speak in Tex-Mex.

From kids and people my own age I picked up *Pachuco*. *Pachuco* (the language of the zoot suiters) is a language of rebellion, both against Standard Spanish and Standard English. It is a secret language. Adults of the culture and outsiders cannot understand it. It is made up of slang words from both English and Spanish. *Ruca* means girl or woman, *vato* means guy or dude, *chale* means no, *simón* means yes, *churro* is sure, talk is *periquiar, pigionear* means petting, *que gacho* means how nerdy, *ponte águila* means watch out, death is called *la pelona*. Through lack of practice and not having others who can speak it, I've lost most of the *Pachuco* tongue.

NICHOLASA MOHR

Nicholasa Mohr was born in New York City in 1935 to Puerto Rican parents. She is the author of several novels and says: "I, as a Puerto Rican child, never existed in North American letters. Our struggles as displaced migrants, working-class descendants of the tabaqueros *(tobacco workers) who began coming here in 1916, were invisible in North American literature. As I proceeded to record who we were, I addressed myself both to adults and children – and, of course, to women."*

A VERY SPECIAL PET

THE Fernández family kept two pets in their small five-room apartment. One was a large female alley cat who was a good mouser when she wasn't in heat. She was very large and had a rich coat of grey fur with black stripes and a long bushy tail. Her eyes were yellow and she had long white whiskers. Her name was Maríalu.

If they would listen carefully to what Maríalu said, Mrs. Fernández assured the children, they would hear her calling her husband Raúl.

"Raúl . . . Raúl . . . this is Maríalu . . . Raúl . . . Raúl . . . this is Maríalu," the children would sing loudly. They all felt sorry for Maríalu, because no matter how long and hard she howled, or how many times she ran off, she could never find her real husband, Raúl.

The second pet was not really supposed to be a pet at all. She was a small, skinny white hen with a red crest and a yellow beak. Graciela and Eugenio Fernández had bought her two years ago, to provide them and their eight children with good fresh eggs.

Her name was Joncrofo, after Graciela Fernández's favorite Hollywood movie star, Joan Crawford. People would repeat the hen's name as she pronounced it, "Joncrofo la gallina."

Joncrofo la gallina lived in the kitchen. She had one foot tied with a very long piece of twine to one of the legs of the kitchen sink. The twine was long enough for Joncrofo to wander all over the kitchen and even to hop onto the large window with a fire escape.

98

Under the sink Mrs. Fernández kept clean newspapers, water, and cornmeal for the hen, and a wooden box lined with some soft flannel cloth and packing straw. It was there that they hoped Joncrofo would lay her eggs. The little hen slept and rested there, but perhaps because she was nervous, she had never once laid an egg.

Graciela and Eugenio Fernández had come to the Bronx six years ago and moved into the small apartment. Except for a trip once before to the seaport city of Mayagüez in Puerto Rico, they had never left their tiny village in the mountains. To finance their voyage to New York, Mr. and Mrs. Fernández had sold their small plot of land, the little livestock they had, and their wooden cabin. The sale had provided the fare and expenses for them and their five children. Since then, three more children had been born. City life was foreign to them, and they had to learn everything, even how to get on a subway and travel. Graciela Fernández had been terribly frightened at first of the underground trains, traffic, and large crowds of people. Although she finally adjusted, she still confined herself to the apartment and seldom went out.

She would never complain; she would pray at the small altar she had set up in the kitchen, light her candles and murmur that God would provide and not forget her and her family. She was proud of the fact that they did not have to ask for welfare or home relief, as so many other families did.

"Papi provides for us. We are lucky and we have to thank Jesus Christ," she would say, making the sign of the cross.

Eugenio Fernández had found a job as a porter in one of the large buildings in the garment center in Manhattan. He still held the same job, but he hoped to be promoted someday to freight-elevator operator. In the meantime, he sold newspapers and coffee on the side, ran errands for people in the building, and was always available for extra work. Still, the money he brought home was barely enough to support ten people.

"Someday I'm gonna get that job. I got my eye on it, and Mr. Friedlander, he likes me . . . so we gotta be patient. Besides the increase in salary, my God! – I could do a million things on the side, and we could make a lotta money. Why I could . . . " Mr. Fernández would tell his family this story several times a week.

"Oh, wow! Papi, we are gonna be rich when you get that job!" the children would shriek.

"Can we get a television when we get rich, Papi?" Pablito, the oldest boy, would ask. Nellie, Carmen, and Linda wanted a telephone.

"Everybody on the block got a telephone but us." Nellie, the oldest girl, would speak for them.

The younger children, William, Olgita, and Freddie, would request lots of toys and treats. Baby Nancy would smile and babble happily with everybody.

"We gonna get everything and we gonna leave El Bronx," Mr. Fernández would assure them. "We even gonna save enough to buy our farm in Puerto Rico—a big one! With lots of land, maybe a hundred acres, and a chicken house, pigs, goats, even a cow. We can plant coffee and some sugar, and have all the fruit trees—mangoes, sweet oranges, everything!" Mr. Fernández would pause and tell the children all about the wonderful food they could eat back home in his village. "All you need to get the farm is a good start."

"We gonna take Joncrofo, right?" the kids would ask. "And Maríalu? Her too?"

"Sure," Mr. Fernández would say good-naturedly, "even Raúl, her husband, when she finds him, eh?" He would wink, laughing. "And Joncrofo don't have to be tied up like a prisoner no more—she could run loose."

It was the dream of Graciela and Eugenio Fernández to go back to their village as owners of their own farm, with the faith that the land would provide for them.

This morning Mrs. Fernández sat in her kitchen, thinking that things were just not going well. Now that the holidays were coming and Christmas would soon be here, money was scarcer than ever and prices were higher than ever. Things had been hard for Eugenio Fernández; he was still working as a porter and lately had been sick with a bad throat. They had not saved one cent toward their farm. In fact, they still owed the dry-goods salesman for the kitchen curtains and two bedspreads; even insurance payments were long overdue. She wanted to find a job and help out, but there were still three small preschool children at home to care for. Lately, she had begun to worry; it was hard to put meat on the table.

Graciela Fernández sighed, looking about her small, clean kitchen, and caught sight of Joncrofo running frantically after a stray cockroach. The hen quickly jerked her neck and snapped up the insect with her beak. In spite of all the fumigation and daily scrubbing, it seemed there was always a cockroach or two in sight.

Joncrofo was always searching for a tasty morsel—spiders, ants, even houseflies. She was quick and usually got her victim.

The little white hen had a wicked temper and would snap at anyone she felt was annoying her. Even Maríalu knew better; she had a permanent scar on her right ear as a result of Joncrofo's sharp yellow beak. Now the cat carefully kept her distance.

In spite of Joncrofo's cantankerous ways, the children loved her. They were proud of her because no one else on the block had such a pet. Whenever other children teased them about not having a television, the Fernández children would remind them that Joncrofo was a very special pet. Even Baby Nancy would laugh and clap when she saw Joncrofo rushing toward one of her tiny victims.

For some time now, Mrs. Fernández had given up any hope of Joncrofo producing eggs and had also accepted her as a house pet. She had tried everything: warm milk, fresh grass from the park, relining the wooden box. She had even consulted the spiritualist and followed the instructions faithfully, giving the little hen certain herbs to eat and reciting the prayers; and yet nothing ever worked. She had even tried to fatten her up, but the more Joncrofo ate, it seemed, the less she gained.

After thinking about it for several days, this morning Graciela Fernández reached her decision. Tonight, her husband would have good fresh chicken broth for his cold, and her children a full plate of rice with chicken. This silly hen was really no use alive to anyone, she concluded.

It had been six long years since Mrs. Fernández had killed a chicken, but she still remembered how. She was grateful that the older children were in school, and somehow she would find a way to keep the three younger ones at the other end of the apartment.

Very slowly she got up and found the kitchen cleaver. Feeling it with her thumb, she decided it should be sharper, and taking a flat stone, she carefully sharpened the edge as she planned the best way to finish off the hen.

It was still quite early. If she worked things right, she could be through by noontime and have supper ready before her husband got home. She would tell the children that Joncrofo flew away. Someone had untied the twine on her foot and when she opened the window to the fire escape to bring in the mop, Joncrofo flew out and disappeared. That's it, she said to herself, satisfied.

The cleaver was sharp enough and the small chopping block was set up on the kitchen sink. Mrs. Fernández bent down and looked Joncrofo right in the eye. The hen stared back without any fear or much interest. Good, thought Mrs. Fernández, and she walked back into the apartment where Olgita, Freddie, and Baby Nancy were playing.

"I'm going to clean the kitchen, and I don't want you to come inside. Understand?" The children looked at her and nodded. "I mean it—you stay here. If I catch you coming to the kitchen when I am cleaning, you get it with this," she said, holding out her hand with an open palm, gesturing as if she were spanking them. "Now, I'm going to put the chair across the kitchen entrance so that Baby Nancy can't come in. O.K.?" The children nodded again. Their mother very often put one of the kitchen chairs across the kitchen entrance so the baby could not come inside. "Now," she said, "you listen and you stay here!" The children began to play, interested only in their game.

Mrs. Fernández returned to the kitchen, smoothed down her hair, readjusted her apron, and rolled up her sleeves. She put one of the chairs across the threshold to block the entrance, then found a couple of extra rags and old newspapers.

"Joncrofo," she whispered and walked over to the hen. To her surprise, the hen ran under the sink and sat in her box. Mrs. Fernández bent down, but before she could grab her, Joncrofo jumped out of her box and slid behind one of the legs of the kitchen sink. She extended her hand and felt the hen's sharp beak nip one of her fingers. "Ave María!" she said, pulling away and putting the injured finger in her mouth. "O.K., you wanna play games. You dumb hen!"

She decided to untie the twine that was tied to the leg of the sink and then pull the hen toward her. Taking a large rag, she draped it over one hand and then, bending down once more, untied the twine and began to pull. Joncrofo resisted, and Mrs. Fernández pulled. Harder and harder she tugged and pulled, at the same time making sure she held the rag securely, so that she could protect herself against Joncrofo's sharp beak. Quickly she pulled, and with one fast jerk of the twine, the hen was up in the air. Quickly Mrs. Fernández draped the rag over the hen. Frantically, Joncrofo began to cackle and jump, flapping her wings and snapping her beak. Mrs. Fernández found herself spinning as she struggled to hold on to Joncrofo, who kept wriggling and jumping. With great effort, Joncrofo got her head loose and sank her beak into Mrs. Fernández's arm. In an instant she released the hen.

Joncrofo ran around the kitchen cackling loudly, flapping her wings and ruffling her feathers. The hen kept an eye on Mrs. Fernández, who also watched her as she held on to her injured arm. White feathers were all over the kitchen; some still floated softly in the air.

Each time Mrs. Fernández went toward Joncrofo, she fled swiftly, cackling even louder and snapping wildly with her beak.

Mrs. Fernández remained still for a moment, then went over to the far end of the kitchen and grabbed a broom. Using the handle, she began to hit the hen, swatting her back and forth like a tennis ball. Joncrofo kept running and trying to dodge the blows, but Mrs. Fernández kept landing the broom each time. The hen began to lose her footing, and Mrs. Fernández vigorously swung the broom, hitting the small hen until her cackles became softer and softer. Not able to stand any longer, Joncrofo wobbled, moving with slow jerky movement, and dropped to the floor. Mrs. Fernández let go of the broom and rushed over to the hen. Grabbing her by the neck, she lifted her into the air and spun her around a few times, dropping her on the floor. Near exhaustion, Mrs. Fernández could hear her own heavy breathing.

"Mami . . . Mamita. What are you doing to Joncrofo?" Turning, she saw Olgita, Freddie, and Baby Nancy staring at her wide-eyed. "Ma . . . Mami . . . what are you doing to Joncrofo?" they shouted and began to cry. In her excitement, Mrs. Fernández had forgotten completely about the children and the noise the hen had made.

"Oooo . . . is she dead?" Olgita cried, pointing. "Is she dead?" She began to whine.

"You killed Joncrofo, Mami! You killed her. She's dead." Freddie joined his sister, sobbing loudly. Baby Nancy watched her brother and sister and began to cry too. Shrieking, she threw herself on the floor in a tantrum.

"You killed her! You're bad, Mami. You're bad," screamed Olgita.

"Joncrofo . . . I want Joncrofo . . . ," Freddie sobbed. "I'm gonna tell Papi," he screamed, choking with tears.

"Me too! I'm gonna tell too," cried Olgita. "I'm telling Nellie, and she'll tell teacher on you," she yelled.

Mrs. Fernández watched her children as they stood looking in at her, barricaded by the chair. Then she looked down at the floor where Joncrofo lay, perfectly still. Walking over to the chair, she removed it from the entrance, and before she could say anything, the children ran to the back of the apartment, still yelling and crying.

"Joncrofo. . . . We want Joncrofo. . . . You're bad . . . you're bad. . . . "

Mrs. Fernández felt completely helpless as she looked about her kitchen. What a mess! she thought. Things were overturned, and there were white feathers everywhere. Feeling the tears coming to her eyes, she sat down and began to cry quietly. What's the use now? She sighed and thought, I should have taken her to the butcher. He would have done it for a small fee. Oh, this life, she said to herself, wiping her eyes. Now my children hate me. She remembered that when she was just about Olgita's age she was already helping her mother kill chickens and never thought much about slaughtering animals for food.

Graciela Fernández took a deep breath and began to wonder what she would do with Joncrofo now that she was dead. No use cooking her. They won't eat her, she thought, shaking her head. As she contemplated what was to be done, she heard a low grunt. Joncrofo was still alive!

Mrs. Fernández reached under the sink and pulled out the wooden box. She put the large rag into the box and placed the hen inside. Quickly she went over to a cabinet and took out an eyedropper, filling it with water. Then she forced open Joncrofo's beak and dropped some water inside. She put a washcloth into lukewarm water and washed down the hen, smoothing her feathers.

"Joncrofo," she cooed softly, "cro . . . cro . . . Joncrofita," and stroked the hen gently. The hen was still breathing, but her eyes were closed. Mrs. Fernández went over to the cupboard and pulled out a small bottle of rum that Mr. Fernández saved only for special occasions and for guests. She gave some to Joncrofo. The hen opened her eyes and shook her head, emitting a croaking sound.

"What a good little hen," said Mrs. Fernández. "That's right, come on . . . come, wake up, and I'll give you something special. How about if I get you some nice dried corn? . . . Come on." She continued to pet the hen and talk sweetly to her. Slowly, Joncrofo opened her beak and tried to cackle, and again she made a croaking sound. Blinking her eyes, she sat up in her box, ruffled her feathers, and managed a low soft cackle.

"Is she gonna live, Mami?" Mrs. Fernández turned and saw Olgita, Freddie, and Baby Nancy standing beside her.

"Of course she's going to live. What did you think I did, kill her?

Tsk, tsk . . . did you really think that? You are all very silly children," she said, and shook her finger at them. They stared back at her with bewilderment, not speaking. "All that screaming at me was not nice." She went on, "I was only trying to save her. Joncrofo got very sick, and see?" She held up the eyedropper. "I had to help her get well. I had to catch her in order to cure her. Understand?"

Olgita and Freddie looked at each other and then at their mother.

"When I saw that she was getting sick, I had to catch her. She was running all around, jumping and going crazy. Yes." Mrs. Fernández opened her eyes and pointed to her head, making a circular movement with her right index finger. "She went cuckoo! If I didn't stop her, Joncrofo would have really killed herself," she said earnestly. "So I gave her some medicine—and now . . . "

"Is that why you got her drunk, Mami?" interrupted Olgita.

"What?" asked Mrs. Fernández.

"You gave her Papi's rum . . . in the eyedropper. We seen you," Freddie said. Olgita nodded.

"Well," Mrs. Fernández said, "that don't make her drunk. It . . . it . . . ah . . . just calms her down. Sometimes it's used like a medicine."

"And makes her happy again?" Olgita asked. "Like Papi? He always gets happy when he drink some."

"Yes, that's right. You're right. To make Joncrofo happy again," Mrs. Fernández said.

"Why did she get sick, Mami, and go crazy?" asked Freddie.

"I don't know why. Those things just happen," Mrs. Fernández responded.

"Do them things happen on the farm in Puerto Rico?"

"That's right," she said. "Now let me be. I gotta finish cleaning here. Go on, go to the back of the house; take Baby Nancy . . . go on."

The children left the kitchen, and Mrs. Fernández barricaded the entrance once more. She picked up the box with Joncrofo, who sat quietly blinking, and shoved it under the sink. Then she put the cleaver and the chopping board away. Picking up the broom, she began to sweep the feathers and torn newspaper that were strewn all about the kitchen.

In the back of the apartment, where the children played, they could hear their mother singing a familiar song. It was about a beautiful island where the tall green palm trees swayed under a golden sky and the flowers were always in bloom.

ALBERTO ALVARO RÍOS

Alberto Alvaro Ríos was born in 1952 in Nogales, Arizona. His latest book, Teodoro Luno's Two Kisses, *was published in 1990. He writes poetry and short stories and teaches at Arizona State University in Tempe.*

THE IGUANA KILLER

S APITO HAD turned eight two weeks before and was, at this time, living in Villahermosa, the capital city of Tabasco. He had earned his nickname because his eyes bulged to make him look like a frog, and besides, he was the best fly-catcher in all Villahermosa. This was when he was five. Now he was eight, but his eyes still bulged and no one called him anything but "Sapito."

Among their many duties, all the boys had to go down to the Río Grijalva every day and try to sell or trade off whatever homemade things were available and could be carried on these small men's backs. It was also the job of these boys to fish, capture snails, trick tortoises, and kill the iguanas.

Christmas had just passed, and it had been celebrated as usual, very religious with lots of candle smoke and very solemn church masses. There had been no festivities yet, no laughing, but today would be different. Today was the fifth of January, the day the children of Villahermosa wait for all year. Tomorrow would be the *Día de los Reyes Magos*, the Day of the Wise Kings, when presents of all sorts were brought by the Kings and given to friends. Sapito's grandmother, who lived in Nogales in the United States, had sent him two packages. He had seen them, wrapped in blue paper with bearded red clown faces. Sapito's grandmother always sent presents to his family, and she always seemed to know just what Sapito would want, even though they had never met.

That night, Sapito's mother put the packages under the bed where he slept. It was not a cushioned bed, but rather, a hammock, made with soft rattan leaves. Huts in Villahermosa were not rented to visitors by the number of rooms, but, instead, by the number of hooks in each place. On these hooks were hung the hammocks of a family. People in this town were born and nursed, then slept and died in these hanging beds. Sapito could remember his grandfather, and how they found him one afternoon after lunch. They had eaten mangoes together. Sapito dreamed about him now, about how his face would turn colors when he told his stories, always too loud.

When Sapito woke up, he found the packages. He played up to his mother, the way she wanted, claiming that the *Reyes* had brought him all these gifts. *Look and look, and look here*! he shouted, but this was probably the last time he would do this, for Sapito was now eight, and he knew better, but did not tell. He opened the two packages from Nogales, finding a baseball and a baseball bat. Sapito held both gifts and smiled, though he wasn't clearly sure what the things were. Sapito had not been born in nor ever visited the United States, and he had no idea what baseball was. He was sure he recognized and admired the ball and knew what it was for. He could certainly use that. But he looked at the baseball bat and was puzzled for some seconds.

It was an iguana-killer. "¡*Mira, mamá! un palo para matar iguanas!*" It was beautiful, a dream. It was perfect. His grandmother always knew what he would like.

In Villahermosa, the jungle was not far from where Sapito lived. It started, in fact, at the end of his backyard. It was not dense there, but one could not walk far before a machete became a third hand, sharper, harder, more valuable than the other two in this other world that sometimes kept people.

This strong jungle life was great fun for a boy like Sapito, who especially enjoyed bringing coconuts out of the tangled vines for his mother. He would look for monkeys in the fat palm trees and throw rocks at them, one after the other. To get back, the monkeys would throw coconuts back at him, yelling terrible monkey-words. This was life before the iguana-killer.

Every day for a week after he had gotten the presents, Sapito would walk about half a mile east along the Río Grijalva with Chachi, his best friend. Then they would cut straight south into the hair of the jungle.

There is a correct way to hunt iguanas, and Sapito had been well-skilled even before the bat came. He and Chachi would look at all the trees until the tell-tale movement of an iguana was spotted. When one was found, Sapito would sit at the base of the tree, being as quiet as possible, with baseball bat held high and muscles stiff.

The female iguana would come out first. She moved her head around very quickly, almost jerking, in every direction. Sapito knew that she was not the one to kill. She kept the little iguanas in supply—his father had told him. After a few seconds, making sure everything was safe, she would return to the tree and send her husband out, telling him there was nothing to worry about.

The male iguana is always slower. He comes out and moves his head to one side and just stares, motionless, for several minutes. Now Sapito knew that he must take advantage, but very carefully. Iguanas can see in almost all directions at once. Unlike human eyes, both iguana eyes do not have to center in on the same thing. One eye can look forward, and one backward, like a clown, so that they can detect almost any movement. Sapito knew this and was always careful to check both eyes before striking. Squinting his own eyes which always puffed out even more when he was excited, he would not draw back his club. That would waste time. It was already kept high in the air all these minutes. When he was ready, he would send the bat straight down as hard and as fast as he could. Just like that. And if he had done all these things right, he would take his prize home by the tail to skin him for eating that night.

Iguanas were prepared like any other meat, fried, roasted, or boiled, and they tasted like tough chicken no matter which way they were done. In Tabasco, and especially in Villahermosa, iguanas were eaten by everybody all the time, even tourists, so hunting them was very popular. Iguana was an everyday supper, eaten without frowning at such a thing, eating lizard. It is not different from the other things eaten here, the turtle eggs, *cahuamas*, crocodile meat, river snails. And when iguanas were killed, nobody was supposed to feel sad. Everybody's father said so. Sapito did, though, sometimes. Iguanas had puffed eyes like his.

But, if Sapito failed to kill one of these iguanas, he would run away as fast as he could—being sad was the last thing he would think of. Iguanas look mean, they have bloodshot eyes, and people say that they spit blood. Sapito and his friends thought that, since no one they knew had ever been hurt by these monsters, they must not be so bad. This was what the boys thought in town, talking on a summer afternoon, drinking coconuts. But when he missed, Sapito figured that the real reason no one had ever been hurt was that no one ever hung around afterward to find out what happens. Whether iguanas were really dangerous or not, nobody could say for certain. Nobody's parents had ever heard of an iguana hurting anyone, either. The boys went home one day and asked. So, no one worried, sort of, and iguanas were even tamed and kept as pets by the old sailors in Villahermosa, along with the snakes. But only by the sailors.

The thought of missing a hit no longer bothered Sapito, who now began carrying his baseball bat everywhere. His friends were impressed more by this than by anything else, even candy in tin boxes, especially when he began killing four and five iguanas a day. No one could be that good. Soon, not only Chachi, but the rest of the boys began following Sapito around constantly just to watch the scourge of the iguanas in action.

By now, the bat was proven. Sapito was the champion iguana-provider, always holding his now-famous killer-bat. All his friends would come to copy it. They would come everyday asking for measurements and questioning him as to its design. Chachi and the rest would then go into the jungle and gather fat, straight roots. With borrowed knives and machetes, they tried to whittle out their own iguana-killers, but failed. Sapito's was machine made, and perfect.

This went on for about a week, when Sapito had an idea that was to serve him well for a long time. He began renting out the killer-bat for a *centavo* a day. The boys said yes yes right away, and would go out and hunt at least two or three iguanas to make it worth the price, but really, too, so that they could use the bat as much as possible.

For the next few months, the grown-ups of Villahermosa hated Sapito and his bat because all they ate was iguana. But Sapito was proud. No one would make fun of his bulging eyes now.

Sapito was in Nogales in the United States visiting his grandmother for the first time, before going back to Tabasco, and Villahermosa. His family had come from Chiapas on the other side of the republic on a relative-visiting vacation. It was still winter, but no one in Sapito's family had expected it to be cold. They knew about rain, and winter days, but it was always warm in the jungle, even for these things.

Sapito was sitting in front of the house on Sonoita Avenue, on the sidewalk. He was very impressed by many things in this town, especially the streetlights. Imagine lighting up the inside *and* the outside. It would be easy to catch animals at night here. But most of all, he was impressed by his rather large grandmother, whom he already loved very much. He had remembered to thank her for the iguana-killer and the ball. She had laughed and said, "*Por nada, hijo.*" As he sat and thought about this, he wrapped the two blankets he had brought outside with him tighter around his small body. Sapito could not understand or explain to himself that the weather was cold and that he had to feel it, everyone did, even him. This was almost an unknown experience to him since he had never been out of the tropics before. The sensation, the feeling of cold, then, was very strange, especially since he wasn't even wet. It was actually hurting him. His muscles felt as if he had held his bat up in the air for an hour waiting for an iguana. Of course, Sapito could have gone inside to get warm near the wood-burning stove, but he didn't like the smoke or the smell of the north. It was a different smell, not the jungle.

So Sapito sat there. Cold had never been important in his life before, and he wasn't going to let it start now. With blankets he could cover himself up and it would surely pass. Covered up for escape, he waited for warmness, pulling the blankets over his head. Sometimes he would put out his foot to see if it was okay yet, the way the lady iguana would come out first.

Then, right then in one fast second, Sapito seemed to feel, with his foot on the outside, a very quiet and strange moment, as if everything had slowed. He felt his eyes bulge when he scrunched up his face to hear better. Something scary caught hold of him, and he began to shiver harder. It was different from just being cold, which was scary enough. His heartbeat was pounding so much that he could feel it in his eyes.

He carefully moved one of the blankets from his face. Sapito saw the sky falling, just like the story his grandmother had told him the first day they had been there. He thought she was joking, or that she didn't realize he was already eight, and didn't believe in such things anymore.

Faster than hitting an iguana Sapito threw his blankets off, crying as he had not cried since he was five and they had nicknamed him and teased him. He ran to the kitchen and grabbed his mother's leg. Crying and shivering, he begged, "¡Mamá, por favor, perdóneme!" He kept speaking fast, asking for forgiveness and promising never to do anything wrong in his life ever again. The sky was falling, but he had always prayed, really he had.

His mother looked at him and at first could not laugh. Quietly, she explained that it was *nieve*, snow, that was falling, not the sky. She told him not to be afraid, and that he could go out and play in it, touch it, yes.

Sapito still didn't know exactly what this *nieve* was, but now his mother was laughing and didn't seem worried. In Villahermosa, *nieve* was a good word, it meant ice cream. There was a *nieve* man. Certainly the outside wasn't ice cream, but the white didn't really look bad, he thought, not really. It seemed, in fact, to have great possibilities. Sapito went back outside, sitting again with his blankets, trying to understand. He touched it, and breathed even faster. Then, closing his eyes, which was not easy, he put a little in his mouth.

Sapito's family had been back in Villahermosa for a week now. Today was Sunday. It was the custom here that every Sunday afternoon, since there were no other amusements, the band would play on the *malecón*, an area something like a park by the river, where the boats were all loaded.

Each Sunday it was reserved for this band – that is, the group of citizens that joined together and called themselves a band. It was a favorite time for everyone, as the paddle boat lay resting on the river while its owner played the trumpet and sang loud songs. The instruments were all brass, except for the marimba, which was the only sad sounding instrument. Though it was hit with padded drumsticks, its song was quiet, hidden, always reserved for dusk. Sapito had thought about the marimba as his mother explained about snow. Her voice had its sound for the few minutes she spoke, and held him. Before the marimba, before dusk, however, the brass had full control.

As dusk came, it was time for the *verbenas*, when the girls, young and old, would come in and walk around the park in one direction

and the boys would walk the opposite way, all as the marimba played
its songs easily, almost by itself. On these Sundays no one was a
man or a woman. They were all boys and girls, even the women
who always wore black. This was when all the flirting and the smiling of smiles bigger than people's faces took place. Sapito and Chachi
and the rest of the smaller boys never paid attention to any of this,
except sometimes to make fun of someone's older sister.

An old man, Don Tomasito, the baker, played the tuba. When
he blew into the huge mouthpiece, his face would turn purple and
his thousand wrinkles would disappear as his skin filled out. Sapito
and his friends would choose by throwing fingers, and whoever had
the odd number thrown out, matching no one else, was chosen
to do the best job of the day. This had become a custom all their
own. The chosen one would walk around in front of Don Tomasito
as he played, and cut a lemon. Then slowly, very slowly, squeeze
it, letting the juice fall to the ground. Don Tomasito's lips would
follow.

On this first Sunday afternoon after he had returned, Sapito, after
being chased by Señor Saturnino Cantón, who was normally the
barber but on Sunday was the policeman, pulled out his prize. Sapito
had been preparing his friends all day, and now they were yelling
to see this new surprise. This was no iguana-killer, but Sapito hoped
it would have the same effect.

Some of the people in Villahermosa used to have photographs
of various things. One picture Sapito had particularly remembered.
Some ladies of the town, who always made their own clothes, once
had a picture taken together. They were a group of maybe ten ladies,
in very big dresses and hats, some sitting and some standing. What
Sapito recalled now was that they were all barefoot. They were all
very serious and probably didn't think of it, but now, Sapito, after
traveling to the north and seeing many pictures at his grandmother's
house, thought their bare feet were very funny, even if shoes were
hard to get and couldn't be made like dresses could. Sapito knew
about such things now. He remembered that people in Nogales
laughed at him when he was barefoot in the snow.

But now, Sapito had a photograph, too. This was his surprise.
Well, what it was, really, was a Christmas card picturing a house
with lots of snow around. He had gotten the picture from his grandmother and had taken great care in bringing it back home. He kept
the surprise under his shirt wrapped in blue paper against his

stomach, so it would stay flat. Here was a picture of the *nieve*, just like he had seen for himself, except there was a lot more of it in the picture. An awful lot more.

At the end of this Sunday, making a big deal with his small hands, he showed this prize to his friends, and told them that *nieve*, which means both snow and ice cream in the Spanish of those who have experienced the two, would fall from the sky in Nogales. Any time at all. His bulging eyes widened to emphasize what he was saying, and he held his bat to be even more convincing.

No one believed him.

"*Pues, miren, ¡aquí está!*" He showed them the picture, and added now that it was a picture of his grandmother's house where he had just visited.

When Chachi asked, as Sapito had hoped, if it came down in flavors, he decided that he had gone this far, so why not. "*Vainilla*," he stated.

As the months went by, so did new stories, and strawberry and pistachio, and he was pretty sure that they believed him. After all, none of them had ever been up north. They didn't know the things Sapito knew. And besides, he still owned the iguana-killer.

Three months after the snow-picture stories had worn off, Señora Casimira, with the help of the town midwife, had a baby girl. The custom here was that mother and baby didn't have to do any work for forty days. No one ever complained. Mostly the little girls would help in the house, doing the errands that were not big enough to bother the boys or the big girls with. They'd throw water out front to quiet the dust. Neighbors would wash the clothes.

For the boys, usually because they could yell louder and didn't want to work with the girls, their job was to go and bring charcoal from the river, to bring bananas and coconuts, and whatever other food was needed. Every morning Sapito and his friends would stand outside the door of Señora Casimira's house, with luck before the girls came, and call in to her, asking if she needed anything. She would tell them yes or no, explaining what to bring if something was necessary.

Spring was here now, and today was Saturday. Sapito thought about this, being wise in the way of seasons now, as he looked down on the Casimira *choza*, the palm-thatched hut in which they lived. Señor Casimira was sure to be there today, he figured. There was no need to hang around, probably. Sapito had saved a little money from renting the killer-bat, and he suggested to his friends that they all go to Puerto Alvarado on the paddle boat. They were hitting him on the back and laughing yes! even before he had finished.

The Río Grijalva comes down from the Sierra Madre mountains, down through the state of Tabasco, through Villahermosa, emptying through Puerto Alvarado several miles north into the Gulf of Mexico. The boys looked over at the Casimira *choza*, then backward at this great river, where the paddle boat was getting ready to make its first trip of the day to Puerto Alvarado. They ran after it, fast enough to leave behind their shadows.

Sapito and his friends had been in Alvarado for about an hour when they learned that a *cahuama*, a giant sea turtle, was near by. They were on the rough beach, walking toward the north where the rocks become huge. Some palm trees nodded just behind the beach, followed by the jungle, as always. Sometimes Sapito thought it followed him, always moving closer.

Climbing the mossy rocks, Chachi was the one who spotted the *cahuama*. This was strange because the turtles rarely came so close to shore. In Villahermosa, and Puerto Alvarado, the money situation was such that anything the boys saw, like iguanas or the *cahuama*, they tried to capture. They always tried hard to get something for nothing, and here was their chance—not to mention the adventure involved. They all ran together with the understood intention of dividing up the catch.

They borrowed a rope from the men who were working farther up the shore near the palm trees. "*¡Buena suerte!*" one of the men called, and laughed. Sapito and Chachi jumped in a *cayuco*, a kayak built more like a canoe, which one of the fishermen had left near shore. They paddled out to the floating turtle, jumped out, and managed to get a rope tied around its neck right off. Usually, then, a person had to hop onto the back of the *cahuama* and let it take him down into the water for a little while. Its burst of strength usually went away before the rider drowned or let go. This was the best fun for the boys, and a fairly rare chance, so Sapito, who was closest, jumped on to ride this one. He put up one arm like a tough cowboy. This *cahuama* went nowhere.

The two boys climbed back into the *cayuco* and tried to pull the turtle, but it still wouldn't budge. It had saved its strength, and its strong flippers were more than a match for the two boys now.

Everyone on shore swam over to help them after realizing that yells of how to do it better were doing no good. They all grabbed a part of the rope. With pure strength against strength, the six boys sweated, but finally outpulled the stubborn *cahuama*, dragging it onto the shore. It began flopping around on the sand until they managed to tip it onto its back. The turtle seemed to realize that struggling was a waste of its last fat-man energy, and started moving like a slow motion robot, fighting as before but, now, on its back, the flippers and head moved like a movie going too slow.

The *cahuama* had seemed huge as the boys were pulling it, fighting so strong in the water, but it was only about three feet long when they finally took a breath and looked. Yet, they all agreed, this *cahuama* was very fat. It must have been a grandfather.

Chachi went to call one of the grown-ups to help. Each of the boys was sure that he could kill a *cahuama* and prepare it, but this was everybody's and they wanted it cut right. The men were impressed as the boys explained. The boys were all nervous. Maybe not nervous—not really, just sometimes they were sad when they caught *cahuamas* because they had seen what happens. Like fish, or iguanas, but bigger, and bigger animals are different. Sad, but they couldn't tell anyone, especially not the other boys, or the men. Sapito looked at their catch.

These sailors, or men who used to be sailors, all carried short, heavy machetes, specially made for things taken from the sea. Chachi came back with a man who already had his in hand. The blade was straight because there was no way to shape metal, no anvil in Alvarado. The man looked at Sapito. "*Préstame tu palo,*" he said, looking at Sapito's iguana-killer. Sapito picked it up from where he had left it and handed it to the man, carefully. The fisherman beat the turtle on the head three times fast until it was either dead or unconscious. Then he handed the bat back to Sapito, who was sort of proud, and sort of not.

The man cut the *cahuama's* head off. Some people eat the head and its juice, but Sapito and his friends had been taught not to. No one said anything as it was tossed to the ground. The flippers continued their robot motion.

He cut the side of the turtle, where the underside skin meets the shell. He then pulled a knife out of his pocket, and continued where the machete had first cut, separating the body of the turtle from the shell. As he was cutting he told the boys about the freshwater sac that *cahuamas* have, and how, if they were ever stranded at sea, they could drink it. They had heard the story a hundred times, but nobody knew anybody who really did it. The boys were impatient. Then he separated the underpart from the inside meat, the prize. It looked a little redder than beef. The fins were then cut off—someone would use their leather sometime later.

The man cut the meat into small pieces. The boys took these pieces and washed them in salt water to make the meat last longer. Before cooking them, they would have to be washed again, this time in fresh water to get all the salt off. In the meantime, the salt water would keep the meat from spoiling. One time Sapito forgot, or really he was in too much of a hurry, and he took some *cahuama* home but forgot to tell his mother. It changed colors, and Sapito had to go get some more food, with everybody mad at him. The boys knew that each part of the *cahuama* was valuable, but all they were interested in now was what they could carry. This, of course, was the meat.

The man gave each of the boys some large pieces, and then kept most of it for himself. The boys were young, and could not argue with a grown-up. They were used to this. The fisherman began to throw the shell away.

"*No, por favor, damelo,*" Sapito called to him. The man laughed and handed the shell to Sapito, who put his pieces of meat inside it and, with the rest of the boys, wandered back to the river to wait for the paddle boat. The shell was almost too big for him. The boys were all laughing and joking, proud of their accomplishment. They asked Sapito what he was going to do with the shell, but he said that he wasn't sure yet. This wasn't true. Of course, he was already making big, very big, plans for it.

They got back early in the afternoon, and everyone went home exhausted. Sapito, before going home, went into the jungle and gathered some green branches. He was not very tired yet—he had a new idea, so Sapito spent the rest of the afternoon polishing the shell with sand and the hairy part of some coconuts, which worked just like sandpaper.

When it was polished, he got four of the best branches and whittled them to perfection with his father's knife. Sapito tied these into a rectangle using some *mecate*, something in between rope and string, which his mother had given him. The shell fit halfway down into the opening of the rectangle. It was perfect. Then, onto this frame, he tied two flat, curved branches across the bottom at opposite ends. It moved back and forth like a drunk man. He had made a good, strong crib. It worked, just right for a new-born baby girl.

Sapito had worked hard and fast with the strength of a guilty conscience. Señora Casimira just might have needed something, after all. It was certainly possible that her husband might have had to work today. All the boys had known these facts before they had left, but had looked only at the paddle boat – and it had waved back at them.

Sapito took the crib, hurrying to beat the jungle dusk. Dusk, at an exact moment, even on Sundays, owned the sky and the air in its own strange way. Just after sunset, for about half an hour, the sky blackened more than would be normal for the darkness of early night, and mosquitoes, like pieces of sand, would come up out of the thickest part of the jungle like tornadoes, coming down on the town to take what they could. People always spent this half hour indoors, Sundays, too, even with all the laughing, which stopped then. This was the signal for the marimba's music to take over.

Sapito reached the *choza* as the first buzzings were starting. He listened at the Casimira's door, hearing the baby cry like all babies. The cradle would help. He put it down in front of the wooden door without making any noise, and knocked. Then, as fast as he could, faster than that even, he ran back over the hill, out of sight. He did not turn around. Señora Casimira would find out who had made it. And he would be famous again, thought Sapito, famous like the other times. He felt for the iguana-killer that had been dragging behind him, tied to his belt, and put it over his right shoulder. His face was not strong enough to keep away the smile that pulled his mouth, his fat eyes all the while puffing out.

HELENA MARÍA VIRAMONTES

*Helena María Viramontes, born in Los Angeles in 1954, writes
primarily about women. Her female characters often struggle against
social, cultural, and religious expectations that deny their independence
and creativity. She is an editor and writer, and an important figure in
the new Chicana literature.*

GROWING

THE TWO WALKED down First Street hand in reluctant hand.
The smaller of the two wore a thick, red sweater with a desperately loose button swinging like a pendulum. She carried her
crayons, swinging her arm while humming *Jesus loves little boys and
girls* to the speeding echo of the Saturday morning traffic and was
totally oblivious to her older sister's wrath.

"My eye!" Naomi ground out the words from between her teeth.
She turned to her youngest sister who seemed unconcerned and
quite delighted at the prospect of another adventure. "Chaperone,"
she said with great disdain. "My EYE!" Lucía was chosen by Apá
to be Naomi's chaperone and this infuriated her so much that she
dragged her along impatiently, pulling and jerking at almost every
step. She was 14, almost going on 15 and she thought the idea of
having to be watched by a young snot like Lucía was insulting to
her maturity. She flicked her hair over her shoulder. "Goddamnit,"
she said finally, making sure that the words were low enough so
that neither God nor Lucía would hear them.

There seemed to be no way out of this custom either. Her
arguments were always the same and always turned into pleas. This
morning was no different. Amá, Naomi said, exasperated, but determined not to back out of this one, Amá, América is different. Here

girls don't need chaperones. Mothers trust their daughters. As usual Amá turned to the kitchen sink or the icebox, shrugged her shoulders and said: You have to ask your father. Naomi's nostrils flexed in fury as she said, But Amá, it's so embarrassing. I'm too old for that; I am an adult. And as usual, Apá felt different and in his house, she had absolutely no other choice but to drag Lucía to a sock hop or church carnival or anywhere Apá was sure she would be found around boys. Lucía came along as a spy, a gnat, a pain in the neck.

Well, Naomi debated with herself; it wasn't Lucía's fault, really. She suddenly felt sympathy for the humming little girl who scrambled to keep up with her as they crossed the freeway over-pass. She stopped and tugged Lucía's shorts up, and although her shoelaces were tied, Naomi retied them. No, it wasn't her fault after all, Naomi thought, and she patted her sister's soft light brown and almost blondish hair, it was Apá's. She slowed her pace as they continued their journey to Fierro's house. It was Apá who refused to trust her and she could not understand what she had done to make him so distrustful. *Tú eres mujer*, he thundered, and that was the end of any argument, any question, and the matter was closed because he said those three words as if they were a condemnation from the heavens and so she couldn't be trusted. Naomi tightened her grasp with the thought, shaking her head in disbelief.

"Really," she said out loud.

"Wait up. Wait," Lucía said, rushing behind her.

"Well would you hurry. Would you?" Naomi reconsidered: Lucía did have some fault in the matter after all, and she became irritated at once at Lucía's smile and the way her chaperone had of taking and holding her hand. As they passed El Gallo, Lucía began fussing, grabbing onto her older sister's waist for reassurance and hung onto it.

"Stop it. Would you stop it?" She unglued her sister's grasp and continued pulling her along. "What's wrong with you?" she asked Lucía. I'll tell you what's wrong with you, she thought, as they waited at the corner of an intersection for the light to change: You have a big mouth. That's it. If it wasn't for Lucía's willingness to provide information, she would not have been grounded for three months. Three months, 12 Saturday nights, and two church bazaars later, Naomi still hadn't forgiven her youngest sister. When they crossed the street, a homely young man with a face full of acne honked at her tight purple pedal pushers. The two were startled by the honk.

"Go to hell," she yelled at the man in the blue and white chevy. She indignantly continued her walk.

"Don't be mad, baby," he said, his car crawling across the street, then speeding off leaving tracks on the pavement, "You make me ache," he yelled, and he was gone.

"GO TO HELL, Goddamn you!" she screamed at the top of her lungs forgetting for a moment that Lucía told everything to Apá. What a big mouth her youngest sister had, for christsakes. Three months.

Naomi stewed in anger when she thought of the Salesian Carnival and how she first made eye contact with a Letterman Senior whose eyes, she remembered with a soft smile, sparkled like crystals of brown sugar. She sighed as she recalled the excitement she experienced when she first became aware that he was following them from booth to booth. Joe's hair was greased back to a perfect sculptured ducktail and his dimples were deep. When he finally handed her a stuffed rabbit he had won pitching dimes, she knew she wanted him.

As they continued walking, Lucía waved to the Fruit Man. He slipped his teeth off and again, she was bewildered.

"Would you hurry up!" Naomi ordered Lucía as she had the night at the Carnival. Joe walked beside them and he took out a whole roll of tickets, trying to convince her to leave her youngest sister on the ferris wheel. "You could watch her from behind the gym," he had told her, and his eyes smiled pleasure. "Come on," he said, "have a little fun." They waited in the ferris wheel line of people. Finally:

"Stay on the ride," she instructed Lucía, making sure her sweater was buttoned. "And when it stops again, just give the man another ticket, okay?" Lucía said okay, excited at the prospect of highs and lows and her stomach wheezing in between. After Naomi saw her go up for the first time, she waved to her, then slipped away into the darkness and joined the other hungry couples behind the gym. Occasionally, she would open her eyes to see the lights of the ferris wheel spinning in the air with dizzy speed.

When Naomi returned to the ferris wheel, her hair undone, her lips still tingling from his newly stubbled cheeks, Lucía walked off and vomited. Lucía vomited the popcorn, a hot dog, some chocolate raisins, and a candied apple, and all Naomi knew was that she was definitely in trouble.

"It was the ferris wheel," Lucía said to Apá. "The wheel going like this over and over again." She circled her arms in the air and vomited again at the thought of it.

"Where was your sister?" Apá had asked, his voice rising.

"I don't know," Lucía replied, and Naomi knew she had just committed a major offense, and that Joe would never wait until her prison sentence was completed.

"Owww," Lucía said. "You're pulling too hard."

"You're a slow poke, that's why," Naomi snarled back. They crossed the street and passed the rows of junk yards and the shells of cars which looked like abandoned skull heads. They passed Señora Nuñez's neat, wooden house and Naomi saw her peeking through the curtains of her window. They passed the "TU y YO," the one-room dirt pit of a liquor store where the men bought their beers and sat outside on the curb drinking quietly. When they reached Fourth Street, Naomi spotted the neighborhood kids playing stickball with a broomstick and a ball. Naomi recognized them right away and Tina waved to her from the pitcher's mound.

"Wanna play?" Lourdes yelled from center field. "Come on, have some fun."

"Can't." Naomi replied. "I can't." Kids, kids, she thought. My, my. It wasn't more than a few years ago that she played baseball with Eloy and the rest of them. But she was in high school now, too old now, and it was unbecoming of her. She was an adult.

"I'm tired," Lucía said. "I wanna ice cream."

"You got money?"

"No."

"Then shut up."

Lucía sat on the curb, hot and tired, and she began removing her sweater. Naomi decided to sit down next to her for a few minutes and watch the game. Anyway, she wasn't really in that much of a hurry to get to Fierro's. A few minutes wouldn't make much difference to someone who spent most of his time listening to the radio.

She counted them by names. They were all there. Fifteen of them and their ages varied just as much as their clothes. Pants, skirts, shorts were always too big and had to be tugged up constantly, and shirt sleeves rolled and unrolled, or socks mismatched with shoes that didn't fit. But the way they dressed presented no obstacle for scoring or yelling foul and she enjoyed the zealous abandonment with which they played. She knew that the only decision these kids possibly made was what to play next, and she wished to be younger.

Chano's team was up. The teams were oddly numbered. Chano had nine on his team because everybody wanted to be in a winning team. It was an unwritten law of stickball that anyone who wanted to play joined whatever team they preferred. Tina's team had the family faithful 6. Of course numbers determined nothing. Naomi remembered once playing with Eloy and three of her cousins against ten kids, and still winning by three points.

Chano was at bat and everybody fanned out far and wide. He was a power hitter and Tina's team prepared for him. They couldn't afford a homerun now because Piri was on second, legs apart, waiting to rush home and score a crucial point. And Piri wanted to score it at all costs. It was important for him because his father sat out-side the liquor store with a couple of his uncles and a couple of malt liquors watching the game.

"Steal the base!" his father yelled. "Run, menso!" But Piri hesitated. He was too afraid to take the risk. Tina pitched and Chano swung, missed, strike one.

"Batter, batter, swing!" Naomi yelled from the curb. She stood up to watch the action better.

"I wanna ice cream," Lucía said.

"Come on, Chano!" Piri yelled, bending his knees and resting his hands on them like a true baseball player. He spat, clapped his hands. "Come on."

"Ah, shut up, sissy." This came from Lourdes, Tina's younger sister. Naomi smiled at the rivals. "Can't you see you're making the pitcher nervous?" and she pushed him hard between the shoulder blades, then returned to her position in the outfield, holding her hand over her eyes to shield them from the sun. "Strike the batter out," she screamed at the top of her lungs. "Come on, strike the menso out!" Tina delivered another pitch, but not before going through the motions of a professional preparing for the perfect pitch. Naomi knew she was a much better pitcher than Tina. Strike two. Maybe not, and Lourdes let out such a taunting grito of joy that Piri's father called her a dog.

Chano was angry now, nervous and upset. He put his bat down, spat in his hands and rubbed them together, wiped the sides of his jeans, kicked the dirt for perfect footing.

"Get on with the game!" Naomi shouted impatiently. Chano swung a couple of times to test his swing. He swung so hard he caused Juan, Tina's brother and devoted catcher, to jump back.

"Hey baboso, watch out," he said. "You almost hit my coco." And he pointed to his forehead.

"Well, don't be so stupid," Chano replied, positioning himself once again. "Next time back off when I come to bat."

"Baboso," Juan repeated.

"Say it to my face," Chano said, breaking his stand and turning to Juan, "say it again so I could break this bat over your head."

"Ah, come on, Kiki," the shortstop yelled, "I gotta go home pretty soon."

"Let up," Tina demanded.

"Shut up marrana," Piri said, turning to his father to make sure he heard. "Tinasana, cola de marrana, Tinasana, cola de marrana." Tina became so infuriated that she threw the ball directly to his stomach. Piri folded over in pain.

"No! No!" Sylvia yelled. "Don't get off the base or she'll tag you out!"

"It's a trick!" Miguel yelled from behind home plate.

"That's what you get!" This came from Lourdes. Piri did not move, and for a moment Naomi felt sorry for him, but giggled at the scene anyway.

"I heard the ice cream man," Lucía said.

"You're all right, Tina," Naomi yelled, laughing, "you're A-O-K." And with that compliment, Tina bowed, proud of her performance until everyone began shouting, "STOP WASTING TIME!" Tina was prepared. She pitched and Chano made the connection quick, hard, the ball rising high and flying over her head, Piri's, Lourdes', Naomi's and Lucía's, and landed inside the Chinese Cemetery.

"DON'T JUST STAND THERE!" Tina screamed at Lourdes. "Go get it, stupid!" After Lourdes broke out of her trance, she ran to the tall, chain-link fence which surrounded the cemetery, jumped on the fence and crawled up like a scrambling spider, her dress tearing with a rip roar.

"We saw your calzones, we saw your calzones," Lucía sang.

"Go! Lourdes, go!" Naomi jumped up and down in excitement,

feeling like a player who although benched in the sidelines, was dying to get out there and help her team win. The kids blended into one huge noise, like an untuned orchestra, screaming and shouting Get the Ball, Run in Piri, Go Lourdes, Go throw the ball Chano pick up your feet throw the ballrunrunrunrunthrow the ball. "THROW the ball to me!!" Naomi waved and waved her arms. For that moment she forgot all about 'growing up,' her period, her breasts that bounced with glee. All she wanted was an out on home base. To hell with being benched. "Throw it to me," she yelled.

In the meantime, Lourdes searched frantically for the ball, tiptoeing across the graves saying Excuse me, please excuse me, excuse me, until she found the ball peacefully buried behind a huge gray marble stone, and she yelled to no one in particular, CATCH IT, SOMEONE CATCH IT! She threw the ball up and over the fence and it landed near Lucía. Lucía was about to reach for the ball when Naomi picked it off the ground and threw it straight to Tina. Tina caught the ball, dropped it, picked it up, and was about to throw the ball to Juan at homeplate, when she realized that Juan had picked up the homeplate and ran, zig-zagging across the street while Piri and Chano ran after him. Chano was a much faster runner, but Piri insisted that he be the first to touch the base.

"I gotta touch it first," he kept repeating between pantings, "I gotta."

The kids on both teams grew wild with anger and encouragement. Seeing an opportunity, Tina ran as fast as her stocky legs could take her. Because Chano slowed down to let Piri touch the base first, Tina was able to reach him, and with one quick blow, she thundered OUT! She threw one last desperate throw to Juan so that he could tag Piri out, but she threw it so hard that it struck Piri right in the back of his head, and the blow forced him to stumble just within reach of Juan and homeplate.

"You're out!!" Tina said, out of breath. "O-U-T, out."

"No fair!" Piri immediately screamed. "NO FAIR!!" He stomped his feet in rage like Rumpelstiltskin. "You marrana, you marrana."

"Don't be such a baby," Piri's father said. "Take it like a man," he said as he opened another malt liquor with a can opener. But Piri continued stomping and screaming until his shouts were buried by the honk of an oncoming car and the kids obediently opened up like the red sea to let the car pass.

Naomi felt like a victor. She had helped, once again. Delighted, she giggled, laughed, laughed harder, suppressed her laughter into chuckles, then laughed again. Lucía sat quietly, to her surprise, and her eyes were heavy with sleep. She wiped them, looked at Naomi. "Vamos," Naomi said, offering her hand. By the end of the block, she lifted Lucía and laid her head on her shoulder. As Lucía fell asleep, Naomi wondered why things were always so complicated when you became older. Funny how the old want to be young and the young want to be old. Now that she was older, her obligations became heavier both at home and at school. There were too many demands on her, and no one showed her how to fulfill them, and wasn't it crazy? She cradled Lucía gently, kissed her cheek. They were almost at Fierro's now, and reading to him was just one more thing she dreaded doing, and one more thing she had no control over: it was another one of Apá's thunderous commands.

When she was Lucía's age, she hunted for lizards and played stickball with her cousins until her body began to bleed at 12, and Eloy saw her in a different light. Under the house, he sucked her swelling nipples and became jealous. He no longer wanted to throw rocks at the cars on the freeway with her and she began to act different because everyone began treating her different and wasn't it crazy? She could no longer be herself and her father could no longer trust her because she was a woman. Fierro's gate hung on a hinge and she was almost afraid it would fall off when she opened it. She felt Lucía's warm, deep, breath on her neck and it tickled her momentarily. Enjoy, she whispered to Lucía, enjoy being a young girl, because you will never enjoy being a woman.

JUAN DELGADO

Juan Delgado's poems have appeared in Best New Chicano Literature 1989, *an annual that recognizes the work of emerging writers. He attended the University of California, Irvine, and is the author of* My Green Army.

THE PHONE BOOTH
AT THE CORNER

Grandfather took a walk
down to the neighborhood bar.
That day mother had placed me
under his care—
at sixty he was visiting us
for the first time.

We stopped near a phone booth.
Outside the bar in a cage
a parrot whistled back at us.

The phone began to ring.
Grandfather pushed the door,
forgetting he spoke only Spanish.
He raised the phone to his ear:
there was nothing he could do.

Again, he pushed the door.
He didn't understand
it was divided by hinges
and would only open by pulling in.
He pushed even harder—I could see
the fear in his face grow with his effort.

We were both unable to speak
as we pushed for what seemed minutes.
He finally stopped—exhausted
and the door opened.

He stepped out laughing.
I began to laugh with him
and the bird whistled.
All three of us
broke the air with our voices.

ROSALINDA HERNÁNDEZ

Rosalinda Hernández was one of the 1989 winners in the Chicano Literary Contest, sponsored each year by the University of California at Irvine. The contest recognizes the work of emerging writers.

A P Á

Calloused hands and sun-chapped skin
in the fields of ripened harvest
awakening the dawn
returning not 'till the sun came down
The aroma of tossed-up dirt
fertile soil on your boots
a familiar scent of labor
though fatigued and dismayed
the battle remained within

   "Go to school m'ija," you'd say
   "I work hard for you could be
   all I was not able
   learn to use your head and not your back
   like me
   who could only fight this battle with stones"

Then speaking of the hunger
the death of the twins
A story well recorded in my mind
of your many past seasons of tears
with a father lost in the bars
a brother behind them
a man at twelve with a struggle ahead
wearing shoes too big
too small

with six sisters under your years
a lonely walk in a boisterous wind

"Go to school m'ija,
learn to use your head and not your back
like me
who could only fight this battle with stones"

A lacerated heart
open wounds which never healed
a well-petrified man through your time
hardened and cold
A storm of bitterness escaping your breath
as you relived the days
when the world gave you its back
"Sorry Meskin, there's no job for you here"
A sting eternally felt
Charcoaled eyes
the inferno of your fury
now smoldered with helplessness

"Go to school m'ija"
now more a plea than a demand
"Learn to use your head and not your back
like me
who fought all my days with a handful of stones"

Still grieving past seasons
of picking and plowing
from state to shack
shack to state
a temporary existence
of a migrant of time
reaping the harvest
of a lifeblood of famine
plagued by shadow
a darkness you could not escape
owning nothing but the clothes in a sack
and a pocketful of stones
to fight back with

It is your life Apá
a story told by a pauper's silent shout

A shout that grew to be my own
yet here I am today
learning to use my head and not my back
but like you
only able to fight this battle with stones

JUANITA M. SÁNCHEZ

*Juanita Sánchez is a native New Mexican of mixed Chicana and
American Indian ancestry. Besides being a poet, she has degrees in
psychology and human resource development, and works as a machinist
and union activist. She sponsors "A Festival of Women's Poetry" in
Albuquerque, where she lives with her two dogs and two cats in an
adobe home.*

CIPRIANITA

lita who spoke to the wild
    brought to the river
crickets and their songs
    brought to the river her drum
and the sound of a cat's paw
    beating on my chest

lita
    i wish i could have been with you
in those years when there were no weapons
    that would cause giant mushrooms
on the earth and scars on the faces of the east
    erupting, later, in the hearts of the children

how hateful the times of my years
    my witness to these politics
systems of money above need
    yet

lita
    was it really any better when you were growing,
speaking only spanish, then as a widow
    you had three children to raise
in the united states?

but you had it all
    your oil lamps, metate, flowered apron

and the clothes line with your hanging corn,
    carne seca, red chile
chile so hot our ears burned

remember, lita, when i went with you to sears
    to help you find a dress with pockets
it had to have pockets
    little bolsitas to hold your cigarettes
and leather snap-together coin purse
    remember, lita, we were both afraid of the escalator
the moving stairs made us dizzy
    we weren't ready for high-tech then . . .
oh then, when we were driving home
    us kids in the back seat of the '48 olds
you pulled out bags of chip potatoes
    we thought you were so rich
to give us each a bag
    and i loved playing with the hairs under your chin
you said god gave them to you so why pull them out

lita
    you died too soon
fifty-five year old grandmother
    telling us stories in spanish
that kept us awake all night
    not because they were long
but because they were scary
    i never could sleep in your house
with all the fear i had
    of the ghosts that visited you
the hand of my young dead cousin knocking
    on your bed post and crawling toward your pillow

one time
    when i put paint on my face
you told me that my skin was going to fall off
    and i'd wake up a skeleton
puro huesos y nada más que huesos
    i couldn't sleep because i kept touching my face and hands
to make sure the skin was still there

lita
    you died too soon
remember the pact you made with my mother
    you told her that you would teach me spanish
and she would teach me english
    i learned your language
but you left me too much in the hands
    of the gringo schools
they didn't like what you taught me
    they made me over
it hurt, lita, it hurt so bad
    but i promised you, lita
i promised to remember all you told me
    even the scary stories and sleepless nights
that i would pass them on
    and you could live forever

lita
    you did speak to the wild
i can still hear the songs you whistled
    still smell the tortillas on the iron stove
still taste the ground chile on the stone
    hey lita!
i can speak spanish real good now
    ¡oigame lita!
es tu idioma, ¿recuerdas?
    ¡lita!
i feel the cat on my chest again
    your drum   i imagine

GARY SOTO

Gary Soto was born in Fresno, California in 1952 and worked as a migrant laborer while growing up. "I don't think I had any literary aspirations when I was kid," he says. "I went to a city college, and my intention was to major in geography, but then I gravitated toward literature." He has published numerous collections of poems, including Living up the Street, *which won the American Book Award in 1985, and teaches English and Chicano Studies.*

ORANGES

The first time I walked
With a girl, I was twelve,
Cold, and weighted down
With two oranges in my jacket.
December. Frost cracking
Beneath my steps, my breath
Before me, then gone,
As I walked toward
Her house, the one whose
Porch light burned yellow
Night and day, in any weather.
A dog barked at me, until
She came out pulling
At her gloves, face bright
With rouge. I smiled,
Touched her shoulder, and led
Her down the street, across
A used car lot and a line
Of newly planted trees,
Until we were breathing
Before a drugstore. We
Entered, the tiny bell
Bringing a saleslady
Down a narrow aisle of goods.

I turned to the candies
Tiered like bleachers,
And asked what she wanted—
Light in her eyes, a smile
Starting at the corners
Of her mouth. I fingered
A nickel in my pocket,
And when she lifted a chocolate
That cost a dime,
I didn't say anything.
I took the nickel from
My pocket, then an orange,
And set them quietly on
The counter. When I looked up,
The lady's eyes met mine,
And held them, knowing
Very well what it was all
About.

    Outside,
A few cars hissing past,
Fog hanging like old
Coats between the trees.
I took my girl's hand
In mine for two blocks,
Then released it to let
Her unwrap the chocolate.
I peeled my orange
That was so bright against
The gray of December
That, from some distance
Someone might have thought
I was making a fire in my hands.

FURTHER READINGS

All references are to most recent editions of works cited.

Rudolfo A. Anaya. *Heart of Aztlán*. Albuquerque: University of New Mexico Press, 1988. When the Chávez family is forced to move from a rural village to an Albuquerque barrio, the teenage children face new temptations and challenge old values. The family's spirit is renewed when a magical vision reveals the meaning of the mythical Aztlán. Anaya celebrates the power of imagination in a drab, mechanistic world. An excerpt from another Anaya novel appears on page 85 of this volume.

Ron Arías. *The Road to Tamazunchale*. Tempe, Arizona: Bilingual Press, 1987. An old man spends his last days traveling—in his imagination, that is—to a land where he can be free of restrictions. Reality occasionally barges in, but it soon becomes part of the fantasy.

Best New Chicano Literature 1989. Julian Palley, editor. Tempe, Arizona: Bilingual Press, 1989. This anthology of stories and poems by new and emerging writers includes works in Spanish and English and covers a variety of topics. The selections are chosen through a contest for new writers conducted by the University of California, Irvine. The contest has been conducted annually since the early 1980s.

Nash Candelaria. *Not By the Sword*. Tempe, Arizona: Bilingual Press, 1982. Twin brothers must defend the Rafa family's land during and after the conquest of what is now New Mexico by the United States. Tercerio, a priest, and his reckless brother, Carlos, face challenges to personal and family honor. This historical novel is the second in a series about the Rafa family.

Ana Castillo. *My Father Was a Toltec*. Novato, California: West End Press, 1988. This collection of Castillo's poems is drawn from subjects of everyday life in a Chicago inner-city neighborhood. Some are lyric, some narrative, and the tone ranges from angry to hopeful. She recalls her childhood as the daughter of a street warrior, a member of the Toltec gang, and fights to define herself in her own way.

Denise Chávez. *The Last of the Menu Girls*. Houston: Arte Público, 1986. "There's stories, plenty of them all around," the narrator's mother advises. The stories in this novel center on a young Chicana's first job as hospital menu-girl, her drama class, and observations up and down the street.

Sandra Cisneros. *The House on Mango Street*. New York: Vintage, 1991. The novel is told in the words of a young Chicana girl living in a tough, urban neighborhood. Through her writing she comes to realize her strengths, shortcomings, determination, and losses. Underneath the simple style are complex issues of poverty, discrimination, and individual freedom.

Cuentos: Stories by Latinas. Alma Gómez, Cherríe Moraga, and Mariana Romo-Carmona, editors. Latham, New York: Kitchen Table/Women of Color Press, 1983. An anthology that includes stories by both well-known and less familiar women writers. Most of the stories are in English, but a few appear only in Spanish. Covering a variety of subjects, the stories are firmly rooted in the Southwest and western United States. Two pieces of particular note are Amina Susan Ali's "Teenage Zombie" and Rocky Gámez's "Doña Marciana García."

Mexican American Literature. Charles Tatum, editor. San Diego: Harcourt Brace Jovanovich, 1990. This anthology includes poems by Pat Mora and prose by Sandra Cisneros, among the works of many other contemporary Mexican American authors. An exceptional short story is Gary Soto's "Like Mexicans," which is all about marrying the "right" kind of girl.

Nicholasa Mohr. *El Bronx Remembered*. Houston: Arte Público, 1986. These stories about life in a Puerto Rican neighborhood in

New York City show determination, acceptance, puzzlement, and love. One of the stories, "A Very Special Pet," appears on page 98 of this volume.

Nosotras: Latina Literature Today. Maria Del Carmen Boza, Beverly Silva, and Carmen Valle, editors. Tempe, Arizona: Bilingual Press, 1986. This anthology collects stories and poems by women from Puerto Rico, Cuba, Mexico, and Latin America who are now living and writing in the United States. Achy Obejas' "The Escape" is a particularly moving story about a young Cuban refugee struggling with life-and-death decisions after arriving in Miami.

Alberto Alvaro Ríos. *The Iguana Killer: Twelve Stories of the Heart*. Lewiston, Idaho: Blue Moon Press, 1984. The title story from this collection appears on page 106 of this volume.

Tomás Rivera. . . . *Y no se lo tragó la tierra/ . . . And the Earth Did Not Part*. Herminio Rios, translator. Berkeley: Editorial Justa, 1977. A collage of twelve loosely connected sketches focusing on Chicano migrant workers during the 1950s. Although the events described are often of unspeakable hardships, the characters show that knowledge and wisdom can be salvaged from any experience. Each chapter is told first in Spanish, then in English. This novel won the Quinto Sol literary award in 1970.

Gary Soto. *The Elements of San Joaquin*. Pittsburg: University of Pittsburg Press, 1977. Soto's poems present a compelling view of contemporary Chicano life. The reader is transported southward from Fresno and the San Joaquin Valley farms to Taxco in central Mexico, the town where, as Soto's narrator puts it, "we all begin." This first volume was followed by many others, including *Black Hair* (1985) and *Small Faces* (1986). Soto's poem, "Oranges," appears on page 134 of this volume.

This Bridge Called My Back: Writings by Radical Women of Color. Cherríe Moraga and Gloria Anzaldúa, editors. Latham, New York: Kitchen Table/Women of Color Press, 1983. Gloria Anzaldúa, Cherríe Moraga, and Rosario Morales are among contributors of essays and poems on growing up, invisibility, feminism, and Third World women in the United States. These works, all written in the 1970s, have the raw energy of first-generation politics, but still have much to say about race and gender, and about privilege or the lack of it.

AFRICAN AMERICAN SELECTIONS

THE KALEIDOSCOPE
OF SELF
AN INTRODUCTORY ESSAY

THERE IS an uncommon quality of language and form within the African American tradition that addresses its audience on several levels at once. For example, writers employ lyrics, rhythmic structure, and attitudes from spirituals, ballads, blues, and jazz to convey a diversity of ideas. Dramatic elements of the oral tradition, such as the call and response of the folk sermon, likewise are used to summon images of Black history and orientation.

African American authors offer an astonishing array of subjects, yet it is not content alone that distinguishes this literature, but emphasis, tone, nuance, and the possibilities of interpretation. History, environment, gender, kin, faith and introspection form a matrix from which a stream of ideas flow.

The image of Africa is both concrete reality and metaphor. In many ways the social history of Black people shapes and is shaped by perceptions of a rich, ancient culture.

Every writer's—and every reader's—encounter with American slavery is uniquely transforming. The more we uncover about the history of slavery, the more we stand to learn about slavery's symbolic meanings and its tenacious hold on us. The wrenching of millions of Africans from their homelands to slavery in new environments raises questions about the spiritual foundation of our nation. The reality of bondage, coexisting with democracy, defined freedom in a contradictory way that remains so to this day. This irony has enshrined both faith and cynicism as the household deities of Black writers. The richness with which African American literature presents and embraces this duality is one of its signature qualities.

HOMESCAPES

The significance of place in African American literature is persistent, and geographic references figure prominently in setting, perspective, and characterization. African American migration from the rural South to other regions, as well as to cities, presents a broad framework of contrasting experiences.

Fifty years ago, the most dynamic literary images of Black life focused on the city. Graphic portrayals of social dysfunction, violence, hedonism, and decay seemed to leave no room for recollections of old homesteads or visions of new ones. The terrain of contemporary African American literature recognizes no boundaries, ranging from local to cosmic, shifting from images of an inner-city playground to an alien mothership, drifting through galactic oceans.

BEING FEMALE AND BLACK

The real-life struggles between women and men have never been absent from African American literature. Black women writers have created their own languages for describing the constraints of inequality, while showing the possibilities of justice within their families and society as a whole.

Each generation of writers has chosen its own expressions, forged its own actions, discarded historical assumptions and, in the process, established new rules for intimacy and the inviolable right to relationships. The lives of African American women are being reconstructed from deep experience. Intimacy is not romanticized; neither is the need for intimacy denied. Out of the mouths of their characters, these women writers have extended new invitations for growth and reconciliation.

THE WEB OF KINSHIP

The African American family has survived and adapted to a hostile environment. Black authors draw on a heritage that places kinship at the center of its world view. From this perspective, men's expectations and women's exploitation often exist within the framework of family obligation, which can be stifling as well as reassuring.

African American literature challenges the myth that the Black family was destroyed during slavery, yet does not ignore the psychological and emotional damage caused by racism, poverty, and hopelessness. Instead Black writers are illuminating the strengths of families, showing complex extended kin relations and new configurations of traditional family structure. The very best of these works offer human personalities instead of archetypes, struggle as opposed to defeat, and depth-of-field in contrast to one-dimensional racial philosophy.

KEEPING AND QUESTIONING THE FAITH

Much more has been presumed than understood about the spiritual orientation of Black people in America. Literature reveals both the public act of religious ritual and the profoundly private process of introspection.

Portrayals of religious belief range from devout and hopeful to skeptical and bitter. It could not be otherwise, if one considers not only what was done to African Americans in the name of the Christian God, but also how Christianity has become a part of the struggle for Black liberation.

We must also recognize and celebrate other spiritual orientations, including Islam, animism, and what I would call a reverence for the family of all the elements that constitute our ecosystem. The dedication that African American writers demonstrate toward these themes supports the argument that their literature is universal, in the true sense of the word.

BENEATH THE COLOR LINE

Many contemporary African American writers are writing stories and poems that have not been crafted within the exclusive parameters of race. The extension of personal identity beyond factors of genealogy, physical appearance, and social affiliations has created a vigorous and diverse body of literature and criticism.

The African American literary tradition displays a heightened degree of introspection through which readers may perceive a kaleidoscope of Black selfhood. A series of revelations about ourselves and our nation gives dimension to the work of such authors as Audre Lorde and James Baldwin, who inspire us to question everything we assume about America, while a much different perspective is offered by writers such as Zora Neale Hurston and Langston Hughes.

The works of these writers and others included in this anthology are part of the body of literature designated as African American. The differences within that designation allow us to examine region, class, and gender, along with race, all as expressions of African American identity.

Musa Moore-Foster
St. Paul, Minnesota

JAMES BALDWIN

James Baldwin, born in Harlem in 1924, was a major voice of black America in the 1950s and 1960s through his essays and novels. Books like Notes of a Native Son, The Fire Next Time, Go Tell It on the Mountain, *and* Another Country *have been translated all over the world. He died in 1987.*

SONNY'S BLUES

I READ ABOUT IT in the paper, in the subway, on my way to work. I read it, and I couldn't believe it, and I read it again. Then perhaps I just stared at it, at the newsprint spelling out his name, spelling out the story. I stared at it in the swinging lights of the subway car, and in the faces and bodies of the people, and in my own face, trapped in the darkness which roared outside.

It was not to be believed and I kept telling myself that, as I walked from the subway station to the high school. And at the same time I couldn't doubt it. I was scared, scared for Sonny. He became real to me again. A great block of ice got settled in my belly and kept melting there slowly all day long, while I taught my classes algebra. It was a special kind of ice. It kept melting, sending trickles of ice water all up and down my veins, but it never got less. Sometimes it hardened and seemed to expand until I felt my guts were going to come spilling out or that I was going to choke or scream. This would always be at a moment when I was remembering some specific thing Sonny had once said or done.

When he was about as old as the boys in my class his face had been bright and open, there was a lot of copper in it; and he'd had wonderfully direct brown eyes, and great gentleness and privacy. I wondered what he looked like now. He had been picked up, the evening before, in a raid on an apartment downtown, for peddling and using heroin.

I couldn't believe it: but what I mean by that is that I couldn't find any room for it anywhere inside me. I had kept it outside me for a long time. I hadn't wanted to know. I had had suspicions, but I didn't name them, I kept putting them away. I told myself that Sonny was wild, but he wasn't crazy. And he'd always been a good boy, he hadn't ever turned hard or evil or disrespectful, the way kids can, so quick, so quick especially in Harlem. I didn't want to believe that I'd ever see my brother going down, coming to nothing, all that light in his face gone out, in the condition I'd already seen so many others. Yet it had happened and here I was, talking about algebra to a lot of boys who might, every one of them for all I knew, be popping off needles every time they went to the head. Maybe it did more for them than algebra could.

I was sure that the first time Sonny had ever had horse, he couldn't have been much older than these boys were now. These boys, now, were living as we'd been living then, they were growing up with a rush and their heads bumped abruptly against the low ceiling of their actual possibilities. They were filled with rage. All they really knew were two darknesses, the darkness of their lives, which was now closing in on them, and the darkness of the movies, which had blinded them to that other darkness, and in which they now, vindictively, dreamed, at once more together than they were at any other time, and more alone.

When the last bell rang, the last class ended, I let out my breath. It seemed I'd been holding it for all that time. My clothes were wet—I may have looked as though I'd been sitting in a steam bath, all dressed up, all afternoon. I sat alone in the classroom a long time. I listened to the boys outside, downstairs, shouting and cursing and laughing. Their laughter struck me for perhaps the first time. It was not the joyous laughter which—God knows why—one associates with children. It was mocking and insular, its intent was to denigrate. It was disenchanted, and in this, also, lay the authority of their curses. Perhaps I was listening to them because I was thinking about my brother and in them I heard my brother. And myself.

One boy was whistling a tune, at once very complicated and very simple, it seemed to be pouring out of him as though he were a bird, and it sounded very cool and moving through all that harsh, bright air, only just holding its own through all those other sounds.

I stood up and walked over to the window and looked down into the courtyard. It was the beginning of the spring and the sap was rising in the boys. A teacher passed through them every now and again, quickly, as though he or she couldn't wait to get out of that courtyard, to get those boys out of their sight and off their minds. I started collecting my stuff. I thought I'd better get home and talk to Isabel.

The courtyard was almost deserted by the time I got downstairs. I saw this boy standing in the shadow of a doorway, looking just like Sonny. I almost called his name. Then I saw that it wasn't Sonny, but somebody we used to know, a boy from around our block. He'd been Sonny's friend. He'd never been mine, having been too young for me, and, anyway, I'd never liked him. And now, even though he was a grown-up man, he still hung around that block, still spent hours on the street corners, was always high and raggy. I used to run into him from time to time and he'd often work around to asking me for a quarter or fifty cents. He always had some real good excuse, too, and I always gave it to him, I don't know why.

But now, abruptly, I hated him. I couldn't stand the way he looked at me, partly like a dog, partly like a cunning child. I wanted to ask him what the hell he was doing in the school courtyard.

He sort of shuffled over to me, and he said, "I see you got the papers. So you already know about it."

"You mean about Sonny? Yes. I already know about it. How come they didn't get you?"

He grinned. It made him repulsive and it also brought to mind what he'd looked like as a kid. "I wasn't there. I stay away from them people."

"Good for you." I offered him a cigarette and I watched him through the smoke. "You come all the way down here just to tell me about Sonny?"

"That's right." He was sort of shaking his head and his eyes looked strange, as though they were about to cross. The bright sun deadened his damp dark brown skin and it made his eyes look yellow and showed up the dirt in his kinked hair. He smelled funky. I moved a little away from him and I said, "Well, thanks. But I already know about it and I got to get home."

"I'll walk you a little ways," he said. We started walking. There were a couple of kids still loitering in the courtyard and one of them said goodnight to me and looked strangely at the boy beside me.

"What're you going to do?" he asked me. "I mean, about Sonny?"

"Look, I haven't seen Sonny for over a year, I'm not sure I'm going to do anything. Anyway, what the hell *can* I do?"

"That's right," he said quickly, "ain't nothing you can do. Can't much help old Sonny no more, I guess."

It was what I was thinking and so it seemed to me he had no right to say it.

"I'm surprised at Sonny, though," he went on—he had a funny way of talking, he looked straight ahead as though he were talking to himself—"I thought Sonny was a smart boy, I thought he was too smart to get hung."

"I guess he thought so too," I said sharply, "and that's how he got hung. And now about you? You're pretty goddamn smart, I bet."

Then he looked directly at me, just for a minute. "I ain't smart," he said. "If I was smart, I'd have reached for a pistol a long time ago."

"Look. Don't tell *me* your sad story, if it was up to me, I'd give you one." Then I felt guilty—guilty, probably, for never having supposed that the poor bastard *had* a story of his own, much less a sad one, and I asked quickly, "What's going to happen to him now?"

He didn't answer this. He was off by himself some place. "Funny thing," he said, and from his tone we might have been discussing the quickest way to get to Brooklyn, "when I saw the papers this morning, the first thing I asked myself was if I had anything to do with it. I felt sort of responsible."

I began to listen more carefully. The subway station was on the corner, just before us, and I stopped. He stopped, too. We were in front of a bar and he ducked slightly, peering in, but whoever he was looking for didn't seem to be there. The juke box was blasting away with something black and bouncy and I half watched the barmaid as she danced her way from the juke box to her place behind the bar. And I watched her face as she laughingly responded to something someone said to her, still keeping time to the music. When she smiled one saw the little girl, one sensed the doomed, still-struggling woman beneath the battered face of the semi-whore.

"I never *give* Sonny nothing," the boy said finally, "but a long time ago I come to school high and Sonny asked me how it felt." He paused, I couldn't bear to watch him, I watched the barmaid, and I listened to the music which seemed to be causing the pavement to shake. "I told him it felt great." The music stopped, the barmaid paused and watched the juke box until the music began again. "It did."

All this was carrying me some place I didn't want to go. I certainly didn't want to know how it felt. It filled everything, the people, the houses, the music, the dark, quicksilver barmaid, with menace; and this menace was their reality.

"What's going to happen to him now?" I asked again.

"They'll send him away some place and they'll try to cure him." He shook his head. "Maybe he'll even think he's kicked the habit. Then they'll let him loose"– he gestured, throwing his cigarette into the gutter. "That's all."

"What do you mean, that's *all?*"

But I knew what he meant.

"I *mean*, that's all." He turned his head and looked at me, pulling down the corners of his mouth. "Don't you know what I mean?" he asked, softly.

"How the hell *would* I know what you mean?" I almost whispered it, I don't know why.

"That's right," he said to the air, "how would *he* know what I mean?" He turned toward me again, patient and calm, and yet I somehow felt him shaking, shaking as though he were going to fall apart. I felt that ice in my guts again, the dread I'd felt all afternoon; and again I watched the barmaid, moving about the bar, washing glasses, and singing. "Listen. They'll let him out and then it'll just start all over again. That's what I mean."

"You mean–they'll let him out. And then he'll just start working his way back in again. You mean he'll never kick the habit. Is that what you mean?"

"That's right," he said, cheerfully. "*You* see what I mean."

"Tell me," I said at last, "why does he want to die? He must want to die, he's killing himself, why does he want to die?"

He looked at me in surprise. He licked his lips, "He don't want to die. He wants to live. Don't nobody want to die, ever."

Then I wanted to ask him–too many things. He could not have answered, or if he had, I could not have borne the answers. I started walking. "Well, I guess it's none of my business."

"It's going to be rough on old Sonny," he said. We reached the subway station. "This is your station?" he asked. I nodded. I took one step down. "Damn!" he said suddenly. I looked up at him. He grinned again. "Damn if I didn't leave all my money at home. You ain't got a dollar on you, have you? Just for a couple of days is all."

All at once something inside gave and threatened to come pouring out of me. I didn't hate him any more. I felt that in another moment I'd start crying like a child.

"Sure," I said. "Don't sweat." I looked in my wallet and didn't have a dollar, I only had a five. "Here," I said. "That hold you?"

He didn't look at it—he didn't want to look at it. A terrible, closed look came over his face, as though he were keeping the number on the bill a secret from him and me. "Thanks," he said, and now he was dying to see me go. "Don't worry about Sonny. Maybe I'll write him or something."

"Sure," I said. "You do that. So long."

"Be seeing you," he said. I went on down the steps.

And I didn't write Sonny or send him anything for a long time. When I finally did, it was just after my little girl died, he wrote me back a letter which made me feel like a bastard.

Here's what he said:

Dear brother,

You don't know how much I needed to hear from you. I wanted to write you many a time but I dug how much I must have hurt you and so I didn't write. But now I feel like a man who's been trying to climb up out of some deep, real deep and funky hole and just saw the sun up there, outside. I got to get outside.

I can't tell you much about how I got here. I mean I don't know how to tell you. I guess I was afraid of something or I was trying to escape from something and you know I have never been very strong in the head (smile). I'm glad Mama and Daddy are dead and can't see what's happened to their son and I swear if I'd known what I was doing I would never have hurt you so, you and a lot of other fine people who were nice to me and who believed in me.

I don't want you to think it had anything to do with me being a musician. It's more than that. Or maybe less than that. I can't get anything straight in my head down here and I try not to think about what's going to happen to me when I get outside again. Sometime I think I'm going to flip and *never* get outside and sometime I think I'll come straight back. I tell you one thing, though, I'd rather blow my brains out than go through this again. But that's what they all say, so they tell me. If I tell you when I'm coming to New York and if you could meet me, I sure would appreciate it. Give my love to Isabel and the kids and I was sure sorry to hear about little Gracie. I wish I could be like Mama and say the Lord's will be done, but I don't know it seems to me that trouble is the one thing that never does get stopped and I don't know what good it does to blame it on the Lord. But maybe it does some good if you believe it.

Your brother,
Sonny

Then I kept in constant touch with him and I sent him whatever I could and I went to meet him when he came back to New York. When I saw him many things I thought I had forgotten came flooding back to me. This was because I had begun, finally, to wonder about Sonny, about the life that Sonny lived inside. This life, whatever it was, had made him older and thinner and it had deepened the distant stillness in which he had always moved. He looked very unlike my baby brother. Yet, when he smiled, when we shook hands, the baby brother I'd never known looked out from the depths of his private life, like an animal waiting to be coaxed into the light.

"How you been keeping?" he asked me.

"All right. And you?"

"Just fine." He was smiling all over his face. "It's good to see you again."

"It's good to see you."

The seven years' difference in our ages lay between us like a chasm: I wondered if these years would ever operate between us as a bridge. I was remembering, and it made it hard to catch my breath, that I had been there when he was born; and I had heard the first words he had ever spoken. When he started to walk, he walked from our mother straight to me. I caught him just before he fell when he took the first steps he ever took in this world.

"How's Isabel?"

"Just fine. She's dying to see you."

"And the boys?"

"They're fine, too. They're anxious to see their uncle."

"Oh come on. You know they don't remember me."

"Are you kidding? Of course they remember you."

He grinned again. We got into a taxi. We had a lot to say to each other, far too much to know how to begin.

As the taxi began to move, I asked, "You still want to go to India?"

He laughed. "You still remember that. Hell, no. This place is Indian enough for me."

"It used to belong to them," I said.

And he laughed again. "They damn sure knew what they were doing when they got rid of it."

Years ago, when he was around fourteen, he'd been all hipped on the idea of going to India. He read books about people sitting on rocks, naked, in all kinds of weather, but mostly bad, naturally, and walking barefoot through hot coals and arriving at wisdom. I used to say that it sounded to me as though they were getting away from wisdom as fast as they could. I think he sort of looked down on me for that.

"Do you mind," he asked, "if we have the driver drive alongside the park? On the west side—I haven't seen the city in so long."

"Of course not," I said. I was afraid that I might sound as though I were humoring him, but I hoped he wouldn't take it that way.

So we drove along, between the green of the park and the stony, lifeless elegance of hotels and apartment buildings, toward the vivid, killing streets of our childhood. These streets hadn't changed, though housing projects jutted up out of them now like rocks in the middle of a boiling sea. Most of the houses in which we had grown up had vanished, as had the stores from which we had stolen, the basements in which we had first tried sex, the rooftops from which we had hurled tin cans and bricks. But houses exactly like the houses of our past yet dominated the landscape, boys exactly like the boys we once had been found themselves smothering in these houses, came down into the streets for light and air and found themselves encircled by disaster. Some escaped the trap, most didn't. Those who got out always left something of themselves behind, as some animals amputate a leg and leave it in the trap. It might be said, perhaps, that I had escaped, after all, I was a school teacher; or that Sonny had, he hadn't lived in Harlem for years. Yet, as the cab moved uptown through streets which seemed, with a rush, to darken with dark people, and as I covertly studied Sonny's face, it came to me that what we both were seeking through our separate cab windows was that part of ourselves which had been left behind.

It's always at the hour of trouble and confrontation that the missing member aches.

We hit 110th Street and started rolling up Lenox Avenue. And I'd known this avenue all of my life, but it seemed to me again, as it had seemed on the day I'd first heard about Sonny's trouble, filled with a hidden menace which was its very breath of life.

"We almost there," said Sonny.

"Almost." We were both too nervous to say anything more.

We live in a housing project. It hasn't been up long. A few days after it was up it seemed uninhabitably new, now, of course, it's already rundown. It looks like a parody of the good, clean, faceless life—God knows the people who live in it do their best to make it a parody. The beat-looking grass lying around isn't enough to make their lives green, the hedges will never hold out the streets, and they know it. The big windows fool no one, they aren't big enough to make space out of no space. They don't bother with the windows, they watch the TV screen instead. The playground is most popular with the children who don't play at jacks, or skip rope, or roller skate, or swing, and they can be found in it after dark. We moved in partly because it's not too far from where I teach, and partly for the kids; but it's really just like the houses in which Sonny and I grew up. The same things happen, they'll have the same things to remember. The moment Sonny and I started into the house I had the feeling that I was simply bringing him back into the danger he had almost died trying to escape.

Sonny has never been talkative. So I don't know why I was sure he'd be dying to talk to me when supper was over the first night. Everything went fine, the oldest boy remembered him, and the youngest boy liked him, and Sonny had remembered to bring something for each of them; and Isabel, who is really much nicer than I am, more open and giving, had gone to a lot of trouble about dinner and was genuinely glad to see him. And she's always been able to tease Sonny in a way that I haven't. It was nice to see her face so vivid again and to hear her laugh and watch her make Sonny laugh. She wasn't, or, anyway, she didn't seem to be, at all uneasy or embarrassed. She chatted as though there were no subject which had to be avoided and she got Sonny past his first, faint stiffness. And thank God she was there, for I was filled with that icy dread again. Everything I did seemed awkward to me, and everything I said sounded freighted with hidden meaning. I was trying to

remember everything I'd heard about dope addiction and I couldn't
help watching Sonny for signs. I wasn't doing it out of malice. I
was trying to find out something about my brother. I was dying
to hear him tell me he was safe.

"Safe!" my father grunted, whenever Mama suggested trying to
move to a neighborhood which might be safer for children. "Safe,
hell! Ain't no place safe for kids, nor nobody."

He always went on like this, but he wasn't ever, really as bad as
he sounded, not even on weekends, when he got drunk. As a matter of fact, he was always on the lookout for "something a little better," but he died before he found it. He died suddenly, during a
drunken weekend in the middle of the war, when Sonny was fifteen.
He and Sonny hadn't ever got on too well. And this was partly
because Sonny was the apple of his father's eye. It was because he
loved Sonny so much and was frightened for him, that he was always
fighting with him. It doesn't do any good to fight with Sonny. Sonny
just moves back, inside himself, where he can't be reached. But the
principal reason that they never hit it off is that they were so much
alike. Daddy was big and rough and loud-talking, just the opposite
of Sonny, but they both had—that same privacy.

Mama tried to tell me something about this, just after Daddy died.
I was home on leave from the army.

This was the last time I ever saw my mother alive. Just the same,
this picture gets all mixed up in my mind with pictures I had of
her when she was younger. The way I always see her is the way she
used to be on a Sunday afternoon, say, when the old folks were
talking after the big Sunday dinner. I always see her wearing pale
blue. She'd be sitting on the sofa. And my father would be sitting
in the easy chair, not far from her. And the living room would be
full of church folks and relatives. There they sit, in chairs all around
the living room, and the night is creeping up outside, but nobody
knows it yet. You can see the darkness growing against the win-
dowpanes and you hear the street noises every now and again, or
maybe the jangling beat of a tambourine from one of the churches
close by, but it's real quiet in the room. For a moment nobody's
talking, but every face looks darkening, like the sky outside. And my
mother rocks a little from the waist, and my father's eyes are closed.
Everyone is looking at something a child can't see. For a minute
they've forgotten the children. Maybe a kid is lying on the rug, half
asleep. Maybe somebody's got a kid in his lap and is absent-mindedly

stroking the kid's head. Maybe there's a kid, quiet and big-eyed, curled up in a big chair in the corner. The silence, the darkness coming, and the darkness in the faces frightens the child obscurely. He hopes that the hand which strokes his forehead will never stop— will never die. He hopes that there will never come a time when the old folks won't be sitting around the living room, talking about where they've come from, and what they've seen, and what's happened to them and their kinfolk.

But something deep and watchful in the child knows that this is bound to end, is already ending. In a moment someone will get up and turn on the light. Then the old folks will remember the children and they won't talk any more that day. And when light fills the room, the child is filled with darkness. He knows that every time this happens he's moved just a little closer to that darkness outside. The darkness outside is what the old folks have been talking about. It's what they've come from. It's what they endure. The child knows that they won't talk any more because if he knows too much about what's happened to *them*, he'll know too much too soon, about what's going to happen to *him*.

The last time I talked to my mother, I remembered I was restless. I wanted to get out and see Isabel. We weren't married then and we had a lot to straighten out between us.

There Mama sat, in black, by the window. She was humming an old church song, *Lord, you brought me from a long ways off.* Sonny was out somewhere. Mama kept watching the streets.

"I don't know," she said, "if I'll ever see you again, after you go off from here. But I hope you'll remember the things I tried to teach you."

"Don't talk like that," I said, and smiled. "You'll be here a long time yet."

She smiled, too, but she said nothing. She was quiet for a long time. And I said, "Mama, don't you worry about nothing. I'll be writing all the time, and you be getting the checks. . . . "

"I want to talk to you about your brother," she said, suddenly. "If anything happens to me he ain't going to have nobody to look out for him."

"Mama," I said, "ain't nothing going to happen to you *or* Sonny. Sonny's all right. He's a good boy and he's got good sense."

"It ain't a question of his being a good boy," Mama said, "nor of his having good sense. It ain't only the bad ones, nor yet the dumb ones that gets sucked under." She stopped, looking at me. "Your Daddy once had a brother," she said, and she smiled in a way that made me feel she was in pain. "You didn't never know that, did you?"

"No," I said, "I never knew that," and I watched her face.

"Oh, yes," she said, "your Daddy had a brother." She looked out of the window again. "I know you never saw your Daddy cry. But *I* did—many a time, through all these years."

I asked her, "What happened to his brother? How come nobody's ever talked about him?"

This was the first time I ever saw my mother look old.

"His brother got killed," she said, "when he was just a little younger than you are now. I knew him. He was a fine boy. He was maybe a little full of the devil, but he didn't mean nobody no harm."

Then she stopped and the room was silent, exactly as it had sometimes been on those Sunday afternoons. Mama kept looking out into the streets.

"He used to have a job in the mill," she said, "and, like all young folks, he just liked to perform on Saturday nights. Saturday nights, him and your father would drift around to different places, go to dances and things like that, or just sit around with people they knew, and your father's brother would sing, he had a fine voice, and play along with himself on his guitar. Well, this particular Saturday night, him and your father was coming home from some place, and they were both a little drunk and there was a moon that night, it was bright like day. Your father's brother was feeling kind of good, and he was whistling to himself, and he had his guitar slung over his shoulder. They was coming down a hill and beneath them was a road that turned off from the highway. Well, your father's brother, being always kind of frisky, decided to run down this hill, and he did, with that guitar banging and clanging behind him, and he ran across the road, and he was making water behind a tree. And your father was sort of amused at him and he was still coming down the hill, kind of slow. Then he heard a car motor and that same minute his brother stepped from behind the tree, into the road, in the moonlight. And he started to cross the road. And your father started to run down the hill, he says he don't know why. This car was full of white men. They was all drunk, and when they seen your father's brother they let out a great whoop and holler and they aimed the car straight at him. They was having fun, they just wanted to scare him, the way they do sometimes, you know. But they was drunk. And I guess the boy, being drunk, too, and scared, kind of lost his head. By the time he jumped it was too late. Your father says he heard his brother scream when the car rolled over him, and heard the wood of that guitar when it give, and he heard them strings go flying, and he heard them white men shouting, and the car kept on a-going and it ain't stopped till this day. And, time your father got down the hill, his brother weren't nothing but blood and pulp."

Tears were gleaming on my mother's face. There wasn't anything I could say.

"He never mentioned it," she said, "because I never let him mention it before you children. Your Daddy was like a crazy man that night and for many a night thereafter. He says he never in his life seen anything as dark as that road after the lights of that car had gone away. Weren't nothing, weren't nobody on that road, just your Daddy and his brother and that busted guitar. Oh, yes. Your Daddy never did really get right again. Till the day he died he weren't sure but that every white man he saw was the man that killed his brother."

She stopped and took out her handkerchief and dried her eyes and looked at me.

"I ain't telling you all this," she said, "to make you scared or bitter or to make you hate nobody. I'm telling you this because you got a brother. And the world ain't changed."

I guess I didn't want to believe this. I guess she saw this in my face. She turned away from me, toward the window again, searching those streets.

"But I praise my Redeemer," she said at last, "that He called your Daddy home before me. I ain't saying it to throw no flowers at myself, but, I declare, it keeps me from feeling too cast down to know I helped your father get safely through this world. Your father always acted like he was the roughest, strongest man on earth. And everybody took him to be like that. But if he hadn't had *me* there—to see his tears!"

She was crying again. Still, I couldn't move. I said, "Lord, Lord, Mama, I didn't know it was like that."

"Oh, honey," she said, "there's a lot that you don't know. But you are going to find out." She stood up from the window and came over to me. "You got to hold on to your brother," she said, "and don't let him fall, no matter what it looks like is happening to him and no matter how evil you gets with him. You going to be evil with him many a time. But don't you forget what I told you, you hear?"

"I won't forget," I said. "Don't you worry, I won't forget. I won't let nothing happen to Sonny."

My mother smiled as though she were amused at something she saw in my face. Then, "You may not be able to stop nothing from happening. But you got to let him know you's *there*."

Two days later I was married, and then I was gone. And I had a lot of things on my mind and I pretty well forgot my promise to Mama until I got shipped home on a special furlough for her funeral.

And, after the funeral, with just Sonny and me alone in the empty kitchen, I tried to find out something about him.

"What do you want to do?" I asked him.

"I'm going to be a musician," he said.

For he had graduated, in the time I had been away, from dancing to the juke box to finding out who was playing what, and what they were doing with it, and he bought himself a set of drums.

"You mean, you want to be a drummer?" I somehow had the feeling that being a drummer might be all right for other people but not for my brother Sonny.

"I don't think," he said, looking at me very gravely, "that I'll ever be a good drummer. But I think I can play a piano."

I frowned. I'd never played the role of the older brother quite so seriously before, had scarcely ever, in fact, *asked* Sonny a damn thing. I sensed myself in the presence of something I didn't really know how to handle, didn't understand. So I made my frown a little deeper as I asked: "What kind of musician do you want to be?"

He grinned. "How many kinds do you think there are?"

"Be *serious*," I said.

He laughed, throwing his head back, and then looked at me. "I *am* serious."

"Well, then, for Christ's sake, stop kidding around and answer a serious question. I mean, do you want to be a concert pianist, you want to play classical music and all that, or—or what?" Long before I finished he was laughing again. "For Christ's *sake*, Sonny!"

He sobered, but with difficulty. "I'm sorry. But you sound so— *scared!*" and he was off again.

"Well, you may think it's funny now, baby, but it's not going to be so funny when you have to make your living at it, let me tell you *that*." I was furious because I knew he was laughing at me and I didn't know why.

"No," he said, very sober now, and afraid, perhaps, that he'd hurt me, "I don't want to be a classical pianist. That isn't what interests me. I mean"– he paused, looking hard at me, as though his eyes would help me to understand, and then gestured helplessly, as though perhaps his hand would help–"I mean, I'll have a lot of studying to do, and I'll have to study *everything*, but, I mean, I want to play *with*– jazz musicians." He stopped. "I want to play jazz," he said.

Well, the word had never before sounded as heavy, as real, as it sounded that afternoon in Sonny's mouth. I just looked at him and I was probably frowning a real frown by this time. I simply couldn't see why on earth he'd want to spend his time hanging around nightclubs, clowning around on bandstands, while people pushed each other around a dance floor. It seemed–beneath him, somehow. I had never thought about it before, had never been forced to, but I suppose I had always put jazz musicians in a class with what Daddy called "good-time people."

"Are you *serious*?"

"Hell, *yes*, I'm serious."

He looked more helpless than ever, and annoyed, and deeply hurt.

I suggested, helpfully: "You mean–like Louis Armstrong?"

His face closed as though I'd struck him. "No, I'm not talking about none of that old-time, down home crap."

"Well, look, Sonny, I'm sorry, don't get mad. I just don't altogether get it, that's all. Name somebody–you know, a jazz musician you admire."

"Bird."

"Who?"

"Bird! Charlie Parker! Don't they teach you nothing in the goddamn army?"

I lit a cigarette. I was surprised and then a little amused to discover that I was trembling. "I've been out of touch," I said. "You'll have to be patient with me. Now. Who's this Parker character?"

"He's just one of the greatest jazz musicians alive," said Sonny, sullenly, his hands in his pockets, his back to me. "Maybe *the* greatest," he added, bitterly, "that's probably why *you* never heard of him."

"All right," I said, "I'm ignorant. I'm sorry. I'll go out and buy all the cat's records right away, all right?"

"It don't," said Sonny, with dignity, "make any difference to me. I don't care what you listen to. Don't do me no favors."

I was beginning to realize that I'd never seen him so upset before. With another part of my mind I was thinking that this would probably turn out to be one of those things kids go through and that I shouldn't make it seem important by pushing it too hard. Still, I didn't think it would do any harm to ask: "Doesn't all this take a lot of time? Can you make a living at it?"

He turned back to me and half leaned, half sat, on the kitchen table. "Everything takes time," he said, "and—well, yes, sure, I can make a living at it. But what I don't seem to be able to make you understand is that it's the only thing I want to do."

"Well, Sonny," I said, gently, "you know people can't always do exactly what they *want* to do—"

"*No*, I don't know that," said Sonny, surprising me. "I think people *ought* to do what they want to do, what else are they alive for?"

"You getting to be a big boy," I said desperately, "it's time you started thinking about your future."

"I'm thinking about my future," said Sonny, grimly. "I think about it all the time."

I gave up. I decided, if he didn't change his mind, that we could always talk about it later. "In the meantime," I said, "You got to finish school." We had already decided that he'd have to move in with Isabel and her folks. I knew this wasn't the ideal arrangement because Isabel's folks are inclined to be dicty and they hadn't especially wanted Isabel to marry me. But I didn't know what else to do. "And we have to get you fixed up at Isabel's."

There was a long silence. He moved from the kitchen table to the window. "That's a terrible idea. You know it yourself."

"Do you have a *better* idea?"

He just walked up and down the kitchen for a minute. He was as tall as I was. He had started to shave. I suddenly had the feeling that I didn't know him at all.

He stopped at the kitchen table and picked up my cigarettes. Looking at me with a kind of mocking, amused defiance, he put one between his lips. "You mind?"

"You smoking already?"

He lit the cigarette and nodded, watching me through the smoke.

"I just wanted to see if I'd have the courage to smoke in front of you." He grinned and blew a great cloud of smoke to the ceiling. "It was easy." He looked at my face. "Come on, now. I bet you was smoking at my age, tell the truth."

I didn't say anything but the truth was on my face, and he laughed. But now there was something very strained in his laugh. "Sure. And I bet that ain't all you was doing."

He was frightening me a little. "Cut the crap," I said. "We already decided that you was going to go and live at Isabel's. Now what's got into you all of a sudden?"

"*You* decided it," he pointed out. "*I* didn't decide nothing." He stopped in front of me, leaning against the stove, arms loosely folded. "Look, brother. I don't want to stay in Harlem no more, I really don't." He was very earnest. He looked at me, then over toward the kitchen window. There was something in his eyes I'd never seen before, some thoughtfulness, some worry all his own. He rubbed the muscle of one arm. "It's time I was getting out of here."

"Where do you want to *go*, Sonny?"

"I want to join the army. Or the navy, I don't care. If I say I'm old enough, they'll believe me."

Then I got mad. It was because I was so scared. "You must be crazy. You goddamn fool, what the hell do you want to go and join the *army* for?"

"I just told you. To get out of Harlem."

"Sonny, you haven't even finished *school*. And if you really want to be a musician, how do you expect to study if you're in the *army*?"

He looked at me, trapped, and in anguish. "There's ways. I might be able to work out some kind of deal. Anyway, I'll have the G.I. Bill when I come out."

"*If* you come out." We stared at each other. "Sonny, please. Be reasonable. I know the setup is far from perfect. But we got to do the best we can."

"I ain't learning nothing in school," he said. "Even when I go." He turned away from me and opened the window and threw his cigarette out into the narrow alley. I watched his back. "At least, I ain't learning nothing you'd want me to learn." He slammed the window so hard I thought the glass would fly out, and turned back to me. "And I'm sick of the stink of these garbage cans!"

"Sonny," I said, "I know how you feel. But if you don't finish school now, you're going to be sorry later that you didn't." I grabbed him by the shoulders. "And you only got another year. It ain't so bad. And I'll come back and I swear I'll help you do *whatever* you want to do. Just try to put up with it till I come back. Will you please do that? For me?"

He didn't answer and he wouldn't look at me.

"Sonny. You hear me?"

He pulled away. "I hear you. But you never hear anything I say."

I didn't know what to say to that. He looked out of the window and then back to me. "OK," he said, and sighed. "I'll try."

Then I said, trying to cheer him up a little, "They got a piano at Isabel's. You can practice on it."

And as a matter of fact, it did cheer him up for a minute. "That's right," he said to himself. "I forgot that." His face relaxed a little. But the worry, the thoughtfulness, played on it still, the way shadows play on a face which is staring into the fire.

But I thought I'd never hear the end of that piano. At first, Isabel would write me, saying how nice it was that Sonny was so serious about his music and how, as soon as he came in from school, or wherever he had been when he was supposed to be at school, he went straight to that piano and stayed there until suppertime. And, after supper, he went back to that piano and stayed there until everybody went to bed. He was at the piano all day Saturday and all day Sunday. Then he bought a record player and started playing records. He'd play one record over and over again, all day long sometimes, and he'd improvise along with it on the piano. Or he'd play one section of the record, one chord, one change, one progression, then he'd do it on the piano. Then back to the record. Then back to the piano.

Well, I really don't know how they stood it. Isabel finally confessed that it wasn't like living with a person at all, it was like living with sound. And the sound didn't make any sense to her, didn't make any sense to any of them—naturally. They began, in a way, to be afflicted by this presence that was living in their home. It was as though Sonny were some sort of god, or monster. He moved in an atmosphere which wasn't like theirs at all. They fed him and he ate, he washed himself, he walked in and out of their door; he certainly wasn't nasty or unpleasant or rude, Sonny isn't any of those things; but it was as though he were all wrapped up in some cloud, some fire, some vision all his own; and there wasn't any way to reach him.

At the same time, he wasn't really a man yet, he was still a child, and they had to watch out for him in all kinds of ways. They certainly couldn't throw him out. Neither did they dare to make a great scene about that piano because even they dimly sensed, as I sensed, from so many thousands of miles away, that Sonny was at that piano playing for his life.

But he hadn't been going to school. One day a letter came from the school board and Isabel's mother got it—there had, apparently, been other letters but Sonny had torn them up. This day, when Sonny came in, Isabel's mother showed him the letter and asked where he'd been spending his time. And she finally got it out of him that he'd been down in Greenwich Village, with musicians and other characters, in a white girl's apartment. And this scared her and she started to scream at him and what came up, once she began—though she denies it to this day—was what sacrifices they were making to give Sonny a decent home and how little he appreciated it.

Sonny didn't play the piano that day. By evening, Isabel's mother had calmed down but then there was the old man to deal with, and Isabel herself. Isabel says she did her best to be calm but she broke down and started crying. She says she just watched Sonny's face. She could tell, by watching him, what was happening with him. And what was happening was that they penetrated his cloud, they had reached him. Even if their fingers had been a thousand times more gentle than human fingers ever are, he could hardly help feeling that they had stripped him naked and were spitting on that nakedness. For he also had to see that his presence, that music, which was life or death to him, had been torture for them and that they had endured it, not at all for his sake, but only for mine. And Sonny couldn't take that. He can take it a little better today than he could then but he's still not very good at it and, frankly, I don't know anybody who is.

The silence of the next few days must have been louder than the sound of all the music ever played since time began. One morning, before she went to work, Isabel was in his room for something and she suddenly realized that all of his records were gone. And she knew for certain that he was gone. And he was. He went as far as the navy could carry him. He finally sent me a postcard from some place in Greece and that was the first I knew that Sonny was still alive. I didn't see him any more until we were both back in New York and the war had long been over.

He was a man by then, of course, but I wasn't willing to see it. He came by the house from time to time, but we fought almost every time we met. I didn't like the way he carried himself, loose and dreamlike all the time, and I didn't like his friends, and his music seemed to be merely an excuse for the life he led. It sounded just that weird and disordered.

Then we had a fight, a pretty awful fight, and I didn't see him for months. By and by I looked him up, where he was living, in a furnished room in the Village, and I tried to make it up. But there were lots of other people in the room and Sonny just lay on his bed, and he wouldn't come downstairs with me, and he treated these other people as though they were his family and I weren't. So I got mad and then he got mad, and then I told him that he might just as well be dead as live the way he was living. Then he stood up and he told me not to worry about him any more in life, that he *was* dead as far as I was concerned. Then he pushed me to the door and the other people looked on as though nothing were happening, and he slammed the door behind me. I stood in the hallway, staring at the door. I heard somebody laugh in the room and then the tears came to my eyes. I started down the steps, whistling to keep from crying, I kept whistling to myself, *You going to need me, baby, one of these cold, rainy days.*

I read about Sonny's trouble in the spring. Little Grace died in the fall. She was a beautiful little girl. But she only lived a little over two years. She died of polio and she suffered. She had a slight fever for a couple of days, but it didn't seem like anything and we just kept her in bed. And we would certainly have called the doctor, but the fever dropped, she seemed to be all right. So we thought it had just been a cold. Then, one day, she was up, playing, Isabel was in the kitchen fixing lunch for the two boys when they'd come in from school, and she heard Grace fall down in the living room. When you have a lot of children you don't always start running when one of them falls, unless they start screaming or something. And, this time, Grace was quiet. Yet, Isabel says that when she heard that *thump* and then that silence, something happened in her to make her afraid. And she ran to the living room and there was little Grace on the floor, all twisted-up, and the reason she hadn't screamed was that she couldn't get her breath. And when she did scream, it was the worst sound, Isabel says, that she'd ever heard in all her life, and she still hears it sometimes in her dreams. Isabel will sometimes wake me up with a low, moaning, strangled sound and I have to be quick to awaken her and hold her to me and where Isabel is weeping against me seems a mortal wound.

I think I may have written Sonny the very day that little Grace was buried. I was sitting in the living room in the dark, by myself and I suddenly thought of Sonny. My trouble made his real.

One Saturday afternoon, when Sonny had been living with us, or, anyway, been in our house, for nearly two weeks, I found myself wandering aimlessly about the living room, drinking from a can of beer, and trying to work up the courage to search Sonny's room. He was out, he was usually out whenever I was home, and Isabel had taken the children to see their grandparents. Suddenly I was standing still in front of the living room window, watching Seventh Avenue. The idea of searching Sonny's room made me still. I scarcely dared to admit to myself what I'd been searching for. I didn't know what I'd do if I found it. Or if I didn't.

On the sidewalk across from me, near the entrance to a barbecue joint, some people were holding an old-fashioned revival meeting. The barbecue cook, wearing a dirty white apron, his conked hair reddish and metallic in the pale sun, and a cigarette between his lips, stood in the doorway, watching them. Kids and older people paused in their errands and stood there, along with some older men and a couple of very tough-looking women who watched everything that happened on the avenue, as though they owned it, or were maybe owned by it. Well, they were watching this, too. The revival was being carried on by three sisters in black, and a brother. All they had were their voices and their Bibles and a tambourine. The brother was testifying and while he testified two of the sisters stood together, seeming to say, amen, and the third sister walked around with the tambourine outstretched and a couple of people dropped coins into it. Then the brother's testimony ended and the sister who had been taking up the collection dumped the coins into her palm and transferred them to the pocket of her long black robe. Then she raised both hands, striking the tambourine against the air, and then against one hand, and she started to sing. And the two other sisters and the brother joined in.

It was strange, suddenly, to watch, though I had been seeing these street meetings all my life. So, of course, had everybody else down there. Yet, they paused and watched and listened and I stood still at the window. *"Tis the old ship of Zion,"* they sang, and the sister with the tambourine kept a steady, jangling beat, *"it has rescued many a thousand!"* Not a soul under the sound of their voices was hearing this song for the first time, not one of them had been rescued. Nor had they seen much in the way of rescue work being done around them. Neither did they especially believe in the holiness of the three sisters and the brother, they knew too much about them, knew where they lived, and how. The woman with the tambourine, whose voice dominated the air, whose face was bright with joy, was divided by very little from the woman who stood watching her, a cigarette between her heavy, chapped lips, her hair a cuckoo's nest, her face scarred and swollen from many beatings, and her black eyes glittering like coal. Perhaps they both knew this, which was why, when, as rarely, they addressed each other, they addressed each other as Sister. As the singing filled the air the watching, listening faces underwent a change, the eyes focusing on something within; the music seemed to soothe a poison out of them; and time seemed, nearly, to fall away from the sullen, belligerent, battered faces, as though they were fleeing back to their first condition, while dreaming of their last. The barbecue cook half shook his head and smiled, and dropped his cigarette and disappeared into his joint. A man fumbled in his pockets for change and stood holding it in his hand impatiently, as though he had just remembered a pressing appointment further up the avenue. He looked furious. Then I saw Sonny, standing on the edge of the crowd. He was carrying a wide, flat notebook with a green cover, and it made him look, from where I was standing, almost like a schoolboy. The coppery sun brought out the copper in his skin, he was very faintly smiling, standing very still. Then the singing stopped, the tambourine turned into a collection plate again. The furious man dropped in his coins and vanished, so did a couple of the women, and Sonny dropped some change in the plate, looking directly at the woman with a little smile. He started across the avenue, toward the house. He has a slow, loping walk, something like the way Harlem hipsters walk, only he's imposed on this his own half-beat. I had never really noticed it before.

I stayed at the window, both relieved and apprehensive. As Sonny disappeared from my sight, they began singing again. And they were still singing when his key turned in the lock.

"Hey," he said.

"Hey, yourself. You want some beer?"

"No. Well, maybe." But he came up to the window and stood beside me, looking out. "What a warm voice," he said.

They were singing *If I could only hear my mother pray again!*

"Yes," I said, "and she can sure beat that tambourine."

"But what a terrible song," he said, and laughed. He dropped his notebook on the sofa and disappeared into the kitchen. "Where's Isabel and the kids?"

"I think they went to see their grandparents. You hungry?"

"No." He came back into the living room with his can of beer. "You want to come some place with me tonight?"

I sensed, I don't know how, that I couldn't possibly say no. "Sure. Where?"

He sat down on the sofa and picked up his notebook and started leafing through it. "I'm going to sit in with some fellows in a joint in the Village."

"You mean, you're going to play, tonight?"

"That's right." He took a swallow of his beer and moved back to the window. He gave me a sidelong look. "If you can stand it."

"I'll try," I said.

He smiled to himself and we both watched as the meeting across the way broke up. The three sisters and the brother, heads bowed, were singing *God be with you till we meet again.* The faces around them were very quiet. Then the song ended. The small crowd dispersed. We watched the three women and the lone man walk slowly up the avenue.

"When she was singing before," said Sonny, abruptly, "her voice reminded me for a minute of what heroin feels like sometimes—when it's in your veins. It makes you feel sort of warm and cool at the same time. And distant. And—and sure." He sipped his beer, very deliberately not looking at me. I watched his face. "It makes you feel—in control. Sometimes you've got to have that feeling."

"Do you?" I sat down slowly in the easy chair.

"Sometimes." He went to the sofa and picked up his notebook again. "Some people do."

"In order," I asked, "to play?" And my voice was very ugly, full of contempt and anger.

"Well"—he looked at me with great, troubled eyes, as though, in fact, he hoped his eyes would tell me things he could never otherwise say—"they *think so.* And *if* they think so—!"

"And what do *you* think?" I asked.

He sat on the sofa and put his can of beer on the floor. "I don't know," he said, and I couldn't be sure if he were answering my question or pursuing his thoughts. His face didn't tell me. "It's not so much to *play*. It's to *stand* it, to be able to make it at all. On any level." He frowned and smiled: "In order to keep from shaking to pieces."

"But these friends of yours," I said, "they seem to shake themselves to pieces pretty goddamn fast."

"Maybe." He played with the notebook. And something told me that I should curb my tongue, that Sonny was doing his best to talk, that I should listen. "But of course you only know the ones that've gone to pieces. Some don't—or at least they haven't *yet* and that's just about all *any* of us can say." He paused. "And then there are some who just live, really, in hell, and they know it and they see what's happening and they go right on. I don't know." He sighed, dropped the notebook, folded his arms. "Some guys, you can tell from the way they play, they on something *all* the time. And you can see that, well, it makes something real for them. But of course," he picked up his beer from the floor and sipped it and put the can down again, "they *want* to, too, you've got to see that. Even some of them that say they don't—*some*, not all."

"And what about you?" I asked—I couldn't help it. "What about you? Do *you* want to?"

He stood up and walked to the window and remained silent for a long time. Then he sighed. "Me," he said. Then: "While I was downstairs before, on my way here, listening to that woman sing, it struck me all of a sudden how much suffering she must have had to go through—to sing like that. It's *repulsive* to think you have to suffer that much."

I said: "But there's no way not to suffer—is there, Sonny?"

"I believe not," he said and smiled, "but that's never stopped anyone from trying." He looked at me. "Has it?" I realized, with this mocking look, that there stood between us, forever, beyond the power of time or forgiveness, the fact that I had held silence—so long!—when he had needed human speech to help him. He turned back to the window. "No, there's no way not to suffer. But you try all kinds of ways to keep from drowning in it, to keep on top of it, and to make it seem—well, like *you*. Like you did something, all right, and now you're suffering for it. You know?" I said nothing.

"Well you know," he said, impatiently, "why *do* people suffer? Maybe it's better to do something to give it a reason, *any* reason."

"But we just agreed," I said, "that there's no way not to suffer. Isn't it better, then, just to—take it?"

"But nobody just takes it," Sonny cried, "that's what I'm telling you! *Everybody* tries not to. You're just hung up on the *way* some people try—it's not *your* way!"

The hair on my face began to itch, my face felt wet. "That's not true," I said, "that's not true. I don't give a damn what other people do, I don't even care how they suffer. I just care how *you* suffer." And he looked at me. "Please believe me," I said, "I don't want to see you—die—trying not to suffer."

"I won't," he said, flatly, "die trying not to suffer. At least, not any faster than anybody else."

"But there's no need," I said, trying to laugh, "is there? In killing yourself."

I wanted to say more, but I couldn't. I wanted to talk about will power and how life could be—well, beautiful. I wanted to say that it was all within; but was it? Or, rather, wasn't that exactly the trouble? And I wanted to promise that I would never fail him again. But it would all have sounded—empty words and lies.

So I made the promise to myself and prayed that I would keep it.

"It's terrible sometimes, inside," he said, "that's what's the trouble. You walk these streets, black and funky and cold, and there's not really a living ass to talk to, and there's nothing shaking, and there's no way of getting it out—that storm inside. You can't talk it and you can't make love with it, and when you finally try to get with it and play it, you realize *nobody's* listening. So *you've* got to listen. You got to find a way to listen."

And then he walked away from the window and sat on the sofa again, as though all the wind had suddenly been knocked out of him. "Sometimes you'll do *anything* to play, even cut your mother's throat." He laughed and looked at me. "Or your brother's." Then he sobered. "Or your own." Then: "Don't worry. I'm all right now and I think I'll *be* all right. But I can't forget—where I've been. I don't mean just the physical place I've been, I mean where I've *been*. And *what* I've been."

"What have you been, Sonny?" I asked.

He smiled—but sat sideways on the sofa, his elbow resting on the back, his fingers playing with his mouth and chin, not looking at me. "I've been something I didn't realize, didn't know I could be. Didn't know anybody could be." He stopped, looking inward, looking helplessly young, looking old. "I'm not talking about it now because I feel *guilty* or anything like that—maybe it would be better if I did, I don't know. Anyway, I can't really talk about it. Not to you, not to anybody," and now he turned and faced me. "Sometimes, you know, and it was actually when I was most *out* of the world, I felt that I was in it, that I was *with* it, really, and I could play or I didn't really have to *play*, it just came out of me, it was there. And I don't know how I played, thinking about it now, but I know I did awful things, those times, sometimes, to people. Or it wasn't that I *did* anything to them—it was that they weren't real." He picked up the beer can; it was empty; he rolled it between his palms: "And other times—well, I needed a fix, I needed to find a place to lean, I needed to clear a space to *listen*—and I couldn't find it, and I—went crazy, I did terrible things to *me*, I was terrible *for* me." He began pressing the beer can between his hands, I watched the metal begin to give. It glittered, as he played with it, like a knife, and I was afraid he could cut himself, but I said nothing. "Oh well. I can never tell you. I was all by myself at the bottom of something, stinking and sweating and crying and shaking, and I smelled it, you know? *my* stink, and I thought I'd die if I couldn't get away from it and yet, all the same, I knew that everything I was doing was just locking me in with it. And I didn't know," he paused, still flattening the beer can, "I didn't know, I still *don't* know, something kept telling me that maybe it was good to smell your own stink, but I didn't think that *that* was what I'd been trying to do—and—who can stand it?" and he abruptly dropped the ruined beer can, looking at me with a small, still smile, and then rose, walking to the window as though it were the lodestone rock. I watched his face, he watched the avenue. "I couldn't tell you when Mama died—but the reason I wanted to leave Harlem so bad was to get away from drugs. And then, when I ran away, that's what I was running from—really. When I came back, nothing had changed, *I* hadn't changed, I was just—older." And he stopped, drumming with his fingers on the windowpane. The sun had vanished, soon darkness would fall. I watched his face. "It can come again," he said, almost as though speaking to himself. Then he turned to me. "It can come again," he repeated. "I just want you to know that."

"All right," I said, at last. "So it can come again. All right."

He smiled, but the smile was sorrowful. "I had to try to tell you," he said.

"Yes," I said. "I understood that."

"You're my brother," he said, looking straight at me, and not smiling at all.

"Yes," I repeated, "yes. I understand that."

He turned back to the window, looking out. "All that hatred down there," he said, "all that hatred and misery and love. It's a wonder it doesn't blow the avenue apart."

We went to the only nightclub on a short, dark street, downtown. We squeezed through the narrow, chattering, jampacked bar to the entrance of the big room, where the bandstand was. And we stood there for a moment, for the lights were very dim in this room and we couldn't see. Then, "Hello, boy," said a voice and an enormous black man, much older than Sonny or myself, erupted out of all that atmospheric lighting and put an arm around Sonny's shoulder. "I been sitting right here," he said, "waiting for you."

He had a big voice, too, and heads in the darkness turned toward us.

Sonny grinned and pulled a little away, and said, "Creole, this is my brother. I told you about him."

Creole shook my hand. "I'm glad to meet you, son," he said, and it was clear that he was glad to meet me *there*, for Sonny's sake. And he smiled, "You got a real musician in *your* family," and he took his arm from Sonny's shoulder and slapped him, lightly, affectionately, with the back of his hand.

"Well. Now I've heard it all," said a voice behind us. This was another musician, and a friend of Sonny's, a coal-black, cheerful-looking man, built close to the ground. He immediately began confiding to me, at the top of his lungs, the most terrible things about Sonny, his teeth gleaming like a lighthouse and his laugh coming up out of him like the beginning of an earthquake. And it turned out that everyone at the bar knew Sonny, or almost everyone; some were musicians, working there, or nearby, or not working, some were simply hangers-on, and some were there to hear Sonny play. I was introduced to all of them and they were all very polite to me. Yet, it was clear that, for them, I was only Sonny's brother. Here, I was in Sonny's world. Or, rather: his kingdom.

Here, it was not even a question that his veins bore royal blood.

They were going to play soon and Creole installed me, by myself, at a table in a dark corner. Then I watched them, Creole, and the little black man, and Sonny, and the others, while they horsed around, standing just below the bandstand. The light from the bandstand spilled just a little short of them and, watching them laughing and gesturing and moving about, I had the feeling that they, nevertheless, were being most careful not to step into that circle of light too suddenly: that if they moved into the light too suddenly, without thinking, they would perish in flame. Then, while I watched, one of them, the small, black man, moved into the light and crossed the bandstand and started fooling around with his drums. Then—being funny and being, also, extremely cere-monious—Creole took Sonny by the arm and led him to the piano. A woman's voice called Sonny's name and a few hands started clap-ping. And Sonny, also being funny and being ceremonious, and so touched, I think, that he could have cried, but neither hiding it nor showing it, riding it like a man, grinned, and put both hands to his heart and bowed from the waist.

Creole then went to the bass fiddle and a lean, very bright-skinned brown man jumped up on the bandstand and picked up his horn. So there they were, and the atmosphere on the bandstand and in the room began to change and tighten. Someone stepped up to the microphone and announced them. Then there were all kinds of murmurs. Some people at the bar shushed others. The waitress ran around, frantically getting in the last orders, guys and chicks got closer to each other, and the lights on the bandstand, on the quartet, turned to a kind of indigo. Then they all looked different there. Creole looked about him for the last time, as though he were making certain that all his chickens were in the coop, and then he—jumped and struck the fiddle. And there they were.

All I know about music is that not many people ever really hear it. And even then, on the rare occasions when something opens within, and the music enters, what we mainly hear, or hear cor-roborated, are personal, private, vanishing evocations. But the man who creates the music is hearing something else, is dealing with the roar rising from the void and imposing order on it as it hits the air. What is evoked in him, then, is of another order, more terrible because it has no words, and triumphant, too, for that same reason. And his triumph, when he triumphs, is ours. I just watched

Sonny's face. His face was troubled, he was working hard, but he
wasn't with it. And I had the feeling that, in a way, everyone on the
bandstand was waiting for him, both waiting for him and pushing
him along. But as I began to watch Creole, I realized that it was
Creole who held them all back. He had them on a short rein. Up
there, keeping the beat with his whole body, waiting on the fiddle,
with his eyes half closed, he was listening to everything, but he was
listening to Sonny. He was having a dialogue with Sonny. He
wanted Sonny to leave the shoreline and strike out for the deep
water. He was Sonny's witness that deep water and drowning were
not the same thing—he had been there, and he knew. And he
wanted Sonny to know. He was waiting for Sonny to do the things
on the keys which would let Creole know that Sonny was in the water.

And, while Creole listened, Sonny moved, deep within, exactly
like someone in torment. I had never before thought of how awful
the relationship must be between the musician and his instrument.
He has to fill it, this instrument, with the breath of life, his own.
He has to make it do what he wants it to do. And a piano is just
a piano. It's made out of so much wood and wires and little ham-
mers and big ones, and ivory. While there's only so much you can
do with it, the only way to find this out is to try; to try and make
it do everything.

And Sonny hadn't been near a piano for over a year. And he wasn't
on much better terms with his life, not the life that stretched before
him now. He and the piano stammered, started one way, got scared,
stopped; started another way, panicked, marked time, started again;
then seemed to have found a direction, panicked again, got stuck.
And the face I saw on Sonny I'd never seen before. Everything had
been burned out of it, and, at the same time, things usually hidden were being burned in, by the fire and fury of the battle which
was occuring in him up there.

Yet, watching Creole's face as they neared the end of the first set,
I had the feeling that something had happened, something I hadn't
heard. Then they finished, there was scattered applause, and then,
without an instant's warning, Creole started into something else,
it was almost sardonic, it was *Am I Blue*. And, as though he commanded, Sonny began to play. Something began to happen. And
Creole let out the reins. The dry, low, black man said something
awful on the drums, Creole answered, and the drums talked back.
Then the horn insisted, sweet and high, slightly detached perhaps,

and Creole listened, commenting now and then, dry, and driving, beautiful and calm and old. Then they all came together again, and Sonny was part of the family again. I could tell this from his face. He seemed to have found, right there beneath his fingers, a damn brand-new piano. It seemed that he couldn't get over it. Then, for awhile, just being happy with Sonny, they seemed to be agreeing with him that brand-new pianos certainly were a gas.

Then Creole stepped forward to remind them that what they were playing was the blues. He hit something in all of them, he hit something in me, myself, and the music tightened and deepened, apprehension began to beat the air. Creole began to tell us what the blues were all about. They were not about anything very new. He and his boys up there were keeping it new, at the risk of ruin, destruction, madness, and death, in order to find new ways to make us listen. For, while the tale of how we suffer, and how we are delighted, and how we may triumph is never new, it always must be heard. There isn't any other tale to tell, it's the only light we've got in all this darkness.

And this tale, according to that face, that body, those strong hands on those strings, has another aspect in every country, and a new depth in every generation. Listen, Creole seemed to be saying, listen. Now these are Sonny's blues. He made the little black man on the drums know it, and the bright, brown man on the horn. Creole wasn't trying any longer to get Sonny in the water. He was wishing him Godspeed. Then he stepped back, very slowly, filling the air with the immense suggestion that Sonny speak for himself.

Then they all gathered around Sonny and Sonny played. Every now and again one of them seemed to say, amen. Sonny's fingers filled the air with life, his life. But that life contained so many others. And Sonny went all the way back, he really began with the spare, flat statement of the opening phrase of the song. Then he began to make it his. It was very beautiful because it wasn't hurried and it was no longer a lament. I seemed to hear with what burning he had made it his, with what burning we had yet to make it ours, how we could cease lamenting. Freedom lurked around us and I understood, at last, that he could help us to be free if we would listen, that he would never be free until we did. Yet, there was no battle in his face now. I heard what he had gone through, and would continue to go through until he came to rest in earth. He had made it his: that long line, of which we knew only Mama and

Daddy. And he was giving it back, as everything must be given back, so that, passing through death, it can live forever. I saw my mother's face again, and felt, for the first time, how the stones of the road she had walked on must have bruised her feet. I saw the moonlit road where my father's brother died. And it brought something else back to me, and carried me past it, I saw my little girl again and felt Isabel's tears again, and I felt my own tears begin to rise. And I was yet aware that this was only a moment, that the world waited outside, as hungry as a tiger, and that trouble stretched above us, longer than the sky.

Then it was over. Creole and Sonny let out their breath, both soaking wet, and grinning. There was a lot of applause and some of it was real. In the dark, the girl came by and I asked her to take drinks to the bandstand. There was a long pause, while they talked up there in the indigo light and after a while I saw the girl put a Scotch and milk on top of the piano for Sonny. He didn't seem to notice it, but just before they started playing again, he sipped from it and looked toward me, and nodded. Then he put it back on top of the piano. For me, then, as they began to play again, it glowed and shook above my brother's head like the very cup of trembling.

ZORA NEALE HURSTON

Zora Neale Hurston was not really recognized for her writing until after her death. Her novel celebrating black culture, Their Eyes Were Watching God, *was published in 1937 and rediscovered in 1978. An independent and outspoken woman, she once said: "I do not weep at the world—I am too busy sharpening my oyster knife."*

from
THEIR EYES WERE
WATCHING GOD

JANIE SAW HER life like a great tree in leaf with the things suffered, things enjoyed, things done and undone. Dawn and doom was in the branches.

"Ah know exactly what Ah got to tell yuh, but it's hard to know where to start at.

"Ah ain't never seen my papa. And Ah didn't know 'im if Ah did. Mah mama neither. She was gone from round dere long before Ah wuz big enough tuh know. Mah grandma raised me. Mah grandma and de white folks she worked wid. She had a house out in de back-yard and dat's where Ah wuz born. They was quality white folks up dere in West Florida. Named Washburn. She had four gran'chillun on de place and all of us played together and dat's how come Ah never called mah grandma nothin' but Nanny, 'cause dat's what everybody on de place called her. Nanny used to ketch us in our devilment and lick every youngun on de place and Mis' Washburn did de same. Ah reckon dey never hit us uh lick amiss 'cause dem three boys and us two girls wuz pretty aggravatin', Ah speck.

"Ah was wid dem white chillun so much till Ah didn't know Ah wuzn't white till Ah was round six years old. Wouldn't have found it out then, but a man come long takin' pictures and without askin' anybody, Shelby, dat was de oldest boy, he told him to take us. Round a week later de man brought de picture for Mis' Washburn to see and pay him which she did, then give us all a good lickin'.

"So when we looked at de picture and everybody got pointed out there wasn't nobody left except a real dark little girl with long hair standing by Eleanor. Dat's where Ah wuz s'posed to be, but Ah couldn't recognize dat dark chile as me. So Ah ast, 'where is me? Ah don't see me.'

"Everybody laughed, even Mr. Washburn. Miss Nellie, de Mama of de chillun who come back home after her husband dead, she pointed to de dark one and said, 'Dat's you, Alphabet, don't you know yo' ownself?'

"Dey all useter call me Alphabet 'cause so many people had done named me different names. Ah looked at de picture a long time and seen it was mah dress and mah hair so Ah said:

"'Aw, aw! Ah'm colored!'

"Den dey all laughed real hard. But before Ah seen de picture Ah thought Ah wuz just like de rest.

"Us lived dere havin' fun till de chillun at school got to teasin' me 'bout livin' in de white folks backyard. Dere wuz uh knotty head gal name Mayrella dat useter git mad every time she look at me. Mis' Washburn useter dress me up in all de clothes her gran'chillun didn't need no mo' which still wuz better'n whut de rest uh de colored chillun had. And then she useter put hair ribbon on mah head fuh me tuh wear. Dat useter rile Mayrella uh lot. So she would pick at me all de time and put some others up tuh do de same. They'd push me 'way from de ring plays and make out they couldn't play wid nobody dat lived on premises. Den they'd tell me not to be takin' on over mah looks 'cause they mama told 'em 'bout de hound dawgs huntin' mah papa all night long. 'Bout Mr. Washburn and de sheriff puttin' de bloodhounds on de trail tuh ketch mah papa for whut he done tuh mah mama. Dey didn't tell about how he wuz seen tryin' tuh git in touch wid mah mama later on so he could marry her. Naw, dey didn't talk dat part of it atall. Dey made it sound real bad so as tuh crumple mah feathers. None of 'em didn't even remember whut his name wuz, but dey all knowed de bloodhound part by heart. Nanny didn't love tuh see me wid mah head hung down, so she figgered it would be mo' better fuh me if us had uh house. She got de land and everything and then Mis' Washburn helped out uh whole heap wid things."

Pheoby's hungry listening helped Janie to tell her story. So she went on thinking back to her young years and explaining them to her friend in soft, easy phrases while all around the house, the night time put on flesh and blackness.

She thought awhile and decided that her conscious life had commenced at Nanny's gate. On a late afternoon Nanny had called her to come inside the house because she had spied Janie letting Johnny Taylor kiss her over the gatepost.

It was a spring afternoon in West Florida. Janie had spent most of the day under a blossoming pear tree in the back-yard. She had been spending every minute that she could steal from her chores under that tree for the last three days. That was to say, ever since the first tiny bloom had opened. It had called her to come and gaze on a mystery. From barren brown stems to glistening leaf-buds; from the leaf-buds to snowy virginity of bloom. It stirred her tremendously. How? Why? It was like a flute song forgotten in another existence and remembered again. What? How? Why? This singing she heard that had nothing to do with her ears. The rose of the world was breathing out smell. It followed her through all her waking moments and caressed her in her sleep. It connected itself with other vaguely felt matters that had struck her outside observation and buried themselves in her flesh. Now they emerged and quested about her consciousness.

She was stretched on her back beneath the pear tree soaking in the alto chant of the visiting bees, the gold of the sun and the panting breath of the breeze when the inaudible voice of it all came to her. She saw a dust-bearing bee sink into the sanctum of a bloom; the thousand sister-calyxes arch to meet the love embrace and the ecstatic shiver of the tree from root to tiniest branch creaming in every blossom and frothing with delight. So this was a marriage! She had been summoned to behold a revelation. Then Janie felt a pain remorseless sweet that left her limp and languid.

After a while she got up from where she was and went over the little garden field entire. She was seeking confirmation of the voice and vision, and everywhere she found and acknowledged answers. A personal answer for all other creations except herself. She felt an answer seeking her, but where? When? How? She found herself at the kitchen door and stumbled inside. In the air of the room were flies tumbling and singing, marrying and giving in marriage. When

she reached the narrow hallway she was reminded that her grandmother was home with a sick headache. She was lying across the
bed asleep so Janie tipped on out of the front door. Oh to be a
pear tree—*any* tree in bloom! With kissing bees singing of the beginning of the world! She was sixteen. She had glossy leaves and bursting
buds and she wanted to struggle with life but it seemed to elude
her. Where were the singing bees for her? Nothing on the place
nor in her grandma's house answered her. She searched as much
of the world as she could from the top of the front steps and then
went on down to the front gate and leaned over to gaze up and
down the road. Looking, waiting, breathing short with impatience.
Waiting for the world to be made.

Through pollinated air she saw a glorious being coming up the
road. In her former blindness she had known him as shiftless Johnny
Taylor, tall and lean. That was before the golden dust of pollen had
beglamored his rags and her eyes.

In the last stages of Nanny's sleep, she dreamed of voices. Voices far-
off but persistent, and gradually coming nearer. Janie's voice. Janie talking in whispery snatches with a male voice she couldn't quite place.
That brought her wide awake. She bolted upright and peered out
of the window and saw Johnny Taylor lacerating her Janie with a kiss.

"Janie!"

The old woman's voice was so lacking in command and reproof,
so full of crumbling dissolution,—that Janie half believed that Nanny
had not seen her. So she extended herself outside of her dream and
went inside of the house. That was the end of her childhood.

Nanny's head and face looked like the standing roots of some old
tree that had been torn away by storm. Foundation of ancient power
that no longer mattered. The cooling palma christi leaves that Janie
had bound about her grandma's head with a white rag had wilted
down and become part and parcel of the woman. Her eyes didn't
bore and pierce. They diffused and melted Janie, the room and the
world into one comprehension.

"Janie, youse uh 'oman, now, so—"

"Naw, Nanny, naw Ah ain't no real 'oman yet."

The thought was too new and heavy for Janie. She fought it away.

Nanny closed her eyes and nodded a slow, weary affirmation many
times before she gave it voice.

"Yeah, Janie, youse got yo' womanhood on yuh. So Ah mout ez

well tell yuh whut Ah been savin' up for uh spell. Ah wants to see you married right away."

"Me, married? Naw, Nanny, no ma'am! Whut Ah know 'bout uh husband?"

"Whut Ah seen just now is plenty for me, honey, Ah don't want no trashy nigger, no breath-and-britches, lak Johnny Taylor usin' yo' body to wipe his foots on."

Nanny's words made Janie's kiss across the gatepost seem like a manure pile after a rain.

"Look at me, Janie. Don't set dere wid yo' head hung down. Look at yo' ole grandma!" Her voice began snagging on the prongs of her feelings. "Ah don't want to be talkin' to you lak dis. Fact is Ah done been on mah knees to mah Maker many's de time askin' *please*—for Him not to make de burden too heavy for me to bear."

"Nanny, Ah just—Ah didn't mean nothin' bad."

"Dat's what makes me skeered. You don't mean no harm. You don't even know where harm is at. Ah'm ole now. Ah can't be always guidin' yo' feet from harm and danger. Ah wants to see you married right away."

"Who Ah'm goin' tuh marry off-hand lak dat? Ah don't know nobody."

"De Lawd will provide. He know Ah done bore de burden in de heat uh de day. Somebody done spoke to me 'bout you long time ago. Ah ain't said nothin' 'cause dat wasn't de way Ah placed you. Ah wanted yuh to school out and pick from a higher bush and a sweeter berry. But dat ain't yo' idea, Ah see."

"Nanny, who—who dat been askin' you for me?"

"Brother Logan Killicks. He's a good man, too."

"Naw, Nanny, no ma'am! Is dat whut he been hangin' around here for? He look like some ole skullhead in de grave yard."

The older woman sat bolt upright and put her feet to the floor, and thrust back the leaves from her face.

"So you don't want to marry off decent like, do yuh? You just wants to hug and kiss and feel around with first one man and then another, huh? You wants to make me suck de same sorrow yo' mama did, eh? Mah ole head ain't gray enough. Mah back ain't bowed enough to suit you!"

The vision of Logan Killicks was desecrating the pear tree, but Janie didn't know how to tell Nanny that. She merely hunched over and pouted at the floor.

"Janie."

"Yes, ma'am."

"You answer me when Ah speak. Don't you set dere poutin' wid me after all Ah done went through for you!"

She slapped the girl's face violently, and forced her head back so that their eyes met in struggle. With her hand uplifted for the second blow she saw the huge tear that welled up from Janie's heart and stood in each eye. She saw the terrible agony and the lips tightened down to hold back the cry and desisted. Instead she brushed back the heavy hair from Janie's face and stood there suffering and loving and weeping internally for both of them.

"Come to yo' grandma, honey. Set in her lap lak yo' use tuh. Yo' Nanny wouldn't harm a hair uh yo' head. She don't want nobody else to do it neither if she kin help it. Honey, de white man is de ruler of everything as fur as Ah been able tuh find out. Maybe it's some place way off in de ocean where de black man is in power, but we don't know nothin' but what we see. So de white man throw down de load and tell de nigger man tuh pick it up. He pick it up because he have to, but he don't tote it. He hand it to his womenfolks. De nigger woman is de mule uh de world so fur as Ah can see. Ah been prayin' fuh it tuh be different wid you. Lawd, Lawd, Lawd!"

For a long time she sat rocking with the girl held tightly to her sunken breast. Janie's long legs dangled over one arm of the chair and the long braids of her hair swung low on the other side. Nanny half sung, half sobbed a running chant-prayer over the head of the weeping girl.

"Lawd have mercy! It was a long time on de way but Ah reckon it had to come. Oh Jesus! Do, Jesus! Ah done de best Ah could."

Finally, they both grew calm.

"Janie, how long you been 'lowin' Johnny Taylor to kiss you?"

"Only dis one time, Nanny. Ah don't love him at all. Whut made me do it is—oh, Ah don't know."

"Thank you, Massa Jesus."

"Ah ain't gointuh do it no mo', Nanny. Please don't make me marry Mr. Killicks."

"'Tain't Logan Killicks Ah wants you to have, baby, it's protection. Ah ain't gittin' ole, honey. Ah'm *done* ole. One mornin' soon, now, de angel wid de sword is gointuh stop by here. De day and de hour is hid from me, but it won't be long. Ah ast de Lawd when you was uh infant in mah arms to let me stay here till you got grown.

He done spared me to see de day. Mah daily prayer now is tuh let dese golden moments rolls on a few days longer till Ah see you safe in life."

"Lemme wait, Nanny, please, jus' a lil bit mo'."

"Don't think Ah don't feel wid you, Janie, 'cause Ah do. Ah couldn't love yuh no more if Ah had uh felt yo' birth pains mahself. Fact ud de matter, Ah loves yuh a whole heap more'n Ah do yo' mama, de one Ah did birth. But you got to take in consideration you ain't no everyday chile like most of 'em. You ain't got no papa, you might jus' as well as say no mama, for de good she do yuh. You ain't got nobody but me. And mah head is ole and tilted towards de grave. Neither can you stand along by yo'self. De thought uh you bein' kicked around from pillar tuh post is uh hurtin' thing. Every tear you drop squeezes a cup uh blood outa mah heart. Ah got tuh try and do for you befo' mah head is cold."

A sobbing sigh burst out of Janie. The old woman answered her with little soothing pats of the hand.

"You know, honey, us colored folks is branches without roots and that makes things come round in queer ways. You in particular. Ah was born back dere in slavery so it wasn't for me to fulfill my dreams of whut a woman oughta be and do. Dat's one of de hold-backs of slavery. But nothing can't stop you from wishin'. You can't beat nobody down so low till you can rob 'em of they will. Ah didn't want to be used for a work-ox and a brood-sow and Ah didn't want mah daughter used dat way neither. It sho wasn't mah will for things to happen lak they did. Ah even hated de way you was born. But, all de same Ah said thank God, Ah got another chance. Ah wanted to preach a great sermon about colored women sittin' on high, but they wasn't no pulpit for me. Freedom found me wid a baby daughter in mah arms, so Ah said Ah'd take a broom and a cook-pot and throw up a highway through de wilderness for her. She would expound what Ah felt. But somehow she got lost offa de highway and next thing Ah knowed here you was in de world. So whilst Ah was tendin' you of nights Ah said Ah'd save de text for you. Ah been waitin' a long time, Janie, but nothin' Ah been through ain't too much if you just take a stand on high ground lak Ah dreamed."

Old Nanny sat there rocking Janie like an infant and thinking back and back. Mind-pictures brought feelings, and feelings dragged out dramas from the hollows of her heart.

"Dat mornin' on de big plantation close to Savannah, a rider come in a gallop tellin' 'bout Sherman takin' Atlanta. Marse Robert's son had done been kilt at Chickamauga. So he grabbed his gun and straddled his best horse and went off wid de rest of de gray-headed men and young boys to drive de Yankees back into Tennessee.

"They was all cheerin' and cryin' and shoutin' for de men dat was ridin' off. Ah couldn't see nothin' cause yo' mama wasn't but a week old, and Ah was flat uh my back. But pretty soon he let on he forgot somethin' and run into mah cabin and made me let down mah hair for de last time. He sorta wropped his hand in it, pulled mah big toe, lak he always done, and was gone after de rest lak lightnin'. Ah heard 'em give one last whoop for him. Then de big house and de quarters got sober and silent.

"It was de cool of de evenin' when Mistis come walkin' in mah door. She throwed de door wide open and stood dere lookin' at me outa her eyes and her face look lak she been livin' through uh hundred years in January without one day of spring. She come stood over me in de bed.

"'Nanny, Ah come to see that baby uh yourn.'

"Ah tried not to feel de breeze off her face, but it got so cold in dere dat Ah was freezin' to death under the kivvers. So Ah couldn't move right away lak Ah aimed to. But Ah knowed Ah had to make haste and do it.

"'You better git dat kivver offa dat youngun and dat quick!' she clashed at me. 'Look lak you don't know who is Mistis on dis plantation, Madam. But Ah aims to show you.'

"By dat time I had done managed tuh unkivver mah baby enough for her to see de head and face.

"'Nigger, whut's yo' baby doin' wid gray eyes and yaller hair?' She begin tuh slap mah jaws ever which a'way. Ah never felt the fust ones 'cause Ah wuz too busy gittin' de kivver back over mah chile. But dem last lick burnt me lak fire. Ah had too many feelin's tuh tell which one tuh follow so Ah didn't cry and Ah didn't do nothin' else. But then she kept on askin' me how come mah baby look white. She asted me dat maybe twenty-five or thirty times, lak she got tuh sayin' dat and couldn't help herself. So Ah told her, 'Ah don't know nothin' but what Ah'm told tuh do, 'cause Ah ain't nothin' but uh nigger and uh slave.'

"Instead of pacifyin' her lak Ah thought, look lak she got madder. But Ah reckon she was tired and wore out 'cause she didn't hit me no more. She went to de foot of de bed and wiped her hands on her hand-ksher. 'Ah wouldn't dirty mah hands on yuh. But first thing in de mornin' de overseer will take you to de whippin' post and tie you down on yo' knees and cut de hide offa yo' yaller back. One hundred lashes wid a raw-hide on yo' bare back. Ah'll have you whipped till de blood run down to yo' heels! Ah mean to count de licks mahself. And if it kills you Ah'll stand de loss. Anyhow, as soon as dat brat is a month old Ah'm going to sell it offa dis place.'

"She flounced on off and left her winter time wid me. Ah knowed mah body wasn't healed, but Ah couldn't consider dat. In de black dark Ah wrapped mah baby de best Ah knowed how and made it to de swamp by de river. Ah knowed de place was full uh moccasins and other bitin' snakes, but Ah was more skeered uh whut was behind me. Ah hide in dere day and night and suckled de baby ever time she start to cry, for fear somebody might hear her and Ah'd git found. Ah ain't sayin' uh friend or two didn't feel mah care. And den de Good Lawd seen to it dat Ah wasn't taken. Ah don't see how come mah milk didn't kill mah chile, wid me so skeered and worried all de time. De noise uh de owls skeered me; de limbs of dem cypress trees took to crawlin' and movin' round after dark, and two three times Ah heered panthers prowlin' round. But nothin' never hurt me 'cause de Lawd knowed how it was.

"Den, one night Ah heard de big guns boomin' lak thunder. It kept up all night long. And de next mornin' Ah could see uh big ship at a distance and a great stirrin' round. So Ah wrapped Leafy up in moss and fixed her good in a tree and picked mah way on down to de landin'. The men was all in blue, and Ah heard people say Sherman was comin' to meet de boats in Savannah, and all of us slaves was free. So Ah run got mah baby and got in quotation wid people and found a place Ah could stay.

"But it was a long time after dat befo' de Big Surrender at Richmond. Den de big bell ring in Atlanta and all de men in gray uniforms had to go to Moultrie, and bury their swords in de ground to show they was never to fight about slavery no mo'. So den we knowed we was free.

"Ah wouldn't marry nobody, though Ah could have uh heap uh times, cause Ah didn't want nobody mistreating mah baby. So Ah got with some good white people and come down here in West Florida to work and make de sunshine on both sides of de street for Leafy.

"Mah Madam help me wid her just lak she been doin' wid you. Ah put her in school when it got so it was a school to put her in. Ah was 'spectin' to make a school teacher outa her.

"But one day she didn't come home at de usual time and Ah waited and waited, but she never come all dat night. Ah took a lantern and went round askin' everybody but nobody ain't seen her. De next mornin' she come crawlin' in on her hands and knees. A sight to see. Dat school teacher had done hid her in de woods all night long, and he had done raped mah baby and run on off just before day.

"She was only seventeen, and somethin' lak dat to happen! Lawd a'mussy! Look lak Ah kin see it all over agin. It was a long time before she was well, and by dat time we knowed you was on de way. And after you was born she took to drinkin' likker and stayin' out nights. Couldn't git her to stay here and nowhere else. Lawd knows where she is right now. She ain't dead, 'cause Ah'd know it by mah feelings, but sometimes Ah wish she was at rest.

"And, Janie, maybe it wasn't much, but Ah done de best Ah kin by you. Ah raked and scraped and bought dis lil piece uh land so you wouldn't have to stay in de white folks' yard and tuck yo' head befo' other chillun at school. Dat was all right when you was little. But when you got big enough to understand things, Ah wanted you to look upon yo'self. Ah don't want yo' feathers always crumpled by folks throwin' up things in yo' face. And Ah can't die easy thinkin' maybe de menfolks white or black is makin' a spit cup outa you: Have some sympathy fuh me. Put me down easy, Janie, Ah'm a cracked plate."

AUDRE LORDE

Audre Lorde lives in New York with her two children. She is a professor of English and a poet. She says, "I was born in the middle of New York City of West Indian parents and raised to know that America was not my home."

from
ZAMI: A NEW SPELLING
OF MY NAME

M Y MOTHER WAS different from other women, and sometimes it gave me a sense of pleasure and specialness that was a positive aspect of feeling set apart. But sometimes it gave me pain and I fancied it the reason for so many of my childhood sorrows. *If my mother were like everybody else's maybe they would like me better.* But most often, her difference was like the season or a cold day or a steamy night in June. It just *was*, with no explanation or evocation necessary.

My mother and her two sisters were large and graceful women whose ample bodies seemed to underline the air of determination with which they moved through their lives in the strange world of Harlem and america. To me, my mother's physical substance and the presence and self-possession with which she carried herself were a large part of what made her *different*. Her public air of in-charge competence was quiet and effective. On the street people deferred to my mother over questions of taste, economy, opinion, quality, not to mention who had the right to the first available seat on the bus. I saw my mother fix her blue-grey-brown eyes upon a man scrambling for a seat on the Lenox Avenue bus, only to have him falter midway, grin abashedly, and, as if in the same movement, offer it to the old woman standing on the other side of him. I became aware, early on, that sometimes people would change their actions because of some opinion my mother never uttered, or even particularly cared about.

My mother was a very private woman, and actually quite shy, but with a very imposing, no-nonsense exterior. Full-bosomed, proud, and of no mean size, she would launch herself down the street like a ship under full sail, usually pulling me stumbling behind her. Not too many hardy souls dared cross her prow too closely.

Total strangers would turn to her in the meat market and ask what she thought about a cut of meat as to its freshness and appeal and suitability for such and such, and the butcher, impatient, would nonetheless wait for her to deliver her opinion, obviously quite a little put out but still deferential. Strangers counted upon my mother and I never knew why, but as a child it made me think she had a great deal more power than in fact she really had. My mother was invested in this image of herself also, and took pains, I realize now, to hide from us as children the many instances of her powerlessness. Being Black and foreign and female in New York City in the twenties and thirties was not simple, particularly when she was quite light enough to pass for white, but her children weren't.

In 1936-1938, 125th Street between Lenox and Eighth Avenues, later to become the shopping mecca of Black Harlem, was still a racially mixed area, with control and patronage largely in the hands of white shopkeepers. There were stores into which Black people were not welcomed, and no Black salespersons worked in the shops at all. Where our money was taken, it was taken with reluctance; and often too much was asked. (It was these conditions which young Adam Clayton Powell, Jr., addressed in his boycott and picketing of Blumstein's and Weissbecker's market in 1939 in an attempt, successful, to bring Black employment to 125th Street.) Tensions on the street were high, as they always are in racially mixed zones of transition. As a very little girl, I remember shrinking from a particular sound, a hoarsely sharp, guttural rasp, because it often meant a nasty glob of grey spittle upon my coat or shoe an instant later. My mother wiped it off with the little pieces of newspaper she always carried in her purse. Sometimes she fussed about low-class people who had no better sense nor manners than to spit into the wind no matter where they went, impressing upon me that this humiliation was totally random. It never occurred to me to doubt her.

It was not until years later once in conversation I said to her: "Have you noticed people don't spit into the wind so much the way they used to?" And the look on my mother's face told me that I had blundered into one of those secret places of pain that must never be spoken of again. But it was so typical of my mother when I was young that if she couldn't stop white people from spitting on her children because they were Black, she would insist it was something else. It was so often her approach to the world; to change reality. If you can't change reality, change your perceptions of it.

Both of my parents gave us to believe that they had the whole world in the palms of their hands for the most part, and if we three girls acted correctly—meaning working hard and doing as we were told—we could have the whole world in the palms of our hands also. It was a very confusing way to grow up, enhanced by the insularity of our family. Whatever went wrong in our lives was because our parents had decided that was best. Whatever went right was because our parents had decided that was the way it was going to be. Any doubts as to the reality of that situation were rapidly and summarily put down as small but intolerable rebellions against divine authority.

All our storybooks were about people who were very different from us. They were blond and white and lived in houses with trees around and had dogs named Spot. I didn't know people like that any more than I knew people like Cinderella who lived in castles. Nobody wrote stories about us, but still people always asked my mother for directions in a crowd.

It was this that made me decide as a child we must be rich, even when my mother did not have enough money to buy gloves for her chilblained hands, nor a proper winter coat. She would finish washing clothes and dress me hurriedly for the winter walk to pick up my sisters at school for lunch. By the time we got to St. Mark's School, seven blocks away, her beautiful long hands would be covered with ugly red splotches and welts. Later, I remember my mother rubbing her hands gingerly under cold water, and wringing them in pain. But when I asked, she brushed me off by telling me this was what they did for it at "home," and I still believed her when she said she hated to wear gloves.

At night, my father came home late from the office, or from a political meeting. After dinner, the three of us girls did our home-work sitting around the kitchen table. Then my two sisters went off down the hall to their beds. My mother put down the cot for me in the front bedroom, and supervised my getting ready for bed.

She turned off all the electric lights, and I could see her from my bed, two rooms away, sitting at the same kitchen table, reading the *Daily News* by a kerosene lamp, and waiting for my father. She always said it was because the kerosene lamp reminded her of "home." When I was grown I realized she was trying to save a few pennies of electricity before my father came in and turned on the lights with "Lin, why you sitting in the dark so?" Sometimes I'd go to sleep with the soft chunk-a-ta-chink of her foot-pedal-powered Singer Sewing Machine, stitching up sheets and pillowcases from un-bleached muslin gotten on sale "under the bridge."

I only saw my mother crying twice when I was little. Once was when I was three, and sat on the step of her dental chair at the City Dental Clinic on 23rd Street, while a student dentist pulled out all the teeth on one side of her upper jaw. It was in a huge room full of dental chairs with other groaning people in them, and white-jacketed young men bending over open mouths. The sound of the many dental drills and instruments made the place sound like a street-corner excavation site.

Afterwards, my mother sat outside on a long wooden bench. I saw her lean her head against the back, her eyes closed. She did not respond to my pats and tugs at her coat. Climbing up upon the seat, I peered into my mother's face to see why she should be sleeping in the middle of the day. From under her closed eyelids, drops of tears were squeezing out and running down her cheek toward her ear. I touched the little drops of water on her high cheekbone in horror and amazement. The world was turning over. My mother was crying.

The other time I saw my mother cry was a few years later, one night, when I was supposed to be asleep in their bedroom. The door to the parlor was ajar, and I could see through the crack into the next room. I woke to hear my parents' voices in english. My father had just come home, and with liquor on his breath.

"I hoped I'd never live to see the day when you, Bee, stand up in some saloon and it's drink you drinking with some clubhouse woman."

"But Lin, what are you talking? It's not that way a-tall, you know. In politics you must be friendly-friendly so. It doesn't mean a thing."

"And if you were to go before I did, I would never so much as look upon another man, and I would expect you to do the same."

My mother's voice was strangely muffled by her tears.

These were the years leading up to the Second World War, when Depression took such a terrible toll, and of Black people in particular.

Even though we children could be beaten for losing a penny coming home from the store, my mother fancied a piece of her role as lady bountiful, a role she would accuse me bitterly of playing years later in my life whenever I gave something to a friend. But one of my earlier memories of World War II was just before the beginning, with my mother splitting a one-pound tin of coffee between two old family friends who had come on an infrequent visit.

Although she always insisted that she had nothing to do with politics or government affairs, from somewhere my mother had heard the winds of war, and despite our poverty had set about consistently hoarding sugar and coffee in her secret closet under the sink. Long before Pearl Harbor, I recall opening each cloth five-pound sack of sugar which we purchased at the market and pouring a third of it into a scrubbed tin to store away under the sink, secure from mice. The same thing happened with coffee. We would buy Bokar Coffee at the A&P and have it ground and poured into bags, and then divide the bag between the coffee tin on the back of the stove, and the hidden ones under the sink. Not many people came to our house, ever, but no one left without at least a cupful of sugar or coffee during the war, when coffee and sugar were heavily rationed.

Meat and butter could not be hoarded, and throughout the early war, my mother's absolute refusal to accept butter substitutes (only "other people" used margarine, those same "other people" who fed their children peanut butter sandwiches for lunch, used sandwich spread instead of mayonnaise and ate pork chops and watermelon) had us on line in front of supermarkets all over the city on bitterly cold Saturday mornings, waiting for the store to open so we each could get first crack at buying our allotted quarter-pound of un-rationed butter. Throughout the war, Mother kept a mental list of all the supermarkets reachable by one bus, frequently taking only me because I could ride free. She also noted which were friendly and which were not, and long after the war ended there were meat markets and stores we never shopped in because someone in them had crossed my mother during the war over some precious scarce commodity, and my mother never forgot and rarely forgave.

ALICE WALKER

Alice Walker, best known for The Color Purple, *was born in Mississippi and lived in Massachusetts after graduating from Sarah Lawrence College. She has said that she thinks of the three characters in "Everyday Use" as herself, split into three parts.*

EVERYDAY USE

I WILL WAIT for her in the yard that Maggie and I made so clean and wavy yesterday afternoon. A yard like this is more comfortable than most people know. It is not just a yard. It is like an extended living room. When the hard clay is swept clean as a floor and the fine sand around the edges lined with tiny, irregular grooves anyone can come and sit and look up into the elm tree and wait for the breezes that never come inside the house.

Maggie will be nervous until after her sister goes: she will stand hopelessly in corners homely and ashamed of the burn scars down her arms and legs, eyeing her sister with a mixture of envy and awe. She thinks her sister has held life always in the palm of one hand, that "no" is a word the world never learned to say to her.

You've no doubt seen those TV shows where the child who has "made it" is confronted, as a surprise, by her own mother and father, tottering in weakly from backstage. (A pleasant surprise, of course: What would they do if parent and child came on the show only to curse out and insult each other?) On TV mother and child embrace and smile into each other's faces. Sometimes the mother and father weep, the child wraps them in her arms and leans across the table to tell how she would not have made it without their help. I have seen these programs.

Sometimes I dream a dream in which Dee and I are suddenly brought together on a TV program of this sort. Out of a dark and soft-seated limousine I am ushered into a bright room filled with many people. There I meet a smiling, gray, sporty man like Johnny Carson who shakes my hand and tells me what a fine girl I have. Then we are on the stage and Dee is embracing me with tears in her eyes. She pins on my dress a large orchid, even though she has told me once that she thinks orchids are tacky flowers.

In real life I am a large, big-boned woman with rough, man-working hands. In the winter I wear flannel nightgowns to bed and overalls during the day. I can kill and clean a hog as mercilessly as a man. My fat keeps me hot in zero weather. I can work all day, breaking ice to get water for washing. I can eat pork liver cooked over the open fire minutes after it comes steaming from the hog. One winter I knocked a bull calf straight in the brain between the eyes with a sledge hammer and had the meat hung up to chill before nightfall. But of course all this does not show on television. I am the way my daughter would want me to be: a hundred pounds lighter, my skin like an uncooked barley pancake. My hair glistens in the hot bright lights. Johnny Carson has much to do to keep up with my quick and witty tongue.

But that is a mistake. I know even before I wake up. Who ever knew a Johnson with a quick tongue? Who can even imagine me looking a strange white man in the eye? It seems to me I have talked to them always with one foot raised in flight, with my head turned in whichever way is farthest from them. Dee, though. She would always look anyone in the eye. Hesitation was no part of her nature.

"How do I look, Mama?" Maggie says, showing just enough of her thin body enveloped in pink skirt and red blouse for me to know she's there, almost hidden by the door.

"Come out into the yard," I say.

Have you ever seen a lame animal, perhaps a dog run over by some careless person rich enough to own a car, sidle up to someone who is ignorant enough to be kind to him? That is the way my Maggie walks. She has been like this, chin on chest, eyes on ground, feet in shuffle, ever since the fire that burned the other house to the ground.

Dee is lighter than Maggie, with nicer hair and a fuller figure. She's a woman now, though sometimes I forget. How long ago was it that the other house burned? Ten, twelve years? Sometimes I can still hear the flames and feel Maggie's arm sticking to me, her hair smoking and her dress falling off her in little black papery flakes. Her eyes seemed stretched open, blazed open by the flames reflected in them. And Dee. I see her standing off under the sweet gum tree she used to dig gum out of; a look of concentration on her face as she watched the last dingy gray board of the house fall in toward the red-hot brick chimney. Why don't you do a dance around the ashes? I'd wanted to ask her. She had hated the house that much.

I used to think she hated Maggie, too. But that was before we raised the money, the church and me, to send her to Augusta to school. She used to read to us without pity; forcing words, lies, other folks' habits, whole lives upon us two, sitting trapped and ignorant underneath her voice. She washed us in a river of make-believe, burned us with a lot of knowledge we didn't necessarily need to know. Pressed us to her with the serious way she read, to shove us away at just the moment, like dimwits, we seemed about to understand.

Dee wanted nice things. A yellow organdy dress to wear to her graduation from high school; black pumps to match a green suit she'd made from an old suit somebody gave me. She was determined to stare down any disaster in her efforts. Her eyelids would not flicker for minutes at a time. Often I fought off the temptation to shake her. At sixteen she had a style of her own: and knew what style was.

I never had an education myself. After second grade the school was closed down. Don't ask me why: in 1927 colored asked fewer questions than they do now. Sometimes Maggie reads to me. She stumbles along good-naturedly but can't see well. She knows she is not bright. Like good looks and money, quickness passed her by. She will marry John Thomas (who has mossy teeth in an earnest face) and then I'll be free to sit here and I guess just sing church songs to myself. Although I never was a good singer. Never could carry a tune. I was always better at a man's job. I used to love to milk till I was hoofed in the side in '49. Cows are soothing and slow and don't bother you, unless you try to milk them the wrong way.

I have deliberately turned my back on the house. It is three rooms, just like the one that burned, except the roof is tin; they don't make shingle roofs any more. There are no real windows, just some holes cut in the sides, like the portholes in a ship, but not round and not square, with rawhide holding the shutters up on the outside. This house is in a pasture, too, like the other one. No doubt when Dee sees it she will want to tear it down. She wrote me once that no matter where we "choose" to live, she will manage to come see us. But she will never bring her friends. Maggie and I thought about this and Maggie asked me, "Mama, when did Dee ever *have* any friends?"

She had a few. Furtive boys in pink shirts hanging about on wash-day after school. Nervous girls who never laughed. Impressed with her they worshiped the well-turned phrase, the cute shape, the scalding humor that erupted like bubbles in lye. She read to them.

When she was courting Jimmy T she didn't have much time to pay to us, but turned all her faultfinding power on him. He *flew* to marry a cheap gal from a family of ignorant flashy people. She hardly had time to recompose herself.

When she comes I will meet—but there they are!

Maggie attempts to make a dash for the house, in her shuffling way, but I stay her with my hand. "Come back here," I say. And she stops and tries to dig a well in the sand with her toe.

It is hard to see them clearly through the strong sun. But even the first glimpse of leg out of the car tells me it is Dee. Her feet were always neat-looking, as if God himself had shaped them with a certain style. From the other side of the car comes a short, stocky man. Hair is all over his head a foot long and hanging from his chin like a kinky mule tail. I hear Maggie suck in her breath. "Uhnnnh," is what it sounds like. Like when you see the wriggling end of a snake just in front of your foot on the road. "Uhnnnh."

Dee next. A dress down to the ground, in this hot weather. A dress so loud it hurts my eyes. There are yellows and oranges enough to throw back the light of the sun. I feel my whole face warming from the heat waves it throws out. Earrings, too, gold and hanging down to her shoulders. Bracelets dangling and making noises when she moves her arm up to shake the folds of the dress out of her armpits. The dress is loose and flows, and as she walks closer, I like it. I hear Maggie go "Uhnnnh" again. It is her sister's hair. It stands straight up like the wool on a sheep. It is black as night and around the edges are two long pigtails that rope about like small lizards disappearing behind her ears.

"Wa-su-zo-Tean-o!" she says, coming on in that gliding way the dress makes her move. The short stocky fellow with the hair to his navel is all grinning and he follows up with "Asalamalakim, my mother and sister!" He moves to hug Maggie but she falls back, right up against the back of my chair. I feel her trembling there and when I look up I see the perspiration falling off her chin.

"Don't get up," says Dee. Since I am stout it takes something of a push. You can see me trying to move a second or two before I make it. She turns, showing white heels through her sandals, and goes back to the car. Out she peeks next with a Polaroid. She stoops down quickly and lines up picture after picture of me sitting there in front of the house with Maggie cowering behind me. She never takes a shot without making sure the house is included. When a cow comes nibbling around the edge of the yard she snaps it and me and Maggie *and* the house. Then she puts the Polaroid in the back seat of the car, and comes up and kisses me on the forehead.

Meanwhile Asalamalakim is going through the motions with Maggie's hand. Maggie's hand is as limp as a fish, and probably as cold, despite the sweat, and she keeps trying to pull it back. It looks like Asalamalakim wants to shake hands but wants to do it fancy. Or maybe he don't know how people shake hands. Anyhow, he soon gives up on Maggie.

"Well," I say. "Dee."

"No, Mama," she says. "Not 'Dee,' Wangero Leewanika Kemanjo!"

"What happened to 'Dee'?" I wanted to know.

"She's dead," Wangero said. "I couldn't bear it any longer being named after the people who oppress me."

"You know as well as me you was named after your aunt Dicie," I said. Dicie is my sister. She named Dee. We called her "Big Dee" after Dee was born.

"But who was *she* named after?" asked Wangero.

"I guess after Grandma Dee," I said.

"And who was she named after?" asked Wangero.

"Her mother," I said, and saw Wangero was getting tired. "That's about as far back as I can trace it," I said. Though, in fact, I probably could have carried it back beyond the Civil War through the branches.

"Well," said Asalamalakim, "there you are."

"Uhnnnh," I heard Maggie say.

"There I was not," I said, "before 'Dicie' cropped up in our family, so why should I try to trace it that far back?"

He just stood there grinning, looking down on me like somebody inspecting a Model A car. Every once in a while he and Wangero sent eye signals over my head.

"How do you pronounce this name?" I asked.

"You don't have to call me by it if you don't want to," said Wangero.

"Why shouldn't I?" I asked. "If that's what you want us to call you, we'll call you."

"I know it might sound awkward at first," said Wangero.

"I'll get used to it," I said. "Ream it out again."

Well, soon we got the name out of the way. Asalamalakim had a name twice as long and three times as hard. After I tripped over it two or three times he told me to just call him Hakim-a-barber. I wanted to ask him was he a barber, but I didn't really think he was, so I didn't ask.

"You must belong to those beef-cattle peoples down the road," I said. They said "Asalamalakim" when they met you, too, but they didn't shake hands. Always too busy: feeding the cattle, fixing the fences, putting up salt-lick shelters, throwing down hay. When the white folks poisoned some of the herd the men stayed up all night with rifles in their hands. I walked a mile and a half just to see the sight.

Hakim-a-barber said, "I accept some of their doctrines, but farming and raising cattle is not my style." (They didn't tell me, and I didn't ask, whether Wangero [Dee] had really gone and married him.)

We sat down to eat and right away he said he didn't eat collards and pork was unclean. Wangero, though, went on through the chitlins and corn bread, the greens and everything else. She talked a blue streak over the sweet potatoes. Everything delighted her. Even the fact that we still used the benches her daddy made for the table when we couldn't afford to buy chairs.

"Oh, Mama!" she cried. Then turned to Hakim-a-barber. "I never knew how lovely these benches are. You can feel the rump prints," she said, running her hands underneath her and along the bench. Then she gave a sigh and her hand closed over Grandma Dee's butter dish. "That's it!" she said. "I knew there was something I wanted to ask you if I could have." She jumped up from the table and went over in the corner where the churn stood, the milk in its clabber by now. She looked at the churn and looked at it.

"This churn top is what I need," she said. "Didn't Uncle Buddy whittle it out of a tree you all used to have?"

"Yes," I said.

"Uh huh," she said happily. "And I want the dasher, too."

"Uncle Buddy whittle that, too?" asked the barber.

Dee (Wangero) looked up at me.

"Aunt Dee's first husband whittled the dash," said Maggie so low you almost couldn't hear her. "His name was Henry, but they called him Stash."

"Maggie's brain is like an elephant's," Wangero said, laughing. "I can use the churn top as a centerpiece for the alcove table," she said, sliding a plate over the churn, "and I'll think of something artistic to do with the dasher."

When she finished wrapping the dasher the handle stuck out. I took it for a moment in my hands. You didn't even have to look close to see where hands pushing the dasher up and down to make butter had left a kind of sink in the wood. In fact, there were a lot of small sinks; you could see where thumbs and fingers had sunk into the wood. It was beautiful light yellow wood, from a tree that grew in the yard where Big Dee and Stash had lived.

After dinner Dee (Wangero) went to the trunk at the foot of my bed and started rifling through it. Maggie hung back in the kitchen over the dishpan. Out came Wangero with two quilts. They had been pieced by Grandma Dee and then Big Dee and me had hung them on the quilt frames on the front porch and quilted them. One was in the Lone Star pattern. The other was Walk Around the Mountain. In both of them were scraps of dresses Grandma Dee had worn fifty and more years ago. Bits and pieces of Grandpa Jarell's Paisley shirts. And one teeny faded blue piece, about the size of a penny matchbox, that was from Great Grandpa Ezra's uniform that he wore in the Civil War.

"Mama," Wangero said sweet as a bird. "Can I have these old quilts?"

I heard something fall in the kitchen, and a minute later the kitchen door slammed.

"Why don't you take one or two of the others?" I asked. "These old things was just done by me and Big Dee from some tops your grandma pieced before she died."

"No," said Wangero. "I don't want those. They are stitched around the borders by machine."

"That makes them last better," I said.

"That's not the point," said Wangero. "These are all pieces of dresses Grandma used to wear. She did all this stitching by hand.

Imagine!" She held the quilts securely in her arms, stroking them.

"Some of the pieces, like those lavender ones, come from old clothes her mother handed down to her," I said, moving up to touch the quilts. Dee (Wangero) moved back just enough so that I couldn't reach the quilts. They already belonged to her.

"Imagine!" she breathed again, clutching them closely to her bosom.

"The truth is," I said, "I promised to give them quilts to Maggie, for when she marries John Thomas."

She gasped like a bee had stung her.

"Maggie can't appreciate these quilts!" she said. "She'd probably be backward enough to put them to everyday use."

"I reckon she would," I said. "God knows I been saving 'em for long enough with nobody using 'em. I hope she will!" I didn't want to bring up how I had offered Dee (Wangero) a quilt when she went away to college. Then she had told me they were old-fashioned, out of style.

"But they're *priceless*!" she was saying now, furiously; for she has a temper. "Maggie would put them on the bed and in five years they'd be in rags. Less than that!"

"She can always make some more," I said. "Maggie knows how to quilt."

Dee (Wangero) looked at me with hatred. "You just will not understand. The point is these quilts, *these* quilts!"

"Well," I said, stumped. "What would *you* do with them?"

"Hang them," she said. As if that was the only thing you *could* do with quilts.

Maggie by now was standing in the door. I could almost hear the sound her feet made as they scraped over each other.

"She can have them, Mama," she said, like somebody used to never winning anything, or having anything reserved for her. "I can 'member Grandma Dee without the quilts."

I looked at her hard. She had filled her bottom lip with checker-berry snuff and it gave her face a kind of dopey, hangdog look. It was Grandma Dee and Big Dee who taught her how to quilt herself. She stood there with her scarred hands hidden in the folds of her skirt. She looked at her sister with something like fear but she wasn't mad at her. This was Maggie's portion. This was the way she knew God to work.

When I looked at her like that something hit me in the top of my head and ran down to the soles of my feet. Just like when I'm in church and the spirit of God touches me and I get happy and shout. I did something I never had done before: hugged Maggie to me, then dragged her on into the room, snatched the quilts out of Miss Wangero's hands and dumped them into Maggie's lap. Maggie just sat there on my bed with her mouth open.

"Take one or two of the others," I said to Dee.

But she turned without a word and went out to Hakim-a-barber.

"You just don't understand," she said, as Maggie and I came out to the car.

"What don't I understand?" I wanted to know.

"Your heritage," she said. And then she turned to Maggie, kissed her, and said, "You ought to try to make something of yourself, too, Maggie. It's really a new day for us. But from the way you and Mama still live you'd never know it."

She put on some sunglasses that hid everything above the tip of her nose and her chin.

Maggie smiled; maybe at the sunglasses. But a real smile, not scared. After we watched the car dust settle I asked Maggie to bring me a dip of snuff. And then the two of us sat there just enjoying, until it was time to go in the house and go to bed.

AUGUST WILSON

August Wilson, born in 1945 in Pittsburgh, Pennsylvania, founded a black theater company after dropping out of high school. While living in St. Paul, Minnesota, he wrote Fences, *his Pulitzer Prize-winning play, about a father who forbids his son to accept an athletic scholarship.*

from FENCES

ACT I, SCENE 3

TROY: (*Calling.*) Cory! Get your butt out here, boy!

(TROY *goes over to the pile of wood, picks up a board, and starts sawing.* CORY *enters from the house.*)

TROY: You just now coming in here from leaving this morning?

CORY: Yeah, I had to go to football practice.

TROY: Yeah, what?

CORY: Yessir.

TROY: I ain't but two seconds off you noway. The garbage sitting in there overflowing . . . you ain't done none of your chores . . . and you come in here talking about "Yeah."

CORY: I was just getting ready to do my chores now, Pop . . .

TROY: Your first chore is to help me with this fence on Saturday. Everything else come after that. Now get that saw and cut them boards.

(*CORY takes the saw and begins cutting the boards.* TROY *continues working. There is a long pause.*)

CORY: Hey, Pop . . . why don't you buy a TV?

TROY: What I want with a TV? What I want one of them for?

CORY: Everybody got one. Earl, Ba Bra . . . Jesse!

TROY: I ain't asked you who had one. I say what I want with one?

CORY: So you can watch it. They got lots of things on TV. Baseball games and everything. We could watch the World Series.

TROY: Yeah . . . and how much this TV cost?

CORY: I don't know. They got them on sale for around two hundred dollars.

TROY: Two hundred dollars, huh?

CORY: That ain't that much, Pop.

TROY: Naw, it's just two hundred dollars. See that roof you got over your head at night? Let me tell you something about that roof. It's been over ten years since that roof was last tarred. See now . . . the snow come this winter and sit up there on that roof like it is . . . and it's gonna seep inside. It's just gonna be a little bit . . . ain't gonna hardly notice it. Then the next thing you know, it's gonna be leaking all over the house. Then the wood rot from all that water and you gonna need a whole new roof. Now, how much you think it cost to get that roof tarred?

CORY: I don't know.

TROY: Two hundred and sixty-four dollars . . . cash money. While you thinking about a TV, I got to be thinking about the roof . . . and whatever else go wrong around here. Now if you had two hundred dollars, what would you do . . . fix the roof or buy a TV?

CORY: I'd buy a TV. Then when the roof started to leak . . . When it needed fixing . . . I'd fix it.

TROY: Where you gonna get the money from? You done spent it for a TV. You gonna sit up and watch the water run all over your brand new TV.

CORY: Aw, Pop. You got money. I know you do.

TROY: Where I got it at, huh?

CORY: You got it in the bank.

TROY: You wanna see my bankbook? You wanna see that seventy-three dollars and twenty-two cents I got sitting up in there.

CORY: You ain't got to pay for it all at one time. You can put a down payment on it and carry it on home with you.

TROY: Not me. I ain't gonna owe nobody nothing if I can help it. Miss a payment and they come and snatch it right out your house. Then what you got? Now, soon as I get two hundred dollars clear, then I'll buy a TV. Right now, as soon as I get two hundred and sixty-four dollars, I'm gonna have this roof tarred.

CORY: Aw . . . Pop!

TROY: You go on and get you two hundred dollars and buy one if ya want it. I got better things to do with my money.

CORY: I can't get no two hundred dollars. I ain't never seen two hundred dollars.

TROY: I'll tell you what . . . you get you a hundred dollars and I'll put the other hundred with it.

CORY: Alright, I'm gonna show you.

TROY: You gonna show me how you can cut them boards right now.

(CORY *begins to cut the boards. There is a long pause.*)

CORY: The Pirates won today. That makes five in a row.

TROY: I ain't thinking about the Pirates. Got an all-white team. Got that boy . . . that Puerto Rican boy . . . Clemente. Don't even half-play him. That boy could be something if they give him a chance. Play him one day and sit him on the bench the next.

CORY: He gets a lot of chances to play.

TROY: I'm talking about playing regular. Playing every day so you can get your timing. That's what I'm talking about.

CORY: They got some white guys on the team that don't play every day. You can't play everybody at the same time.

TROY: If they got a white fellow sitting on the bench . . . you can bet your last dollar he can't play! The colored guy got to be twice as good before he get on the team. That's why I don't want you to get all tied up in them sports. Man on the team and what it get him? They got colored on the team and don't use them. Same as not having them. All them teams the same.

CORY: The Braves got Hank Aaron and Wes Covington. Hank Aaron hit two home runs today. That makes forty-three.

TROY: Hank Aaron ain't nobody. That's what you supposed to do. That's how you supposed to play the game. Ain't nothing to it. It's just a matter of timing . . . getting the right follow-through. Hell, I can hit forty-three home runs right now!

CORY: Not off no major-league pitching, you couldn't.

TROY: We had better pitching in the Negro leagues. I hit seven home runs off of Satchel Paige. You can't get no better than that!

CORY: Sandy Koufax. He's leading the league in strike-outs.

TROY: I ain't thinking of no Sandy Koufax.

CORY: You got Warren Spahn and Lew Burdette. I bet you couldn't hit no home runs off of Warren Spahn.

TROY: I'm through with it now. You go on and cut them boards. (*Pause.*)
Your mama tell me you done got recruited by a college football team? Is that right?

CORY: Yeah. Coach Zellman say the recruiter gonna be coming by to talk to you. Get you to sign the permission papers.

TROY: I thought you supposed to be working down there at the A&P. Ain't you suppose to be working down there after school?

CORY: Mr. Stawicki say he gonna hold my job for me until after the football season. Say starting next week I can work weekends.

TROY: I thought we had an understanding about this football stuff? You suppose to keep up with your chores and hold that job down at the A&P. Ain't been around here all day on a Saturday. Ain't none of your chores done . . . and now you telling me you done quit your job.

CORY: I'm gonna be working weekends.

TROY: You damn right you are! And ain't no need for nobody coming around here to talk to me about signing nothing.

CORY: Hey, Pop . . . you can't do that. He's coming all the way from North Carolina.

TROY: I don't care where he coming from. The white man ain't gonna let you get nowhere with that football noway. You go on and get your book-learning so you can work yourself up in that A&P or learn how to fix cars or build houses or something, get you a trade. That way you have something can't nobody take away from you. You go on and learn how to put your hands to some good use. Besides hauling people's garbage.

CORY: I get good grades, Pop. That's why the recruiter wants to talk with you. You got to keep up your grades to get recruited. This way I'll be going to college. I'll get a chance . . .

TROY: First you gonna get your butt down there to the A&P and get your job back.

CORY: Mr. Stawicki done already hired somebody else 'cause I told him I was playing football.

TROY: You a bigger fool than I thought . . . to let somebody take away your job so you can play some football. Where you gonna get your money to take out your girlfriend and whatnot? What kind of foolishness is that to let somebody take away your job?

CORY: I'm still gonna be working weekends.

TROY: Naw . . . naw. You getting your butt out of here and finding you another job.

CORY: Come on, Pop! I got to practice. I can't work after school and play football too. The team needs me. That's what Coach Zellman say . . .

TROY: I don't care what nobody else say. I'm the boss . . . you understand? I'm the boss around here. I do the only saying what counts.

CORY: Come on, Pop!

TROY: I asked you . . . did you understand?

CORY: Yeah . . .

TROY: What?!

CORY: Yessir.

TROY: You go on down there to that A&P and see if you can get your job back. If you can't do both . . . then you quit the football team. You've got to take the crookeds with the straights.

CORY: Yessir.
(*Pause.*)
Can I ask you a question?

TROY: What the hell you wanna ask me? Mr. Stawicki the one you got the questions for.

CORY: How come you ain't never liked me?

TROY: Like you? Who the hell say I got to like you? What law is there say I got to like you? Wanna stand up in my face and ask a damn fool-ass question like that. Talking about liking somebody. Come here, boy, when I talk to you.
(*CORY comes over to where TROY is working. He stands slouched over and TROY shoves him on his shoulder.*)
Straighten up, goddammit! I asked you a question . . . what law is there say I got to like you?

CORY: None.

TROY: Well, alright then! Don't you eat every day?
(*Pause.*)
Answer me when I talk to you! Don't you eat every day?

CORY: Yeah.

TROY: Nigger, as long as you in my house, you put that sir on the end of it when you talk to me!

CORY: Yes . . . sir.

TROY: You eat every day.

CORY: Yessir!

TROY: Got a roof over your head.

CORY: Yessir!

TROY: Got clothes on your back.

CORY: Yessir.

TROY: Why you think that is?

CORY: 'Cause of you.

TROY: Aw, hell I know it's 'cause of me . . . but why do you think that is?

CORY: (*Hesitant.*) 'Cause you like me.

TROY: Like you? I go out of here every morning . . . bust my butt . . . putting up with them crackers every day . . . 'cause I like you? You about the biggest fool I ever saw.
(*Pause.*)
It's my job. It's my responsibility! You understand that? A man got to take care of his family. You live in my house . . . sleep you behind on my bedclothes . . . fill you belly up with my food . . . 'cause you my son. You my flesh and blood. Not 'cause I like you! 'Cause it's my duty to take care of you. I owe a responsibility to you! Let's get this straight right here . . . before it go along any further . . . I ain't got to like you. Mr. Rand don't give me my money come payday 'cause he likes me. He gives me 'cause he owe me. I done give you everything I had to give you. I gave you your life! Me and your mama worked that out between us. And liking your black ass wasn't part of the bargain. Don't you try and go through life worrying about if somebody like you or not. You best be making sure they doing right by you. You understand what I'm saying, boy?

CORY: Yessir.

TROY: Then get the hell out of my face, and get on down to that A&P.

NIKKI GIOVANNI

Nikki Giovanni is a poet and a teacher. Of being a poet, she says: "As a writer I have always sought to do that which I have not done." Of being a teacher, she says: "I think the students don't mind a little old crazy poet expecting them to do something."

EGO TRIPPING

(there may be a reason why)

I was born in the congo
I walked to the fertile crescent and built
    the sphinx
I designed a pyramid so tough that a star
      that only glows every one hundred years falls
      into the center giving divine perfect light
I am bad

I sat on the throne
    drinking nectar with allah
I got hot and sent an ice age to europe
    to cool my thirst
My oldest daughter is nefertiti
    the tears from my birth pains
    created the nile
I am a beautiful woman

I gazed on the forest and burned
    out the sahara desert
    with a packet of goat's meat
    and a change of clothes
I crossed it in two hours
I am a gazelle so swift
    so swift you can't catch me

For a birthday present when he was three
I gave my son hannibal an elephant
    He gave me rome for mother's day
My strength flows ever on

My son noah built new/ark and
I stood proudly at the helm
    as we sailed on a soft summer day
I turned myself into myself and was
    jesus
    men intone my loving name
    All praises All praises
I am the one who would save

I sowed diamonds in my back yard
My bowels deliver uranium
    the filings from my fingernails are
    semi-precious jewels
    On a trip north
I caught a cold and blew
My nose giving oil to the arab world
I am so hip even my errors are correct
I sailed west to reach east and had to round off
    the earth as I went
    The hair from my head thinned and gold was laid
    across three continents

I am so perfect so divine so ethereal so surreal
I cannot be comprehended
    except by my permission

I mean . . . I . . . can fly
    like a bird in the sky . . .

N I K K I - R O S A

childhood remembrances are always a drag
if you're Black
you always remember things like living in Woodlawn
with no inside toilet
and if you become famous or something
they never talk about how happy you were to have your mother
all to yourself and
how good the water felt when you got your bath from one of those
big tubs that folk in chicago barbecue in
and somehow when you talk about home
it never gets across how much you
understood their feelings
as the whole family attended meetings about Hollydale
and even though you remember
your biographers never understand
your father's pain as he sells his stock
and another dream goes
and though you're poor it isn't poverty that
concerns you
and though they fought a lot
it isn't your father's drinking that makes any difference
but only that everybody is together and you
and your sister have happy birthdays and very good christmasses
and I really hope no white person ever has cause to write about me
because they never understand Black love is Black wealth and they'll
probably talk about my hard childhood and never understand that
all the while I was quite happy

LANGSTON HUGHES

Langston Hughes, born in 1902, is perhaps America's best-known African American poet. His plays and poems made him a central figure in the Harlem Renaissance, a burst of creativity in the 1920s. He wrote in almost every conceivable genre—including a humorous newspaper column and slogans of encouragement to black troops during World War II—until his death in 1967.

THEME FOR ENGLISH B

The instructor said,

> Go home and write
> a page tonight.
> And let that page come out of you—
> Then, it will be true.

I wonder if it's that simple?

I am twenty-two, colored, born in Winston-Salem.
I went to school there, then Durham, then here
to this college on the hill above Harlem.
I am the only colored student in my class.
The steps from the hill lead down to Harlem,
through a park, then I cross St. Nicholas,
Eighth Avenue, Seventh, and I come to the Y,
the Harlem Branch Y, where I take the elevator
up to my room, sit down, and write this page:

It's not easy to know what is true for you or me
at twenty-two, my age. But I guess I'm what
I feel and see and hear. Harlem, I hear you:
hear you, hear me—we two—you, me talk on this page.
(I hear New York, too.) Me—who?

Well, I like to eat, sleep, drink, and be in love.
I like to work, read, learn, and understand life.
I like a pipe for a Christmas present,
or records—Bessie, bop, or Bach.

I guess being colored doesn't make me not like
the same things other folks like who are other races.
So will my page be colored that I write?
Being me, it will not be white.
But it will be
a part of you, instructor.
You are white—
yet a part of me, as I am a part of you.
That's American.
Sometimes perhaps you don't want to be a part of me.
Nor do I often want to be a part of you.
But we are, that's true!
As I learn from you,
I guess you learn from me—
although you're older—and white—
and somewhat more free.

This is my page for English B.

DONNA KATE RUSHIN

Donna Kate Rushin grew up in New Jersey and attended Oberlin College. She works as a Poet-in-the-Schools.

THE BRIDGE POEM

I've had enough
I'm sick of seeing and touching
Both sides of things
Sick of being the damn bridge for everybody

Nobody
Can talk to anybody
Without me
Right?

I explain my mother to my father my father to my little sister
My little sister to my brother my brother to the white feminists
The white feminists to the Black church folks the Black church folks
To the ex-hippies the ex-hippies to the Black separatists the
Black separatists to the artists the artists to my friends' parents . . .

Then
I've got to explain myself
To everybody
I do more translating
Than the Gawdamn U.N.

Forget it
I'm sick of it

I'm sick of filling in your gaps
Sick of being your insurance against
The isolation of your self-imposed limitations
Sick of being the crazy at your holiday dinners
Sick of being the odd one at your Sunday Brunches
Sick of being the sole Black friend to 34 individual white people

Find another connection to the rest of the world
Find something else to make you legitimate
Find some other way to be political and hip
I will not be the bridge to your womanhood
Your manhood
Your human-ness

I'm sick of reminding you not to
Close off too tight for too long

I'm sick of mediating with your worst self
On behalf of your better selves

I am sick
Of having to remind you
To breathe
Before you suffocate
Your own fool self

Forget it
Stretch or drown
Evolve or die

The bridge I must be
Is the bridge to my own power
I must translate
My own fears
Mediate
My own weaknesses

I must be the bridge to nowhere
But my true self
And then
I will be useful

MARGARET WALKER

Margaret Walker, born in Alabama in 1915, is of an older generation of African American writers. Her first book of poems, For My People, *was published in 1942, and her novel,* Jubilee, *in 1966. She lives in Jackson, Mississippi, where she has been a professor of English and raised four children.*

FOR MY PEOPLE

For my people everywhere singing their slave songs
    repeatedly: their dirges and their ditties and their blues
    and jubilees, praying their prayers nightly to an unknown
    god, bending their knees humbly to an unseen power;
For my people lending their strength to the years: to the
    gone years and the now years and the maybe years,
    washing ironing cooking scrubbing sewing mending hoeing
    plowing digging planting pruning patching dragging
    along never gaining never reaping never knowing and
    never understanding;
For my playmates in the clay and dust and sand of Alabama
    backyards playing baptizing and preaching, and doctor
    and jail and soldier and school and mama and cooking
    and playhouse and concert and store and Miss Choomby
    and hair and company;
For the cramped bewildered years we went to school to
    learn to know the reasons why and the answers to and
    the people who and the places where and the days when, in
    memory of the bitter hours when we discovered we
    were black and poor and small and different and nobody
    wondered and nobody understood;
For the boys and girls who grew in spite of these things
    to be Man and Woman, to laugh and dance and sing and
    play and drink their wine and religion and success, to

marry their playmates and bear children and then die
   of consumption and anemia and lynching;
For my people thronging 47th Street in Chicago and Lenox
   Avenue in New York and Rampart Street in New
   Orleans, lost disinherited dispossessed and HAPPY
   people filling the cabarets and taverns and other people's
   pockets needing bread and shoes and milk and land
   and money and Something—Something all our own;
For my people walking blindly, spreading joy, losing time
   being lazy, sleeping when hungry, shouting when burdened,
   drinking when hopeless, tied and shackled and tangled
   among ourselves by the unseen creatures who tower
   over us omnisciently and laugh;
For my people blundering and groping and floundering in
   the dark of churches and schools and clubs and societies,
   associations and councils and committees and conventions,
   distressed and disturbed and deceived and devoured
   by money-hungry glory-craving leeches, preyed on by
   facile force of state and fad and novelty by false prophet
   and holy believer;
For my people standing staring trying to fashion a better
   way from confusion from hypocrisy and misunderstanding,
   trying to fashion a world that will hold all the people
   all the faces all the adams and eves and their countless
   generations;
Let a new earth rise. Let another world be born. Let a
   bloody peace be written in the sky. Let a second
   generation full of courage issue forth, let a people loving
   freedom come to growth, let a beauty full of healing
   and a strength of final clenching be the pulsing in our
   spirits and our blood. Let the martial songs be written,
   let the dirges disappear. Let a race of men now rise
   and take control!

FURTHER READINGS

All references are to most recent editions of works cited.

James Baldwin. *Go Tell It on the Mountain*. New York: Dell, 1985. This novel moves from the rural South to Harlem, and contrasts two generations of a family. Central to the story is the destructive relationship between a young boy and his stepfather, a fundamentalist preacher. First published in 1953, this is Baldwin's first and best-known novel. Baldwin's "Sonny's Blues" appears on page 145 of this volume.

Toni Cade Bambara. *Gorilla, My Love*. New York: Vintage, 1981. The stories in this collection are all about characters who are independent, resourceful, unconventional, and defined by self, not by stereotypes. When human suffering surfaces in these stories, it is often cushioned by community support and the ability to survive. Two favorites in this collection are "The Lesson" and "Raymond's Run."

Black-Eyed Susans/Midnight Birds: Stories by and about Black Women. Mary Helen Washington, editor. New York: Anchor Books, 1990. Originally published as two separate volumes, this new edition includes short stories by thirteen women writers, including Gwendolyn Brooks, Toni Morrison, Ntozake Shange, and Toni Cade Bambara.

Breaking Ice: An Anthology of Contemporary African-American Fiction. Terry McMillan, editor. New York: Anchor Books, 1990. A striking collection of stories from both established and emerging authors. It features works by Paule Marshall, Ishmael Reed, Alice Walker, John Edgar Wideman and many other writers.

Rita Dove. *Thomas and Beulah*. Pittsburgh: Carnegie-Mellon University Press, 1986. A series of poems meant to be read in sequence tell the story of the courtship, marriage, and long lives of a husband and a wife. The first half of the book is Thomas' side of the story, and the second half is Beulah's very different version.

W. E. B. DuBois. *The Souls of Black Folk*. New York: Random, 1990. This passionate portrayal of the bitter struggle for survival and self-respect is a classic in the literature of the civil rights movement. First published in 1903, the book describes the "two-ness" of being an African American: "two souls, two thoughts, two unreconciled strivings."

Ralph Ellison. *Invisible Man*. New York: Random, 1989. Reciting his story from an underground cell, the nameless narrator explains that he is invisible because people see his race and poverty, rather than his true personality. In the course of the novel, the young man must discover his own true self before he can emerge from the underground.

Ernest Gaines. *The Autobiography of Miss Jane Pittman*. New York: Bantam, 1982. This novel is based on the recollections of a woman who lived for 110 years, from the days of slavery to the 1960s. In addition to this novel, Gaines is the author of the well-crafted and often anthologized short story, "The Sky is Gray."

Zora Neale Hurston. *Their Eyes Were Watching God*. New York: Harper & Row, 1990. A chapter of this novel is found on page 176 of this volume.

Jamaica Kincaid. *Annie John*. New York: Farrar, Straus & Giroux, 1985. This coming-of-age novel about a girl growing up on the Caribbean island of Antigua portrays the intensity of childhood friends, family loyalty, and the excitement and confusion of adolescence and womanhood.

Audre Lorde. *Zami: A New Spelling of My Name*. Freedom, California: The Crossing Press, 1983. A selection from the book appears on page 186 of this volume.

Memory of Kin: Stories about Family by Black Writers. Mary Helen Washington, editor. New York: Anchor Books, 1991. A collection of prose and poetry by old favorites such as James Baldwin and Langston Hughes, established writers such as Paulette Childress White and Jamaica Kincaid, and also many new writers. These carefully chosen selections explore the many ways that generations, families, and individuals connect.

Toni Morrison. *Sula*. New York: Plume, 1987. This novel, which first appeared in 1973, follows the lives of two women—Sula and Nel—from their childhood together in a small town in Ohio, through their sharply divergent paths as grown women, to their eventual reconciliation. The story moves from 1919 to 1965, and marks the changes in the life of the town and in these two remarkable women who lose and find each other. Morrison's most recent novel, *Beloved*, won the 1988 Pulitzer Prize for fiction.

Talk That Talk: An Anthology of African-American Storytelling. Linda Gross and Marian E. Barnes, editors. New York: Simon & Schuster, 1989. Here is a tremendous range of authentic stories: animal tales, legends, fantastic stories of ghosts and witches, heroic biographies, sermons, raps, and more. Each chapter also includes commentaries by scholars and by storytellers. Among the famous yarn spinners are Leadbelly, Maya Angelou, Martin Luther King, Jr., Langston Hughes, and Zora Neale Hurston.

Sherley Anne Williams. *Dessa Rose*. New York: Berkley Publishing Group, 1987. The novel follows the life of the slave girl Dessa Rose, whose voice is as clear, honest, and direct as her slaveowner's is confused and clouded by his racist beliefs. Through showing multiple and contradictory versions of Dessa Rose's experiences, the novel challenges the accuracy of historical accounts of slavery.

August Wilson. *Fences*. New York: Plume, 1986. An excerpt from this play appears on page 200 of this volume.

Richard Wright. *Native Son*. New York: Harper & Row, 1989. First published in 1940, this powerful novel exposes the pent-up hatred and bitterness of the oppressed. In the book, Bigger Thomas, a poor black youth, accidently murders a wealthy white woman. At his trial, Bigger's lawyer pleads for leniency, arguing that Bigger is being prosecuted not for a murder but for "his very existence."

ASIAN
AMERICAN
SELECTIONS

LIVING IN THE
GLOBAL VILLAGE

AN INTRODUCTORY ESSAY

THE LITERARY delights in these stories and poems will be obvious to most readers. The characters are vivid and interesting, the language charged with lyricism. The works tell moving tales and reflect a wide range of experiences – from love to war, from family life to political life, from Vietnam to a bus stop outside Target in St. Paul.

Despite their traditional pleasures, these works require a different type of reading. They are more than interesting stories and poems to add to the American quilt. They challenge the ways we as Americans see ourselves.

About thirty years ago, the cultural critic Marshall McCluhan coined the term, "global village," to indicate the ways in which human beings from various parts of the planet were communicating with each other in unprecedented ways. Through television, radio, and other media, events in China, for example, could reach a living room in St. Paul within seconds of when they happened. Wars and economic need have also led to migrations and cultural collisions. The emblem of our times is not the family that has lived in one spot for generations. It is the refugee, the immigrant, the exile.

In America, we like to believe people from across the globe, from different cultures, can come together and form a common identity. But who decides what this common identity is going to be? What is the culture that binds us all together?

In the end, no one vision of our American culture can ever describe us all. We come from too many different cultures, too many different histories. The truth is we are not all alike. If we are to understand each other, we must stop thinking that our view of the world is better or more natural or more American. Instead, our vision is one among many others. What I think is important or cool may seem odd or boring to someone else.

In these stories and poems by Asian Americans, you can find certain characters longing for a single way of looking at the world that will explain everything. Invariably, they cannot satisfy this longing.

In Bharati Mukherjee's "Orbiting," Renata, a young Italian American woman, introduces her family to Ro, her Afghani lover. Renata finds herself looking at her family through Ro's eyes and Ro through her family's eyes. When her father and brother-in-law try to talk basketball with Ro, they discover he knows nothing about American sports. Renata senses their bewilderment and disapproval. She wants to defend Ro: "Ro's skied St. Moritz, lost a thousand dollars in a casino in Beirut, knows where to buy Havana cigars without getting hijacked. He's sophisticated, he could make monkeys out of us all, but they think he's a retard."

As Renata has gotten to know Ro, she has learned the history of Afghanistan. She knows about the Russian invasion there and the torture of political prisoners. She has seen the scars on Ro's body. Compared to Ro, Renata and her family have led sheltered, naive lives.

To understand the stories and poems in this volume, we must travel beyond our own backgrounds, just as Renata does. We must break out of our preconceived images of America and the world. We must, like Renata, lose our innocence.

This means we must learn the specific histories behind what we read. Wing Tek Lum's "Local Sensibilities" portrays not simply a locale, Hawaii, but the specific culture and history of Hawaii. For Lum, the pineapple is not just a tropical fruit, but an industry. And unlike a mainland Asian American who would mention the relocation camps, Lum focuses on the "Sand Island roundup" of Japanese Americans living in Hawaii.

Sometimes the work's historical backdrop is readily apparent. Take the collaborative poems by Wendy Larsen and Tran Thi Nga and my poem, "Huy Nguyen: Brothers, Drowning Cries." Both depend upon a knowledge of the Vietnam war and what happened after American troops pulled out of that country.

The internment of Japanese Americans in World War II is the subject of Dwight Okita's poem, "In Response to Executive Order 9066," and Janice Mirikitani's poem, "Breaking Silence." Racism was a prime fuel for the internment orders. Despite the military's cries of internal security, not one of the 110,000 Japanese Americans was ever convicted of espionage. Few people know that another motivation for removing Japanese Americans from the West Coast was economic—many people wanted the land owned by Japanese Americans.

Readers must also discover the differences between Asian Americans of different generations. Maxine Hong Kingston was born and educated in America. She is both bewildered and fascinated by the culture of her mother, who was raised in China. The mother in "No Name Woman" will not tell her American-born daughter the story of an aunt's adultery back in China. The daughter has to imagine the details of her aunt's life and recreate it on her own.

In Hisaye Yamamoto's "Seventeen Syllables" the mother is an Issei or first-generation Japanese American. She is much more tied to Japanese culture than the Nisei or second generation, like the girl who speaks in Dwight Okita's poem. The second generation wanted to assimilate and many were reluctant after the war to talk about the re-location camps. When Janice Mirikitani's Nisei mother testifies about the camps, it is a brave act that goes against years of silence and shame. Because Mirikitani is a Sansei—a third-generation Japanese American—she displays an anger about the camps that many Nisei did not express.

These descriptions of generations may seem complicated, but Asian American reality is complicated. Contrary to what the movies or television often tell us, there is no generic Asian American experience. All Asian Americans are not alike. Each story and poem has its own particular history and reflects the individual vision of the writer.

Reading works from other cultures can show us our own strangeness, our own limited viewpoint. At the same time, for Asian American readers, these stories and poems by Asian American writers also help tell us who we are. Their voices say that our lives matter, that we have important stories to tell. Finally, these works insist that all of us are both individuals and members of a group, and it is through our membership in various groups that our individuality emerges.

David Mura
St. Paul, Minnesota

MAXINE HONG KINGSTON

Maxine Hong Kingston grew up in California, but both of her parents were born in China. She weaves together family history and Chinese myth. When asked if her parents encouraged her writing, Kingston said, "Not directly. I'd just say that I was doing homework."

No Name Woman

"YOU MUST not tell anyone," my mother said, "what I am about to tell you. In China your father had a sister who killed herself. She jumped into the family well. We say that your father has all brothers because it is as if she had never been born.

"In 1924 just a few days after our village celebrated seventeen hurry-up weddings—to make sure that every young man who went 'out on the road' would responsibly come home—your father and his brothers and your grandfather and his brothers and your aunt's new husband sailed for America, the Gold Mountain. It was your grandfather's last trip. Those lucky enough to get contracts waved goodbye from the decks. They fed and guarded the stowaways and helped them off in Cuba, New York, Bali, Hawaii. 'We'll meet in California next year,' they said. All of them sent money home.

"I remember looking at your aunt one day when she and I were dressing; I had not noticed before that she had such a protruding melon of a stomach. But I did not think, 'She's pregnant,' until she began to look like other pregnant women, her shirt pulling and the white tops of her black pants showing. She could not have been pregnant, you see, because her husband had been gone for years. No one said anything. We did not discuss it. In early summer she was ready to have the child, long after the time when it could have been possible.

"The village had also been counting. On the night the baby was to be born the villagers raided our house. Some were crying. Like a great saw, teeth strung with lights, files of people walked zigzag across our land, tearing the rice. Their lanterns doubled in the disturbed black water, which drained away through the broken bunds. As the villagers closed in, we could see that some of them, probably men and women we knew well, wore white masks. The people with long hair hung it over their faces. Women with short hair made it stand up on end. Some had tied white bands around their foreheads, arms, and legs.

"At first they threw mud and rocks at the house. Then they threw eggs and began slaughtering our stock. We could hear the animals scream their deaths—the roosters, the pigs, a last great roar from the ox. Familiar wild heads flared in our night windows; the villagers encircled us. Some of the faces stopped to peer at us, their eyes rushing like searchlights. The hands flattened against the panes, framed heads, and left red prints.

"The villagers broke in the front and the back doors at the same time, even though we had not locked the doors against them. Their knives dripped with the blood of our animals. They smeared blood on the doors and walls. One woman swung a chicken, whose throat she had slit, splattering blood in red arcs about her. We stood together in the middle of our house, in the family hall with the pictures and tables of the ancestors around us, and looked straight ahead.

"At that time the house had only two wings. When the men came back, we would build two more to enclose our courtyard and a third one to begin a second courtyard. The villagers pushed through both wings, even your grandparents' rooms, to find your aunt's, which was also mine until the men returned. From this room a new wing for one of the younger families would grow. They ripped up her clothes and shoes and broke her combs, grinding them underfoot. They tore her work from the loom. They scattered the cooking fire and rolled the new weaving in it. We could hear them in the kitchen breaking our bowls and banging the pots. They overturned the great waist-high earthenware jugs; duck eggs, pickled fruits, vegetables burst out and mixed in acrid torrents. The old woman from the next field swept a broom through the air and loosed the spirits-of-the-broom over our heads. 'Pig.' 'Ghost.' 'Pig,' they sobbed and scolded while they ruined our house.

"When they left, they took sugar and oranges to bless themselves. They cut pieces from the dead animals. Some of them took bowls that were not broken and clothes that were not torn. Afterward we swept up the rice and sewed it back up into sacks. But the smells from the spilled preserves lasted. Your aunt gave birth in the pigsty that night. The next morning when I went for the water, I found her and the baby plugging up the family well.

"Don't let your father know that I told you. He denies her. Now that you have started to menstruate, what happened to her could happen to you. Don't humiliate us. You wouldn't like to be forgotten as if you had never been born. The villagers are watchful."

Whenever she had to warn us about life, my mother told stories that ran like this one, a story to grow up on. She tested our strength to establish realities. Those in the emigrant generations who could not reassert brute survival died young and far from home. Those of us in the first American generations have had to figure out how the invisible world the emigrants built around our childhoods fits in solid America.

The emigrants confused the gods by diverting their curses, misleading them with crooked streets and false names. They must try to confuse their offspring as well, who, I suppose, threaten them in similar ways—always trying to get things straight, always trying to name the unspeakable. The Chinese I know hide their names; sojourners take new names when their lives change and guard their real names with silence.

Chinese-Americans, when you try to understand what things in you are Chinese, how do you separate what is peculiar to childhood, to poverty, insanities, one family, your mother who marked your growing with stories, from what is Chinese? What is Chinese tradition and what is the movies?

If I want to learn what clothes my aunt wore, whether flashy or ordinary, I would have to begin, "Remember Father's drowned-in-the-well sister?" I cannot ask that. My mother has told me once and for all the useful parts. She will add nothing unless powered by Necessity, a riverbank that guides her life. She plants vegetable gardens rather than lawns; she carries the odd-shaped tomatoes home from the fields and eats food left for the gods.

Whenever we did frivolous things, we used up energy; we flew high kites. We children came up off the ground over the melting cones our parents brought home from work and the American movie on New Year's Day—*Oh, You Beautiful Doll* with Betty Grable one year, and *She Wore a Yellow Ribbon* with John Wayne another year. After the one carnival ride each, we paid in guilt; our tired father counted his change on the dark walk home.

Adultery is extravagance. Could people who hatch their own chicks and eat the embryos and the heads for delicacies and boil the feet in vinegar for party food, leaving only the gravel, eating even the gizzard lining—could such people engender a prodigal aunt? To be a woman, to have a daughter in starvation time was a waste enough. My aunt could not have been the lone romantic who gave up everything for sex. Women in the old China did not choose. Some man had commanded her to lie with him and be his secret evil. I wonder whether he masked himself when he joined the raid on her family.

Perhaps she had encountered him in the fields or on the mountain where the daughters-in-law collected fuel. Or perhaps he first noticed her in the marketplace. He was not a stranger because the village housed no strangers. She had to have dealings with him other than sex. Perhaps he worked an adjoining field, or he sold her the cloth for the dress she sewed and wore. His demand must have surprised, then terrified her. She obeyed him; she always did as she was told.

When the family found a young man in the next village to be her husband, she had stood tractably beside the best rooster, his proxy, and promised before they met that she would be his forever. She was lucky that he was her age and she would be the first wife, an advantage secure now. The night she first saw him, he had sex with her. Then he left for America. She had almost forgotten what he looked like. When she tried to envision him, she only saw the black and white face in the group photograph the men had had taken before leaving.

The other man was not, after all, much different from her husband. They both gave orders: she followed. "If you tell your family, I'll beat you. I'll kill you. Be here again next week." No one talked sex, ever. And she might have separated the rapes from the rest of living if only she did not have to buy her oil from him or gather wood in the same forest. I want her fear to have lasted just as long as rape lasted so that the fear could have been contained. No drawn-out fear. But women at sex hazarded birth and hence lifetimes. The fear did not stop but permeated everywhere. She told the man, "I think I'm pregnant." He organized the raid against her.

On nights when my mother and father talked about their life back home, sometimes they mentioned an "outcast table" whose business they still seemed to be settling, their voices tight. In a commensal tradition, where food is precious, the powerful older people made wrongdoers eat alone. Instead of letting them start separate new lives like the Japanese, who could become samurais and geishas, the Chinese family, faces averted but eyes glowering sideways, hung on to the offenders and fed them leftovers. My aunt must have lived in the same house as my parents and eaten at an outcast table. My mother spoke about the raid as if she had seen it, when she and my aunt, a daughter-in-law to a different household, should not have been living together at all. Daughters-in-law lived with their husbands' parents, not their own; a synonym for marriage in Chinese is "taking a daughter-in-law." Her husband's parents could have sold her, mortgaged her, stoned her. But they had sent her back to her own mother and father, a mysterious act hinting at disgraces not told me. Perhaps they had thrown her out to deflect the avengers.

She was the only daughter; her four brothers went with her father, husband, and uncles "out on the road" and for some years became western men. When the goods were divided among the family, three of the brothers took land, and the youngest, my father, chose an education. After my grandparents gave their daughter away to her husband's family, they had dispensed all the adventure and all the property. They expected her alone to keep the traditional ways, which her brothers, now among the barbarians, could fumble without detection. The heavy, deep-rooted women were to maintain the past against the flood, safe for returning. But the rare urge west had fixed upon our family, and so my aunt crossed boundaries not delineated in space.

The work of preservation demands that the feelings playing about in one's guts not be turned into action. Just watch their passing like cherry blossoms. But perhaps my aunt, my forerunner, caught in a slow life, let dreams grow and fade and after some months or years went toward what persisted. Fear at the enormities of the forbidden kept her desires delicate, wire and bone. She looked at a man because she liked the way the hair was tucked behind his ears, or she liked the question-mark line of a long torso curving at the shoulder and straight at the hip. For warm eyes or a soft voice or a slow walk—that's all—a few hairs, a line, a brightness, a sound, a pace, she gave up family. She offered us up for a charm that vanished with tiredness, a pigtail that didn't toss when the wind died. Why, the wrong lighting could erase the dearest thing about him.

It could very well have been, however, that my aunt did not take subtle enjoyment of her friend, but, a wild woman, kept rollicking company. Imagining her free with sex doesn't fit, though. I don't know any women like that, or men either. Unless I see her life branching into mine, she gives me no ancestral help.

To sustain her being in love, she often worked at herself in the mirror, guessing at the colors and shapes that would interest him, changing them frequently in order to hit on the right combination. She wanted him to look back.

On a farm near the sea, a woman who tended her appearance reaped a reputation for eccentricity. All the married women blunt-cut their hair in flaps about their ears or pulled it back in tight buns. No nonsense. Neither style blew easily into heart-catching tangles. And at their weddings they displayed themselves in their long hair for the last time. "It brushed the backs of my knees," my mother tells me. "It was braided, and even so, it brushed the backs of my knees."

At the mirror my aunt combed individuality into her bob. A bun could have been contrived to escape into black streamers blowing in the wind or in quiet wisps about her face, but only the older women in our picture album wear buns. She brushed her hair back from her forehead, tucking the flaps behind her ears. She looped a piece of thread, knotted into a circle between her index fingers and thumbs, and ran the double strand across her forehead. When she closed her fingers as if she were making a pair of shadow geese bite, the string twisted together catching the little hairs. Then she pulled the thread away from her skin, ripping the hairs out neatly, her eyes watering from the needles of pain. Opening her fingers, she cleaned the thread, then rolled it along her hairline and the tops of her eyebrows. My mother did the same to me and my sisters and herself. I used to believe that the expression "caught by the short hairs" meant a captive held with a depilatory string. It especially hurt at the temples, but my mother said we were lucky we didn't have to have our feet bound when we were seven. Sisters used to sit on their beds and cry together, she said, as their mothers or their slave removed the bandages for a few minutes each night and let the blood gush back into their veins. I hope that the man my aunt loved appreciated a smooth brow, that he wasn't just a tits-and-ass man.

Once my aunt found a freckle on her chin, at a spot that the almanac said predestined her for unhappiness. She dug it out with a hot needle and washed the wound with peroxide.

More attention to her looks than these pullings of hair and pick-ings at spots would have caused gossip among the villagers. They owned work clothes and good clothes, and they wore good clothes for feasting the new seasons. But since a woman combing her hair hexes beginnings, my aunt rarely found an occasion to look her best. Women looked like great sea snails – the corded wood, babies, and laundry they carried were the whorls on their backs. The Chinese did not admire a bent back; goddesses and warriors stood straight. Still there must have been a marvelous freeing of beauty when a worker laid down her burden and stretched and arched.

Such commonplace loveliness, however, was not enough for my aunt. She dreamed of a lover for the fifteen days of New Year's, the time for families to exchange visits, money, and food. She plied her secret comb. And sure enough she cursed the year, the family, the village, and herself.

Even as her hair lured her imminent lover, many other men looked at her. Uncles, cousins, nephews, brothers would have looked, too, had they been home between journeys. Perhaps they had already been restraining their curiosity, and they left, fearful that their glances, like a field of nesting birds, might be startled and caught. Poverty hurt, and that was their first reason for leaving. But another, final reason for leaving the crowded house was the never-said.

She may have been unusually beloved, the precious only daughter, spoiled and mirror gazing because of the affection the family lavished on her. When her husband left, they welcomed the chance to take her back from the in-laws; she could live like the little daughter for just a while longer. There are stories that my grandfather was different from other people, "crazy ever since the little Jap bayoneted him in the head." He used to put his naked penis on the dinner table, laughing. And one day he brought home a baby girl, wrapped up inside his brown western-style greatcoat. He had traded one of his sons, probably my father, the youngest, for her. My grandmother made him trade back. When he finally got a daughter of his own, he doted on her. They must have all loved her except perhaps my father, the only brother who never went back to China, having once been traded for a girl.

Brothers and sisters, newly men and women, had to efface their sexual color and present plain miens. Disturbing hair and eyes, a smile like no other, threatened the ideal of five generations living under one roof. To focus blurs, people shouted face to face and yelled from room to room. The immigrants I know have loud voices, un-modulated to American tones even after years away from the village where they called their friendships out across the fields. I have not been able to stop my mother's screams in public libraries or over telephones. Walking erect (knees straight, toes pointed forward, not pigeon-toed, which is Chinese-feminine) and speaking in an inaudible voice, I have tried to turn myself American-feminine. Chinese communication was loud, public. Only sick people had to whisper. But at the dinner table, where the family members came nearest one another, no one could talk, not the outcasts nor any eaters. Every word that falls from the mouth is a coin lost. Silently they gave and accepted food with both hands. A preoccupied child who took his bowl with one hand got a sideways glare. A complete moment of total attention is due everyone alike. Children and lovers have no singularity here, but my aunt used a secret voice, a separate attentiveness.

She kept the man's name to herself throughout her labor and dying; she did not accuse him that he be punished with her. To save her inseminator's name she gave silent birth.

He may have been somebody in her own household, but intercourse with a man outside the family would have been no less abhorrent. All the village were kinsmen, and the titles shouted in loud country voices never let kinship be forgotten. Any man within visiting distance would have been neutralized as a lover–"brother," "younger brother," "older brother"–one hundred and fifteen relationship titles. Parents researched birth charts probably not so much to assure good fortune as to circumvent incest in a population that has but one hundred surnames. Everybody has eight million relatives. How useless then sexual mannerisms, how dangerous.

As if it came from an atavism deeper than fear, I used to add "brother" silently to boys' names. It hexed the boys, who would or would not ask me to dance, and made them less scary and as familiar and deserving of benevolence as girls.

But, of course, I hexed myself also—no dates. I should have stood up, both arms waving, and shouted out across libraries, "Hey, you! Love me back." I had no idea, though, how to make attraction selective, how to control its direction and magnitude. If I made myself American-pretty so that the five or six Chinese boys in the class fell in love with me, everyone else—the Caucasian, Negro, and Japanese boys—would too. Sisterliness, dignified and honorable, made much more sense.

Attraction eludes control so stubbornly that whole societies designed to organize relationships among people cannot keep order, not even when they bind people to one another from childhood and raise them together. Among the very poor and the wealthy, brothers married their adopted sisters, like doves. Our family allowed some romance, paying adult brides' prices and providing dowries so that their sons and daughters could marry strangers. Marriage promises to turn strangers into friendly relatives—a nation of siblings.

In the village structure, spirits shimmered among the live creatures, balanced and held in equilibrium by time and land. But one human being flaring up into violence could open up a black hole, a maelstrom that pulled in the sky. The frightened villagers, who depended on one another to maintain the real, went to my aunt to show her a personal, physical representation of the break she had made in the "roundness." Misallying couples snapped off the future, which was to be embodied in true offspring. The villagers punished her for acting as if she could have a private life, secret and apart from them.

If my aunt had betrayed the family at a time of large grain yields and peace, when many boys were born, and wings were being built on many houses, perhaps she might have escaped such severe punishment. But the men—hungry, greedy, tired of planting in dry soil—had been forced to leave the village in order to send food-money home. There were ghost plagues, bandit plagues, wars with the Japanese, floods. My Chinese brother and sister had died of an unknown sickness. Adultery, perhaps only a mistake during good times, became a crime when the village needed food.

The round moon cakes and round doorways, the round tables of graduated size that fit one roundness inside another, round windows and rice bowls—these talismans had lost their power to warn this family of the law: a family must be whole, faithfully keeping the descent line by having sons to feed the old and the dead, who in turn look after the family. The villagers came to show my aunt and her lover-in-hiding a broken house. The villagers were speeding up the circling of events because she was too shortsighted to see that her infidelity had already harmed the village, that waves of consequences would return unpredictably, sometimes in disguise, as now, to hurt her. This roundness had to be made coin-sized so that she would see its circumference: punish her at the birth of her baby. Awaken her to the inexorable. People who refused fatalism because they could invent small resources insisted on culpability. Deny accidents and wrest fault from the stars.

After the villagers left, their lanterns now scattering in various directions toward home, the family broke their silence and cursed her. "Aiaa, we're going to die. Death is coming. Death is coming. Look what you've done. You've killed us. Ghost! Dead ghost! Ghost! You've never been born." She ran out into the fields, far enough from the house so that she could no longer hear their voices, and pressed herself against the earth, her own land no more. When she felt the birth coming, she thought that she had been hurt. Her body seized together. "They've hurt me too much," she thought. "This is gall, and it will kill me." With forehead and knees against the earth, her body convulsed and then relaxed. She turned on her back, lay on the ground. The black well of sky and stars went out and out and out forever; her body and her complexity seemed to disappear. She was one of the stars, a bright dot in blackness, without home, without a companion, in eternal cold and silence. An agoraphobia rose in her, speeding higher and higher, bigger and bigger; she would not be able to contain it; there would be no end to fear.

Flayed, unprotected against space, she felt pain return, focusing her body. This pain chilled her—a cold, steady kind of surface pain. Inside, spasmodically, the other pain, the pain of the child, heated her. For hours she lay on the ground, alternately body and space. Sometimes a vision of normal comfort obliterated reality: she saw the family in the evening gambling at the dinner table, the young people massaging their elders' backs. She saw them congratulating one another, high joy on the mornings the rice shoots came up. When these pictures burst, the stars drew yet further apart. Black space opened.

She got to her feet to fight better and remembered that old-fashioned women gave birth in their pigsties to fool the jealous, pain-dealing gods, who do not snatch piglets. Before the next spasms could stop her, she ran to the pigsty, each step a rushing out into emptiness. She climbed over the fence and knelt in the dirt. It was good to have a fence enclosing her, a tribal person alone.

Laboring, this woman who had carried her child as a foreign growth that sickened her every day, expelled it at last. She reached down to touch the hot, wet, moving mass, surely smaller than anything human, and could feel that it was human after all—fingers, toes, nails, nose. She pulled it up on to her belly, and it lay curled there, butt in the air, feet precisely tucked one under the other. She opened her loose shirt and buttoned the child inside. After resting, it squirmed and thrashed and she pushed it up to her breast. It turned its head this way and that until it found her nipple. There, it made little snuffling noises. She clenched her teeth at its preciousness, lovely as a young calf, a piglet, a little dog.

She may have gone to the pigsty as a last act of responsibility: she would protect this child as she had protected its father. It would look after her soul, leaving supplies on her grave. But how would this tiny child without family find her grave when there would be no marker for her anywhere, neither in the earth nor the family hall? No one would give her a family hall name. She had taken the child with her into the wastes. At its birth the two of them had felt the same raw pain of separation, a wound that only the family pressing tight could close. A child with no descent line would not soften her life but only trail after her, ghost-like, begging her to give it purpose. At dawn the villagers on their way to the fields would stand around the fence and look.

Full of milk, the little ghost slept. When it awoke, she hardened her breasts against the milk that crying loosens. Toward morning she picked up the baby and walked to the well.

Carrying the baby to the well shows loving. Otherwise abandon it. Turn its face into the mud. Mothers who love their children take them along. It was probably a girl; there is some hope of forgiveness for boys.

"Don't tell anyone you had an aunt. Your father does not want to hear her name. She has never been born." I have believed that sex was unspeakable and words so strong and fathers so frail that "aunt" would do my father mysterious harm. I have thought that my family, having settled among immigrants who had also been their neighbors in the ancestral land, needed to clean their name, and a wrong word would incite the kinspeople even here. But there is more to this silence: they want me to participate in her punishment. And I have.

In the twenty years since I heard this story I have not asked for details nor said my aunt's name; I do not know it. People who can comfort the dead can also chase after them to hurt them further—a reverse ancestor worship. The real punishment was not the raid swiftly inflicted by the villagers, but the family's deliberately forgetting her. Her betrayal so maddened them, they saw to it that she would suffer forever, even after death. Always hungry, always needing, she would have to beg food from other ghosts, snatch and steal it from those whose living descendants give them gifts. She would have to fight the ghosts massed at crossroads for the buns a few thoughtful citizens leave to decoy her away from village and home so that the ancestral spirits could feast unharassed. At peace, they could act like gods, not ghosts, their descent lines providing them with paper suits and dresses, spirit money, paper houses, paper automobiles, chicken, meat, and rice into eternity—essences delivered up in smoke and flames, steam and incense rising from each rice bowl. In an attempt to make the Chinese care for people outside the family, Chairman Mao encourages us now to give our paper replicas to the spirits of outstanding soldiers and workers, no matter whose ancestors they may be. My aunt remains forever hungry. Goods are not distributed evenly among the dead.

My aunt haunts me—her ghost drawn to me because now, after fifty years of neglect, I alone devote pages of paper to her, though not origamied into houses and clothes. I do not think she always means me well. I am telling on her, and she was a spite suicide, drowning herself in the drinking water. The Chinese are always very frightened of the drowned one, whose weeping ghosts, wet hair hanging and skin bloated, waits silently by the water to pull down a substitute.

BHARATI MUKHERJEE

Bharati Mukherjee was born in Calcutta, India in 1940, has been a Canadian citizen since 1972, and a resident of the United States since 1980. "Changing citizenship is easy," she says, "swapping cultures is not."

ORBITING

ON THANKSGIVING morning I'm still in my nightgown thinking of Vic when Dad raps on my apartment door. Who's he rolling joints for, who's he initiating now into the wonders of his inner space? What got me on Vic is remembering last Thanksgiving and his famous cranberry sauce with Grand Marnier, which Dad had interpreted as a sign of permanence in my life. A man who cooks like Vic is ready for other commitments. Dad cannot imagine cooking as self-expression. You cook *for* someone. Vic's sauce was a sign of his permanent isolation, if you really want to know.

Dad's come to drop off the turkey. It's a seventeen-pounder. Mr. Vitelli knows to reserve a biggish one for us every Thanksgiving and Christmas. But this November what with Danny in the Marines, Uncle Carmine having to be very careful after the bypass, and Vic taking off for outer space as well, we might as well have made do with one of those turkey rolls you pick out of the freezer. And in other years, Mr. Vitelli would not have given us a frozen bird. We were proud of that, our birds were fresh killed. I don't bring this up to Dad.

"Your mama took care of the thawing," Dad says. "She said you wouldn't have room in your Frigidaire."

"You mean Mom said Rindy shouldn't be living in a dump, right?"

Mom has the simple, immigrant faith that children should do better than their parents, and her definition of better is comfortingly
rigid. Fair enough—I believed it, too. But the fact is all I can afford
is this third-floor studio with an art deco shower. The fridge fits
under the kitchenette counter. The room has potential. I'm content with that. And I *like* my job even though it's selling, not design-
ing, jewelry made out of seashells and semiprecious stones out of
a boutique in Bellevue Plaza.

Dad shrugs. "You're an adult, Renata." He doesn't try to lower
himself into one of my two deck chairs. He was a minor league
catcher for a while and his knees went. The fake zebra-skin cushions
piled as seats on the rug are out of the question for him. My futon
bed folds up into a sofa, but the satin sheets are still lasciviously
tangled. My father stands in a slat of sunlight, trying not to look
embarrassed.

"Dad, I'd have come to the house and picked it up. You didn't
have to make the extra trip out from Verona." A sixty-five-year-old
man in wingtips and a Borsalino hugging a wet, heavy bird is so
poignant I have to laugh.

"You wouldn't have gotten out of bed until noon, Renata." But
Dad smiles. I know what he's saying. He's saying *he's* retired and
he should be able to stay in bed till noon if he wants to, but he
can't and he'd rather drive twenty miles with a soggy bird than read
the *Ledger* one more time.

Grumbling and scolding are how we deMarcos express love. It's
the North Italian way, Dad used to tell Cindi, Danny, and me when
we were kids. Sicilians and Calabrians are emotional; we're contained.
Actually, he's contained, the way Vic was contained for the most
part. Mom's a Calabrian and she was born and raised there. Dad's
very American, so Italy's a safe source of pride for him. I once figured
it out: *his* father, Arturo deMarco, was a fifteen-week-old fetus when
his mother planted her feet on Ellis Island. Dad, a proud son of
North Italy had one big adventure in his life, besides fighting in
the Pacific, and that was marrying a Calabrian peasant. He made
it sound as though Mom was a Korean or something, and their
marriage was a kind of taming of the West, and that everything about
her could be explained as a cultural deficiency. Actually, Vic could
talk beautifully about his feelings. He'd brew espresso, pour it into
tiny blue pottery cups and analyze our relationship. I should have

listened. I mean really listened. I thought he was talking about us, but I know now he was only talking incessantly about himself. I put too much faith in mail-order nightgowns and bras.

"Your mama wanted me out of the house," Dad goes on. "She didn't used to be like this, Renata."

Renata and Carla are what we were christened. We changed to Rindy and Cindi in junior high. Danny didn't have to make such leaps, unless you count dropping out of Montclair State and joining the Marines. He was always Danny, or Junior.

I lug the turkey to the kitchen sink where it can drip away at a crazy angle until I have time to deal with it.

"Your mama must have told you girls I've been acting funny since I retired."

"No, Dad, she hasn't said anything about you acting funny." What she *has* said is do we think she ought to call Doc Brunetti and have a chat about Dad? Dad wouldn't have to know. He and Doc Brunetti are, or were, on the same church league bowling team. So is, or was, Vic's dad, Vinny Riccio.

"Your mama thinks a man should have an office to drive to every day. I sat at a desk for thirty-eight years and what did I get? Ask Doc, I'm too embarrassed to say." Dad told me once Doc—his real name was Frankie, though no one ever called him that—had been called Doc since he was six years old and growing up with Dad in Little Italy. There was never a time in his life when Doc wasn't Doc, which made his professional decision very easy. Dad used to say, no one ever called me Adjuster when I was a kid. Why didn't they call me something like Sarge or Teach? Then I would have known better.

I wish I had something breakfasty in my kitchen cupboard to offer him. He wants to stay and talk about Mom, which is the way old married people have. Let's talk about me means: What do you think of Mom? I'll take the turkey over means: When will Rindy settle down? I wish this morning I had bought the Goodwill sofa for ten dollars instead of letting Vic haul off the fancy deck chairs from Fortunoff's. Vic had flash. He'd left Jersey a long time before he actually took off.

"I can make you tea."

"None of that herbal stuff."

We don't talk about Mom, but I know what he's going through. She's just started to find herself. He's not burned out, he's merely stuck. I remember when Mom refused to learn to drive, wouldn't leave the house even to mail a letter. Her litany those days was: when you've spent the first fifteen years of your life in a mountain village, when you remember candles and gaslight and carrying water from a well, not to mention holding in your water at night because of wolves and the unlit outdoor privy, you *like* being housebound. She used those wolves for all they were worth, as though imaginary wolves still nipped her heels in the Clifton Mall.

Before Mom began to find herself and signed up for a class at Paterson, she used to nag Cindi and me about finding the right men. "Men," she said; she wasn't coy, never. Unembarrassed, she'd tell me about her wedding night, about her first sighting of Dad's "thing" ("Land Ho!" Cindi giggled. "Thar she blows!" I chipped in.) and she'd giggle at our word for it, the common word, and she'd use it around us, never around Dad. Mom's peasant, she's earthy but never coarse. If I could get that across to Dad, how I admire it in men or in women, I would feel somehow redeemed of all my little mistakes with them, with men, with myself. Cindi and Brent were married on a cruise ship by the ship's captain. Tony, Vic's older brother, made a play for me my senior year. Tony's solid now. He manages a funeral home but he's invested in crayfish ponds on the side.

"You don't even own a dining table." Dad sounds petulant. He uses "even" a lot around me. Not just a judgment, but a comparative judgment. Other people have dining tables. *Lots* of dining tables. He softens it a bit, not wanting to hurt me, wanting more for me to judge him a failure. "We've always had a sit-down dinner, hon."

Okay, so traditions change. This year dinner's potluck. So I don't have real furniture. I eat off stack-up plastic tables as I watch the evening news. I drink red wine and heat a pita bread on the gas burner and wrap it around alfalfa sprouts or green linguine. The Swedish knockdown dresser keeps popping its sides because Vic didn't glue it properly. Swedish engineering, he said, doesn't need glue. Think of Volvos, he said, and Ingmar Bergman. He isn't good with directions that come in four languages. At least he wasn't.

"Trust me, Dad." This isn't the time to spring new lovers on him. "A friend made me a table. It's in the basement."

"How about chairs?" Ah, my good father. He could have said, friend? What friend?

Marge, my landlady, has all kinds of junky stuff in the basement.

"Jorge and I'll bring up what we need. You'd strain your back, Dad."
Shot knees, bad back: daily pain but nothing fatal. Not like Carmine.

"Jorge? Is that the new boyfriend?"

Shocking him makes me feel good. It would serve him right if
Jorge were my new boyfriend. But Jorge is Marge's other roomer.
He gives Marge Spanish lessons, and does the heavy cleaning and
the yard work. Jorge has family in El Salvador he's hoping to bring
up. I haven't met Marge's husband yet. He works on an offshore
oil rig in some emirate with a funny name.

"No, Dad." I explain about Jorge.

"El Salvador!" he repeats. "That means 'the Savior.'" He passes
on the information with a kind of awe. It makes Jorge's homeland,
which he's shown me pretty pictures of, seem messy and exotic,
at the very rim of human comprehension.

After Dad leaves, I call Cindi, who lives fifteen minutes away on
Upper Mountainside Road. She's eleven months younger and almost
a natural blond, but we're close. Brent wasn't easy for me to take,
not at first. He owns a discount camera and electronics store on
Fifty-fourth in Manhattan. Cindi met him through Club Med. They
sat on a gorgeous Caribbean beach and talked of hogs. His father
is an Amish farmer in Kalona, Iowa. Brent, in spite of the obvious
hairpiece and the gold chain, is a rebel. He was born Schwartzendruber, but changed his name to Schwartz. Now no one believes
the Brent, either. They call him Bernie on the street and it makes
everyone more comfortable. His father's never taken their buggy
out of the county.

The first time Vic asked me out, he talked of feminism and holism
and macrobiotics. Then he opened up on cinema and literature,
and I was very impressed, as who wouldn't be? Ro, my current lover,
is very different. He picked me up in an uptown singles bar that
I and sometimes Cindi go to. He bought me a Cinzano and touched
my breast in the dark. He was direct, and at the same time weirdly
courtly. I took him home though usually I don't, at first. I learned
in bed that night that the tall brown drink with the lemon twist
he'd been drinking was Tab.

I went back on the singles circuit even though the break with
Vic should have made me cautious. Cindi thinks Vic's a romantic.
I've told her how it ended. One Sunday morning in March he kissed
me awake as usual. He'd brought in the *Times* from the porch and
was reading it. I made us some cinnamon rose tea. We had a ritual,

starting with the real estate pages, passing remarks on the latest tacky towers. Not for us, we'd say, the view is terrible! No room for the servants, things like that. And our imaginary children's imaginary nanny. "Hi, gorgeous," I said. He is gorgeous, not strong, but showy. He said, "I'm leaving, babe. New Jersey doesn't do it for me anymore." I said, "Okay, so where're we going?" I had an awful job at the time, taking orders for MCI. Vic said, "I didn't say we, babe." So I asked, "You mean it's over? Just like that?" And he said, "Isn't that the best way? No fuss, no hang-ups." Then I got a little whiny. "But *why?*" I wanted to know. But he was macrobiotic in lots of things, including relationships. Yin and yang, hot and sour, green and yellow. "You know, Rindy, there are *places*. You don't fall off the earth when you leave Jersey, you know. Places you see pictures of and read about. Different weathers, different trees, different everything. Places that get the Cubs on cable instead of the Mets." He was into that. For all the sophisticated things he liked to talk about, he was a very local boy. "Vic," I pleaded, "you're crazy. You need help." "I need help because I want to get out of Jersey? You gotta be kidding!" He stood up and for a moment I thought he would do something crazy, like destroy something, or hurt me. "Don't ever call me crazy, got that? And give me the keys to the van."

He took the van. Danny had sold it to me when the Marines sent him overseas. I'd have given it to him anyway, even if he hadn't asked.

"Cindi, I need a turkey roaster," I tell my sister on the phone.
"I'll be right over," she says. "The brat's driving me crazy."
"Isn't Franny's visit working out?"
"I could kill her. I think up ways. How does that sound?"
"Why not send her home?" I'm joking. Franny is Brent's twelve-year-old and he's shelled out a lot of dough to lawyers in New Jersey and Florida to work out visitation rights.
"Poor Brent. He feels so *divided*," Cindi says. "He shouldn't have to take sides."
I want her to ask who my date is for this afternoon, but she doesn't. It's important to me that she like Ro, that Mom and Dad more than tolerate him.

All over the country, I tell myself, women are towing new lovers home to meet their families. Vic is simmering cranberries in somebody's kitchen and explaining yin and yang. I check out the stuffing recipe. The gravy calls for cream and freshly grated nutmeg. Ro brought me six whole nutmegs in a Ziplock bag from his friend, a Pakistani, who runs a spice store in SoHo. The nuts look hard and ugly. I take one out of the bag and sniff it. The aroma's so exotic my head swims. On an impulse I call Ro.

The phone rings and rings. He doesn't have his own place yet. He has to crash with friends. He's been in the States three months, maybe less. I let it ring fifteen, sixteen, seventeen times.

Finally someone answers. "Yes?" The voice is guarded, the accent obviously foreign even though all I'm hearing is a one-syllable word. Ro has fled here from Kabul. He wants to take classes at NJIT and become an electrical engineer. He says he's lucky his father got him out. A friend of Ro's father, a man called Mumtaz, runs a fried chicken restaurant in Brooklyn in a neighborhood Ro calls "Little Kabul," though probably no one else has ever noticed. Mr. Mumtaz puts the legal immigrants to work as waiters out front. The illegals hide in a backroom as pluckers and gutters.

"Ro? I miss you. We're eating at three, remember?"

"Who is speaking, please?"

So I fell for the accent, but it isn't a malicious error. I *can* tell one Afghan tribe from another now, even by looking at them or by their names. I can make out some Pashto words. "Tell Ro it's Rindy. Please? I'm a friend. He wanted me to call this number."

"Not knowing any Ro."

"Hey, wait. Tell him it's Rindy deMarco."

The guy hangs up on me.

I'm crumbling cornbread into a bowl for the stuffing when Cindi honks half of "King Cotton" from the parking apron in the back. Brent bought her the BMW on the gray market and saved a bundle—once discount, always discount—then spent three hundred dollars to put in a horn that beeps a Sousa march. I wave a potato masher at her from the back window. She doesn't get out of the car. Instead she points to the pan in the back seat. I come down, wiping my hands on a dish towel.

"I should stay and help." Cindi sounds ready to cry. But I don't want her with me when Ro calls back.

"You're doing too much already, kiddo." My voice at least sounds comforting. "You promised one veg and the salad."

"I ought to come up and help. That or get drunk." She shifts the stick. When Brent bought her the car, the dealer threw in driving gloves to match the upholstery.

"Get Franny to shred the greens," I call as Cindi backs up the car. "Get her involved."

The phone is ringing in my apartment. I can hear it ring from the second-floor landing.

"Ro?"

"You're taking a chance, my treasure. It could have been any other admirer, then where would you be?"

"I don't have any other admirers." Ro is not a conventionally jealous man, not like the types I have known. He's totally unlike any man I have ever known. He wants men to come on to me. Lately when we go to a bar he makes me sit far enough from him so some poor lonely guy thinks I'm looking for action. Ro likes to swagger out of a dark booth as soon as someone buys me a drink. I go along. He comes from a macho culture.

"How else will I know you are as beautiful as I think you are? I would not want an unprized woman," he says. He is asking me for time, I know. In a few more months he'll know I'm something of a catch in my culture, or at least I've never had trouble finding boys. Even Brent Schwartzendruber has begged me to see him alone.

"I'm going to be a little late," Ro says. "I told you about my cousin, Abdul, no?"

Ro has three or four cousins that I know of in Manhattan. They're all named Abdul something. When I think of Abdul, I think of a giant black man with goggles on, running down a court. Abdul is the teenage cousin whom immigration officials nabbed as he was gutting chickens in Mumtaz's backroom. Abdul doesn't have the right papers to live and work in this country, and now he's been locked up in a detention center on Varick Street. Ro's afraid Abdul will be deported back to Afghanistan. If that happens, he'll be tortured.

"I have to visit him before I take the DeCamp bus. He's talking nonsense. He's talking of starting a hunger fast."

"A hunger strike! God!" When I'm with Ro I feel I am looking at America through the wrong end of a telescope. He makes it sound like a police state, with sudden raids, papers, detention centers, deportations, and torture and death waiting in the wings. I'm not a political person. Last fall I wore the Ferraro button because she's a woman and Italian.

"Rindy, all night I've been up and awake. All night I think of your splendid breasts. Like clusters of grapes, I think. I am stroking and fondling your grapes this very minute. My talk gets you excited?"

I tell him to test me, please get here before three. I remind him he can't buy his ticket on the bus.

"We got here too early, didn't we?" Dad stands just outside the door to my apartment, looking embarrassed. He's in his best dark suit, the one he wears every Thanksgiving and Christmas. This year he can't do up the top button of his jacket.

"Don't be so formal, Dad." I give him a showy hug and pull him indoors so Mom can come in.

"As if your papa ever listens to me!" Mom laughs. But she sits primly on the sofa bed in her velvet cloak with her tote bag and evening purse on her lap. Before Dad started courting her, she worked as a seamstress. Dad rescued her from a sweatshop. He married down, she married well. That's the family story.

"She told me to rush."

Mom isn't in a mood to squabble. I think she's reached the point of knowing she won't have him forever. There was Carmine, at death's door just a month ago. Anything could happen to Dad. She says, "Renata, look what I made! Crostolis." She lifts a cake tin out of her tote bag. The pan still feels warm. And for dessert, I know, there'll be a jar of super-thick, super-rich Death by Chocolate.

The story about Grandma deMarco, Dad's mama, is that every Thanksgiving she served two full dinners, one American with the roast turkey, candied yams, pumpkin pie, the works, and another with Grandpa's favorite pastas.

Dad relaxes. He appoints himself bartender. "Don't you have more ice cubes, sweetheart?"

I tell him it's good Glenlivet. He shouldn't ruin it with ice, just a touch of water if he must. Dad pours sherry in Vic's pottery espresso cups for his women. Vic made them himself, and I used to think they were perfect blue jewels. Now I see they're lumpy, uneven in color.

"Go change into something pretty before Carla and Brent come." Mom believes in dressing up. Beaded dresses lift her spirits. She's wearing a beaded green dress today.

I take the sherry and vanish behind a four-panel screen, the kind long-legged showgirls change behind in black and white movies while their moustached lovers keep talking. My head barely shows above the screen's top, since I'm no long-legged showgirl. My best points, as Ro has said, are my clusters of grapes. Vic found the screen at a country auction in the Adirondacks. It had filled the van. Now I use the panels as a bulletin board and I'm worried Dad'll spot the notice for the next meeting of Amnesty International, which will bother him. He will think the two words stand for draft dodger and communist. I was going to drop my membership, a legacy of Vic, when Ro saw it and approved. Dad goes to the Sons of Italy Anti-Defamation dinners. He met Frank Sinatra at one. He voted for Reagan last time because the Democrats ran an Italian woman.

Instead of a thirties lover, it's my moustached papa talking to me from the other side of the screen. "So where's this dining table?"

"Ro's got the parts in the basement. He'll bring it up, Dad."

I hear them whispering. "Bo? Now she's messing with a Southerner?" and "Shh, it's her business."

I'm just smoothing on my pantyhose when Mom screams for the cops. Dad shouts too, at Mom for her to shut up. It's my fault, I should have warned Ro not to use his key this afternoon.

I peek over the screen's top and see my lover the way my parents see him. He's a slight, pretty man with hazel eyes and a tufty moustache, so whom can he intimidate? I've seen Jews and Greeks, not to mention Sons of Italy, darker-skinned than Ro. Poor Ro resorts to his Kabuli prep-school manners.

"How do you do, Madam! Sir! My name is Roashan."

Dad moves closer to Ro but doesn't hold out his hand. I can almost read his mind: *he speaks*. "Come again!" he says, baffled.

I cringe as he spells his name. My parents are so parochial. With each letter he does a graceful dip and bow. "Try it syllable by syllable, sir. Then it is not so hard."

Mom stares past him at me. The screen doesn't hide me because I've strayed too far in to watch the farce. "Renata, you're wearing only your camisole."

I pull my crew neck over my head, then kiss him. I make the kiss really sexy so they'll know I've slept with this man. Many times. And if he asks me, I will marry him. I had not known that till now. I think my mother guesses.

He's brought flowers: four long-stemmed, stylish purple blossoms in a florist's paper cone. "For you, madam." He glides over the dirty broadloom to Mom who fills up more than half the sofa bed. "This is my first Thanksgiving dinner, for which I have much to give thanks, no?"

"He was born in Afghanistan," I explain. But Dad gets continents wrong. He says, "We saw your famine camps on TV. Well, you won't starve this afternoon."

"They smell good," Mom says. "Thank you very much but you shouldn't spend a fortune."

"No, no, madam. What you smell good is my cologne. Flowers in New York have no fragrance."

"His father had a garden estate outside Kabul." I don't want Mom to think he's putting down American flowers, though in fact he is. Along with American fruits, meats, and vegetables. "The Russians bulldozed it," I add.

Dad doesn't want to talk politics. He senses, looking at Ro, this is not the face of Ethiopian starvation. "Well, what'll it be, Roy? Scotch and soda?" I wince. It's not going well.

"Thank you but no. I do not imbibe alcoholic spirits, though I have no objection for you, sir." My lover goes to the fridge and reaches down. He knows just where to find his Tab. My father is quietly livid, staring down at his drink.

In my father's world, grown men bowl in leagues and drink the best whiskey they can afford. Dad whistles "My Way." He must be under stress. That's his usual self-therapy: how would Francis Albert handle this?

"Muslims have taboos, Dad." Cindi didn't marry a Catholic, so he has no right to be upset about Ro, about us.

"Jews," Dad mutters. "So do Jews." He knows because catty-corner from Vitelli's is a kosher butcher. This isn't the time to parade new words before him, like *halal*, the Muslim kosher. An Italian-American man should be able to live sixty-five years never having heard the word, I can go along with that. Ro, fortunately, is cosmopolitan. Outside of pork and booze, he eats anything else I fix.

Brent and Cindi take forever to come. But finally we hear his MG squeal in the driveway. Ro glides to the front window; he seems to blend with the ficus tree and hanging ferns. Dad and I wait by the door.

"Party time!" Brent shouts as he maneuvers Cindi and Franny

ahead of him up three flights of stairs. He looks very much the head of the family, a rich man steeply in debt to keep up appearances, to compete, to head off middle age. He's at that age—and Cindi's nowhere near that age—when people notice the difference and quietly judge it. I know these things from Cindi—I'd never guess it from looking at Brent. If he feels divided, as Cindi says he does, it doesn't show. Misery, anxiety, whatever, show on Cindi though; they bring her cheekbones out. When I'm depressed, my hair looks rough, my skin breaks out. Right now, I'm lustrous.

Brent does a lot of whooping and hugging at the door. He even hugs Dad who looks grave and funereal like an old-world Italian gentleman because of his outdated, pinched dark suit. Cindi makes straight for the fridge with her casserole of squash and browned marshmallow. Franny just stands in the middle of the room holding two biggish Baggies of salad greens and vinaigrette in an old Dijon mustard jar. Brent actually bought the mustard in Dijon, a story that Ro is bound to hear and not appreciate. Vic was mean enough last year to tell him that he could have gotten it for more or less the same price at the Italian specialty foods store down on Watchung Plaza. Franny doesn't seem to have her own winter clothes. She's wearing Cindi's car coat over a Dolphins sweatshirt. Her mother moved down to Florida the very day the divorce became final. She's got a Walkman tucked into the pocket of her cords.

"You could have trusted me to make the salad dressing at least," I scold my sister.

Franny gives up the Baggies and the jar of dressing to me. She scrutinizes us—Mom, Dad, me and Ro, especially Ro, as though she can detect something strange about him—but doesn't take off her earphones. A smirk starts twitching her tanned, feral features. I see what she is seeing. Asian men carry their bodies differently, even these famed warriors from the Khyber Pass. Ro doesn't stand like Brent or Dad. His hands hang kind of stiffly from the shoulder joints, and when he moves, his palms are tucked tight against his thighs, his stomach sticks out like a slightly pregnant woman's. Each culture establishes its own manly posture, different ways of claiming space. Ro, hiding among my plants, holds himself in a way that seems both too effeminate and too macho. I hate Franny for what she's doing to me. I am twenty-seven years old, I should be more mature. But I see now how wrong Ro's clothes are. He shows too much white collar and cuff. His shirt and his wool-blend flare-leg pants were made to measure in Kabul. The jacket comes from a discount store on Canal Street, part of a discontinued line of two-trousered suits. I ought to know, I took him there. I want to shake Franny or smash the earphones.

Cindi catches my exasperated look. "Don't pay any attention to her. She's unsociable this weekend. We can't compete with the Depeche Mode."

I intend to compete.

Franny, her eyes very green and very hostile, turns on Brent. "How come she never gets it right, Dad?"

Brent hi-fives his daughter, which embarrasses her more than anyone else in the room. "It's a Howard Jones, hon," Brent tells Cindi.

Franny, close to tears, runs to the front window where Ro's been hanging back. She has an ungainly walk for a child whose support payments specify weekly ballet lessons. She bores in on Ro's hidey hole like Russian artillery. Ro moves back to the perimeter of family intimacy. I have no way of helping yet. I have to set out the dips and Tostitos. Brent and Dad are talking sports, Mom and Cindi are watching the turkey. Dad's going on about the Knicks. He's in despair, so early in the season. He's on his second Scotch. I see Brent try. "What do you think, Roy?" He's doing his best to get my lover involved. "Maybe we'll get lucky, huh? We can always hope for a top draft pick. End up with Patrick Ewing!" Dad brightens. "That guy'll change the game. Just wait and see. He'll fill the lane better than Russell." Brent gets angry, since for some strange Amish reason he's a Celtics fan. So was Vic. "Bird'll make a monkey out of him." He looks to Ro for support.

Ro nods. Even his headshake is foreign. "You are undoubtedly correct, Brent," he says. "I am deferring to your judgment because currently I have not familiarized myself with these practices."

Ro loves squash, but none of my relatives have ever picked up a racket. I want to tell Brent that Ro's skied in St. Moritz, lost a thousand dollars in a casino in Beirut, knows where to buy Havana cigars without getting hijacked. He's sophisticated, he could make monkeys out of us all, but they think he's a retard.

Brent drinks three Scotches to Dad's two; then all three men go down to the basement. Ro and Brent do the carrying, negotiating sharp turns in the stairwell. Dad supervises. There are two trestles and a wide, splintery plywood top. "Try not to take the wall down!" Dad yells.

When they make it back in, the men take off their jackets to assemble the table. Brent's wearing a red lamb's wool turtleneck under his camel hair blazer. Ro unfastens his cuff links—they are 24-karat gold and his father's told him to sell them if funds run low—and pushes up his very white shirt sleeves. There are scars on both arms, scars that bubble against his dark skin, scars like lightning flashes under his thick black hair. Scar tissue on Ro is the color of freshwater pearls. I want to kiss it.

Cindi checks the turkey one more time. "You guys better hurry. We'll be ready to eat in fifteen minutes."

Ro, the future engineer, adjusts the trestles. He's at his best now. He's become quite chatty. From under the plywood top, he's holding forth on the Soviet menace in Kabul. Brent may actually have an idea where Afghanistan is, in a general way, but Dad is lost. He's talking of being arrested for handing out pro-American pamphlets on his campus. Dad stiffens at "arrest" and blanks out the rest. He talks of this "so-called leader," this "criminal" named Babrak Karmal and I hear other buzz-words like Kandāhar and Pamir, words that might have been Polish to me a month ago, and I can see even Brent is slightly embarrassed. It's his first exposure to Third World passion. He thought only Americans had informed political opinion—other people staged coups out of spite and misery. It's an unwelcome revelation to him that a reasonably educated and rational man like Ro would die for things that he, Brent, has never heard of and would rather laugh about. Ro was tortured in jail. Franny has taken off her earphones. Electrodes, canes, freezing tanks. He leaves nothing out. Something's gotten into Ro.

Dad looks sick. The meaning of Thanksgiving should not be so explicit. But Ro's in a daze. He goes on about how—*inshallah*—his father, once a rich landlord, had stashed away enough to bribe a guard, sneak him out of this cell and hide him for four months in a tunnel dug under a servant's adobe hut until a forged American visa could be bought. Franny's eyes are wide, Dad joins Mom on the sofa bed, shaking his head. Jail, bribes, forged, what is this? I can read his mind. "For six days I must orbit one international airport to another," Ro is saying. "The main trick is having a valid ticket, that way the airline has to carry you, even if the country won't take you in. Colombo, Seoul, Bombay, Geneva, Frankfurt, I know too

too well the transit lounges of many airports. We travel the world
with our gym bags and prayer rugs, unrolling them in the transit
lounges. The better airports have special rooms."

Brent tries to ease Dad's pain. "Say, buddy," he jokes, "you
wouldn't be ripping us off, would you?"

Ro snakes his slender body from under the makeshift table. He
hasn't been watching the effect of his monologue. "I am a working
man," he says stiffly. I have seen his special permit. He's one of the
lucky ones, though it might not last. He's saving for NJIT. Meantime he's gutting chickens to pay for room and board in Little Kabul.
He describes the gutting process. His face is transformed as he sticks
his fist into imaginary roasters and grabs for gizzards, pulls out the
squishy stuff. He takes an Afghan dagger out of the pocket of his
pants. You'd never guess, he looks like such a victim. "This," he
says, eyes glinting. "This is all I need."

"Cool," Franny says.

"Time to eat," Mom shouts. "I made the gravy with the nutmeg
as you said, Renata."

I lead Dad to the head of the table. "Everyone else sit where you
want to."

Franny picks out the chair next to Ro before I can put Cindi there.
I want Cindi to know him, I want her as an ally.

Dad tests the blade of the carving knife. Mom put the knife where
Dad always sits when she set the table. He takes his thumb off the
blade and pushes the switch. "That noise makes me feel good."

But I carry in the platter with the turkey and place it in front of
Ro. "I want you to carve," I say.

He brings out his dagger all over again. Franny is practically lick-
ing his fingers. "You mean this is a professional job?"

We stare fascinated as my lover slashes and slices, swiftly, confi-
dently, at the huge, browned, juicy breast. The dagger scoops out
flesh.

Now I am the one in a daze. I am seeing Ro's naked body as though
for the first time, his nicked, scarred, burned body. In his body,
the blemishes seem embedded, more beautiful, like wood. I am
seeing character made manifest. I am seeing Brent and Dad for the
first time, too. They have their little scars, things they're proud of,
football injuries and bowling elbows they brag about. Our scars are
so innocent; they are invisible and come to us from rough-housing
gone too far. Ro hates to talk about his scars. If I trace the puckered

tissue on his left thigh and ask "How, Ro?" he becomes shy, dismissive: a pack of dogs attacked him when he was a boy. The skin on his back is speckled and lumpy from burns, but when I ask he laughs. A crazy villager whacked him with a burning stick for cheekiness, he explains. He's ashamed that he comes from a culture of pain.

The turkey is reduced to a drying, whitened skeleton. On our plates, the slices are symmetrical, elegant. I realize all in a rush how much I love this man with his blemished, tortured body. I will give him citizenship if he asks. Vic was beautiful, but Vic was self-sufficient. Ro's my chance to heal the world.

I shall teach him how to walk like an American, how to dress like Brent but better, how to fill up a room as Dad does instead of melting and blending but sticking out in the Afghan way. In spite of the funny way he holds himself and the funny way he moves his head from side to side when he wants to say yes, Ro is Clint Eastwood, scarred hero and survivor. Dad and Brent are children. I realize Ro's the only circumcised man I've slept with.

Mom asks, "Why are you grinning like that, Renata?"

HISAYE YAMAMOTO

Hisaye Yamamoto was born in California in 1921 and is of Japanese American descent. She started writing when she was fourteen and first published her work in the Poston Chronicle, *the newspaper of the relocation camp where she spent three years during World War II. The mother of seven children, she says she writes "to reaffirm certain basic truths which seem to get lost in the shuffle from generation to generation."*

SEVENTEEN SYLLABLES

THE FIRST ROSIE knew that her mother had taken to writing poems was one evening when she finished one and read it aloud for her daughter's approval. It was about cats, and Rosie pretended to understand it thoroughly and appreciate it no end, partly because she hesitated to disillusion her mother about the quantity and quality of Japanese she had learned in all the years now that she had been going to Japanese school every Saturday (and Wednesday, too, in the summer). Even so, her mother must have been skeptical about the depth of Rosie's understanding, because she explained afterwards about the kind of poem she was trying to write.

See, Rosie, she said, it was a *haiku*, a poem in which she must pack all her meaning into seventeen syllables only, which were divided into three lines of five, seven, and five syllables. In the one she had just read, she had tried to capture the charm of a kitten, as well as comment on the superstition that owning a cat of three colors meant good luck.

"Yes, yes, I understand. How utterly lovely," Rosie said, and her mother, either satisfied or seeing through the deception and resigned, went back to composing.

The truth was that Rosie was lazy; English lay ready on the tongue but Japanese had to be searched for and examined, and even then put forth tentatively (probably to meet with laughter). It was so much easier to say yes, yes, even when one meant no, no. Besides, this was what was in her mind to say: I was looking through one of your magazines from Japan last night, Mother, and towards the back I found some *haiku* in English that delighted me. There was one that made me giggle off and on until I fell asleep—

> It is morning, and lo!
> I lie awake, comme il faut,
> sighing for some dough.

Now, how to reach her mother, how to communicate the melancholy song? Rosie knew formal Japanese by fits and starts, her mother had even less English, no French. It was much more possible to say yes, yes.

It developed that her mother was writing the *haiku* for a daily newspaper, the *Mainichi Shimbun*, that was published in San Francisco. Los Angeles, to be sure, was closer to the farming community in which the Hayashi family lived and several Japanese vernaculars were printed there, but Rosie's parents said they preferred the tone of the northern paper. Once a week, the *Mainichi* would have a section devoted to *haiku*, and her mother became an extravagant contributor, taking for herself the blossoming pen name, Ume Hanazono.

So Rosie and her father lived for awhile with two women, her mother and Ume Hanazono. Her mother (Tome Hayashi by name) kept house, cooked, washed, and, along with her husband and the Carrascos, the Mexican family hired for the harvest, did her ample share of picking tomatoes out in the sweltering fields and boxing them in tidy strata in the cool packing shed. Ume Hanazono, who came to life after the dinner dishes were done, was an earnest, muttering stranger who often neglected speaking when spoken to and stayed busy at the parlor table as late as midnight scribbling with pencil on scratch paper or carefully copying characters on good paper with her fat, pale green Parker.

The new interest had some repercussions on the household routine. Before, Rosie had been accustomed to her parents and herself taking their hot baths early and going to bed almost immediately afterwards, unless her parents challenged each other to a game of flower cards or unless company dropped in. Now if her father wanted to play cards, he had to resort to solitaire (at which he always cheated fearlessly), and if a group of friends came over, it was bound to contain someone who was also writing *haiku*, and the small assemblage would be split in two, her father entertaining the non-literary members and her mother comparing ecstatic notes with the visiting poet.

If they went out, it was more of the same thing. But Ume Hanazono's life span, even for a poet's, was very brief—perhaps three months at most.

One night they went over to see the Hayano family in the neighboring town to the west, an adventure both painful and attractive to Rosie. It was attractive because there were four Hayano girls, all lovely and each one named after a season of the year (Haru, Natsu, Aki, Fuyu), painful because something had been wrong with Mrs. Hayano ever since the birth of her first child. Rosie would sometimes watch Mrs. Hayano, reputed to have been the belle of her native village, making her way about a room, stooped, slowly shuffling, violently trembling (*always* trembling), and she would be reminded that this woman, in this same condition, had carried and given issue to three babies. She would look wonderingly at Mr. Hayano, handsome, tall, and strong, and she would look at her four pretty friends. But it was not a matter she could come to any decision about.

On this visit, however, Mrs. Hayano sat all evening in the rocker, as motionless and unobtrusive as it was possible for her to be, and Rosie found the greater part of the evening practically anaesthetic. Too, Rosie spent most of it in the girls' room, because Haru, the garrulous one, said almost as soon as the bows and other greetings were over, "Oh, you must see my new coat!"

It was a pale plaid of grey, sand, and blue, with an enormous collar, and Rosie, seeing nothing special in it, said, "Gee, how nice."

"Nice?" said Haru, indignantly. "Is that all you can say about it? It's gorgeous! And so cheap, too. Only seventeen-ninety-eight, because it was a sale. The saleslady said it was twenty-five dollars regular."

"Gee," said Rosie. Natsu, who never said much and when she said anything said it shyly, fingered the coat covetously and Haru pulled it away.

"Mine," she said, putting it on. She minced in the aisle between the two large beds and smiled happily. "Let's see how your mother likes it."

She broke into the front room and the adult conversation, and went to stand in front of Rosie's mother, while the rest watched from the door. Rosie's mother was properly envious. "May I inherit it when you're through with it?"

Haru, pleased, giggled and said yes, she could, but Natsu reminded gravely from the door, "You promised me, Haru."

Everyone laughed but Natsu, who shamefacedly retreated into the bedroom. Haru came in laughing, taking off the coat. "We were only kidding, Natsu," she said. "Here, you try it on now."

After Natsu buttoned herself into the coat, inspected herself solemnly in the bureau mirror, and reluctantly shed it, Rosie, Aki, and Fuyu got their turns, and Fuyu, who was eight, drowned in it while her sisters and Rosie doubled up in amusement. They all went into the front room later, because Haru's mother quaveringly called to her to fix the tea and rice cakes and open a can of sliced peaches for everybody. Rosie noticed that her mother and Mr. Hayano were talking together at the little table – they were discussing a *haiku* that Mr. Hayano was planning to send to the *Mainichi*, while her father was sitting at one end of the sofa looking through a copy of *Life*, the new picture magazine. Occasionally, her father would comment on a photograph, holding it toward Mrs. Hayano and speaking to her as he always did – loudly, as though he thought someone such as she must surely be at least a trifle deaf also.

The five girls had their refreshments at the kitchen table, and it was while Rosie was showing the sisters her trick of swallowing peach slices without chewing (she chased each slippery crescent down with a swig of tea) that her father brought his empty teacup and untouched saucer to the sink and said, "Come on, Rosie, we're going home now."

"Already?" asked Rosie.

"Work tomorrow," he said.

He sounded irritated, and Rosie, puzzled, gulped one last yellow slice and stood up to go, while the sisters began protesting, as was their wont.

"We have to get up at five-thirty," he told them, going into the front room quickly, so that they did not have their usual chance to hang onto his hands and plead for an extension of time.

Rosie, following, saw that her mother and Mr. Hayano were sipping tea and still talking together, while Mrs. Hayano concentrated, quivering, on raising the handleless Japanese cup to her lips with both her hands and lowering it back to her lap. Her father, saying nothing, went out the door, onto the bright porch, and down the steps. Her mother looked up and asked, "Where is he going?"

"Where is he going?" Rosie said. "He said we were going home now."

"Going home?" Her mother looked with embarrassment at Mr. Hayano and his absorbed wife and then forced a smile. "He must be tired," she said.

Haru was not giving up yet. "May Rosie stay overnight?" she asked, and Natsu, Aki, and Fuyu came to reinforce their sister's plea by helping her make a circle around Rosie's mother. Rosie, for once having no desire to stay, was relieved when her mother, apologizing to the perturbed Mr. and Mrs. Hayano for her father's abruptness at the same time, managed to shake her head no at the quartet, kindly but adamant, so that they broke their circle and let her go.

Rosie's father looked ahead into the windshield as the two joined him. "I'm sorry," her mother said. "You must be tired." Her father, stepping on the starter, said nothing. "You know how I get when it's *haiku*," she continued, "I forget what time it is." He only grunted.

As they rode homeward silently, Rosie, sitting between, felt a rush of hate for both—for her mother for begging, for her father for denying her mother. I wish this old Ford would crash, right now, she thought, then immediately, no, no, I wish my father would laugh, but it was too late: already the vision had passed through her mind of the green pick-up crumpled in the dark against one of the mighty eucalyptus trees they were just riding past, of the three contorted, bleeding bodies, one of them hers.

Rosie ran between two patches of tomatoes, her heart working more rambunctiously than she had ever known it to. How lucky it was that Aunt Taka and Uncle Gimpachi had come tonight, though, how very lucky. Otherwise she might not have really kept her half-promise to meet Jesus Carrasco. Jesus was going to be a senior in September at the same school she went to, and his parents were the ones helping with the tomatoes this year. She and Jesus, who hardly remembered seeing each other at Cleveland High where there were so many other people and two whole grades between them, had become great friends this summer—he always had a joke for her when he periodically drove the loaded pick-up up from the fields to the shed where she was usually sorting while her mother and father did the packing, and they laughed a great deal together over infinitesimal repartee during the afternoon break for chilled watermelon or ice cream in the shade of the shed.

What she enjoyed most was racing him to see which could finish picking a double row first. He, who could work faster, would tease her by slowing down until she thought she would surely pass him this time, then speeding up furiously to leave her several sprawling vines behind. Once he had made her screech hideously by crossing over, while her back was turned, to place atop the tomatoes in her green-stained bucket a truly monstrous, pale green worm (it had looked more like an infant snake). And it was when they had finished a contest this morning, after she had pantingly pointed a green finger at the immature tomatoes evident in the lugs at the end of his row and he had returned the accusation (with justice), that he had startlingly brought up the matter of their possibly meeting outside the range of both their parents' dubious eyes.

"What for?" she had asked.

"I've got a secret I want to tell you," he said.

"Tell me now," she demanded.

"It won't be ready till tonight," he said.

She laughed. "Tell me tomorrow then."

"It'll be gone tomorrow," he threatened.

"Well, for seven hakes, what is it?" she had asked, more than twice, and when he had suggested that the packing shed would be an appropriate place to find out, she had cautiously answered maybe. She had not been certain she was going to keep the appointment until the arrival of Mother's sister and her husband. Their coming seemed a sort of signal of permission, of grace, and she had definitely made up her mind to lie and leave as she was bowing them welcome.

So as soon as everyone appeared settled back for the evening, she announced loudly that she was going to the privy outside, "I'm going to the *benjo*!" and slipped out the door. And now that she was actually on her way, her heart pumped in such an undisciplined way that she could hear it with her ears. It's because I'm running, she told herself, slowing to a walk. The shed was up ahead, one more patch away, in the middle of the fields. Its bulk, looming in the dimness, took on a sinisterness that was funny when Rosie reminded herself that it was only a wooden frame with a canvas roof and three canvas walls that made a slapping noise on breezy days.

Jesus was sitting on the narrow plank that was the sorting platform and she went around to the other side and jumped backwards to seat herself on the rim of a packing stand. "Well, tell me," she said, without greeting, thinking her voice sounded reassuringly familiar.

"I saw you coming out the door," Jesus said. "I heard you running part of the way, too."

"Uh-huh," Rosie said. "Now tell me the secret."

"I was afraid you wouldn't come," he said.

Rosie delved around on the chicken-wire bottom of the stall for number two tomatoes, ripe, which she was sitting beside, and came up with a left-over that felt edible. She bit into it and began sucking out the pulp and seeds. "I'm here," she pointed out.

"Rosie, are you sorry you came?"

"Sorry? What for?" she said. "You said you were going to tell me something."

"I will, I will," Jesus said, but his voice contained disappointment, and Rosie fleetingly felt the older of the two, realizing a brand-new power which vanished without category under her recognition.

"I have to go back in a minute," she said. "My aunt and uncle are here from Wintersburg. I told them I was going to the privy."

Jesus laughed. "You funny thing," he said. "You slay me!"

"Just because you have a bathroom *inside*," Rosie said. "Come on, tell me."

Chuckling, Jesus came around to lean on the stand facing her. They still could not see each other very clearly, but Rosie noticed that Jesus became very sober again as he took the hollow tomato from her hand and dropped it back into the stall. When he took hold of her empty hand, she could find no words to protest; her vocabulary had become distressingly constricted and she thought desperately that all that remained intact now was yes and no and oh, and even these few sounds would not easily out. Thus, kissed by Jesus, Rosie fell, for the first time entirely victim to a helplessness delectable beyond speech. But the terrible, beautiful sensation lasted no more than a second, and the reality of Jesus' lips and tongue and teeth and hands made her pull away with such strength that she nearly tumbled.

Rosie stopped running as she approached the lights from the windows of home. How long since she had left? She could not guess, but gasping yet, she went to the privy in back and locked herself in. Her own breathing deafened her in the dark, close space, and she sat and waited until she could hear at last the nightly calling of the frogs and crickets. Even then, all she could think to say was oh, my, and the pressure of Jesus' face against her face would not leave.

No one had missed her in the parlor, however, and Rosie walked in and through quickly, announcing that she was next going to take a bath. "Your father's in the bathhouse," her mother said, and Rosie, in her room, recalled that she had not seen him when she entered. There had been only Aunt Taka and Uncle Gimpachi with her mother at the table, drinking tea. She got her robe and straw sandals and crossed the parlor again to go outside. Her mother was telling them about the *haiku* competition in the *Mainichi* and the poem she had entered.

Rosie met her father coming out of the bathhouse. "Are you through, Father?" she asked. "I was going to ask you to scrub my back."

"Scrub your own back," he said shortly, going toward the main house.

"What have I done now?" she yelled after him. She suddenly felt like doing a lot of yelling. But he did not answer, and she went into the bathhouse. Turning on the dangling light, she removed her denims and T-shirt and threw them in the big carton for dirty clothes standing next to the washing machine. Her other things she took with her into the bath compartment to wash after her bath. After she had scooped a basin of hot water from the square wooden tub, she sat on the grey cement of the floor and soaped herself at exaggerated leisure, singing "Red Sails in the Sunset" at the top of her voice and using da-da-da where she suspected her words. Then, standing up, still singing, for she was possessed by the notion that any attempt now to analyze would result in spoilage and she believed that the larger her volume the less she would be able to hear herself think, she obtained more hot water and poured it on until she was free of lather. Only then did she allow herself to step into the steaming vat, one leg first, then the remainder of her body inch by inch until the water no longer stung and she could move around at will.

She took a long time soaking, afterwards remembering to go around outside to stoke the embers of the tin-lined fireplace beneath the tub and to throw on a few more sticks so that the water might keep its heat for her mother, and when she finally returned to the parlor, she found her mother still talking *haiku* with her aunt and uncle, the three of them on another round of tea. Her father was nowhere in sight.

At Japanese school the next day (Wednesday, it was), Rosie was grave and giddy by turns. Preoccupied at her desk in the row for students on Book Eight, she made up for it at recess by performing wild mimicry for the benefit of her friend Chizuko. She held her nose and whined a witticism or two in what she considered was the manner of Fred Allen; she assumed intoxication and a British accent to go over the climax of the Rudy Vallee recording of the pub conversation about William Ewart Gladstone; she was the child Shirley Temple piping, "On the Good Ship Lollipop;" she was the gentleman soprano of the Four Inkspots trilling, "If I Didn't Care." And she felt reasonably satisfied when Chizuko wept and gasped, "Oh, Rosie, you ought to be in the movies!"

Her father came after her at noon, bringing her sandwiches of minced ham and two nectarines to eat while she rode, so that she could pitch right into the sorting when they got home. The lugs were piling up, he said, and the ripe tomatoes in them would probably have to be taken to the cannery tomorrow if they were not ready for the produce haulers tonight. "This heat's not doing them any good. And we've got no time for a break today."

It *was* hot, probably the hottest day of the year, and Rosie's blouse stuck damply to her back even under the protection of the canvas. But she worked as efficiently as a flawless machine and kept the stalls heaped, with one part of her mind listening in to the parental murmuring about the heat and the tomatoes and with another part planning the exact words she would say to Jesus when he drove up with the first load of the afternoon. But when at last she saw that the pick-up was coming, her hands went berserk and the tomatoes started falling in the wrong stalls, and her father said, "Hey, hey! Rosie, watch what you're doing!"

"Well, I have to go to the *benjo*," she said, hiding panic.

"Go in the weeds over there," he said, only half-joking.

"Oh, Father!" she protested.

"Oh, go on home," her mother said. "We'll make out for awhile."

In the privy Rosie peered through a knothole toward the fields, watching as much as she could of Jesus. Happily she thought she saw him look in the direction of the house from time to time before he finished unloading and went back toward the patch where his mother and father worked. As she was heading for the shed, a very presentable black car purred up the dirt driveway to the house and its driver motioned to her. Was this the Hayashi home, he wanted to know. She nodded. Was she a Hayashi? Yes, she said, thinking that he was a good-looking man. He got out of the car with a huge, flat package and she saw that he warmly wore a business suit. "I have something here for your mother then," he said, in a more elegant Japanese than she was used to.

She told him where her mother was and he came along with her, patting his face with an immaculate white handkerchief and saying something about the coolness of San Francisco. To her surprised mother and father, he bowed and introduced himself as, among other things, the *haiku* editor of the *Mainichi Shimbun*, saying that since he had been coming as far as Los Angeles anyway, he had decided to bring her the first prize she had won in the recent contest.

"First prize?" her mother echoed, believing and not believing, pleased and overwhelmed. Handed the package with a bow, she bobbed her head up and down numerous times to express her utter gratitude.

"It is nothing much," he added, "but I hope it will serve as a token of our great appreciation for your contributions and our great admiration of your considerable talent."

"I am not worthy," she said, falling easily into his style. "It is I who should make some sign of my humble thanks for being permitted to contribute."

"No, no, to the contrary," he said, bowing again.

But Rosie's mother insisted, and then saying that she knew she was being unorthodox, she asked if she might open the package because her curiosity was so great. Certainly she might. In fact, he would like her reaction to it, for personally, it was one of his favorite *Hiroshiges*.

Rosie thought it was a pleasant picture, which looked to have been sketched with delicate quickness. There were pink clouds, containing some graceful calligraphy, and a sea that was a pale blue except at the edges, containing four sampans with indications of people in them. Pines edged the water and on the far-off beach there was a cluster of thatched huts towered over by pine-dotted mountains of grey and blue. The frame was scalloped and gilt.

After Rosie's mother pronounced it without peer and somewhat prodded her father into nodding agreement, she said Mr. Kuroda must at least have a cup of tea after coming all this way, and although Mr. Kuroda did not want to impose, he soon agreed that a cup of tea would be refreshing and went along with her to the house, carrying the picture for her.

"Ha, your mother's crazy!" Rosie's father said, and Rosie laughed uneasily as she resumed judgment on the tomatoes. She had emptied six lugs when he broke into an imaginary conversation with Jesus to tell her to go and remind her mother of the tomatoes, and she went slowly.

Mr. Kuroda was in his shirtsleeves expounding some *haiku* theory as he munched a rice cake, and her mother was rapt. Abashed in the great man's presence, Rosie stood next to her mother's chair until her mother looked up inquiringly, and then she started to whisper the message, but her mother pushed her gently away and reproached, "You are not being very polite to our guest."

"Father says the tomatoes . . . " Rosie said aloud, smiling foolishly.

"Tell him I shall only be a minute," her mother said, speaking the language of Mr. Kuroda.

When Rosie carried the reply to her father, he did not seem to hear and she said again, "Mother says she'll be back in a minute."

"All right, all right," he nodded, and they worked again in silence. But suddenly, her father uttered an incredible noise, exactly like the cork of a bottle popping, and the next Rosie knew, he was stalking angrily toward the house, almost running in fact, and she chased after him crying, "Father! Father! What are you going to do?"

He stopped long enough to order her back to the shed. "Never mind!" he shouted. "Get on with the sorting!"

And from the place in the fields where she stood, frightened and vacillating, Rosie saw her father enter the house. Soon Mr. Kuroda came out alone, putting on his coat. Mr. Kuroda got into his car and backed out down the driveway onto the highway. Next her father emerged, also alone, something in his arms (it was the picture, she realized), and, going over to the bathhouse woodpile, he threw the picture on the ground and picked up the axe. Smashing the picture, glass and all (she heard the explosion faintly), he reached over for the kerosene that was used to encourage the bath fire and poured it over the wreckage. I am dreaming, Rosie said to herself, I am dreaming, but her father, having made sure that his act of cremation was irrevocable, was even then returning to the fields.

Rosie ran past him and toward the house. What had become of her mother? She burst into the parlor and found her mother at the back window watching the dying fire. They watched together until there remained only a feeble smoke under the blazing sun. Her mother was very calm.

"Do you know why I married your father?" she said without turning.

"No," said Rosie. It was the most frightening question she had ever been called upon to answer. Don't tell me now, she wanted to say, tell me tomorrow, tell me next week, don't tell me today. But she knew she would be told now, that the telling would combine with the other violence of the hot afternoon to level her life, her world to the very ground.

It was like a story out of the magazines illustrated in sepia, which she had consumed so greedily for a period until the information had somehow reached her that those wretchedly unhappy autobiographies, offered to her as the testimonials of living men and women, were largely inventions: Her mother, at nineteen, had come to America and married her father as an alternative to suicide.

At eighteen she had been in love with the first son of one of the well-to-do families in her village. The two had met whenever and wherever they could, secretly, because it would not have done for his family to see him favor her—her father had no money; he was a drunkard and a gambler besides. She had learned she was with child; an excellent match had already been arranged for her lover. Despised by her family, she had given premature birth to a stillborn son, who would be seventeen now. Her family did not turn her out, but she could no longer project herself in any direction without refreshing in them the memory of her indiscretion. She wrote to Aunt Taka, her favorite sister in America, threatening to kill herself if Aunt Taka would not send for her. Aunt Taka hastily arranged a marriage with a young man of whom she knew, but lately arrived from Japan, a young man of simple mind, it was said, but of kindly heart. The young man was never told why his unseen betrothed was so eager to hasten the day of meeting.

The story was told perfectly, with neither groping for words nor untoward passion. It was as though her mother had memorized it by heart, reciting it to herself so many times over that its nagging vileness had long since gone.

"I had a brother then?" Rosie asked, for this was what seemed to matter now; she would think about the other later, she assured herself, pushing back the illumination which threatened all that darkness that had hitherto been merely mysterious or even glamorous. "A half-brother?"

"Yes."

"I would have liked a brother," she said.

Suddenly, her mother knelt on the floor and took her by the wrists. "Rosie," she said urgently, "promise me you will never marry!" Shocked more by the request than the revelation, Rosie stared at her mother's face. Jesus, Jesus, she called silently, not certain whether she was invoking the help of the son of the Carrascos or of God, until there returned sweetly the memory of Jesus' hand, how it had touched her and where. Still her mother waited for an answer, holding her wrists so tightly that her hands were going numb. She tried to pull free. "Promise," her mother whispered fiercely, "promise." "Yes, yes, I promise," Rosie said. But for an instant she turned away, and her mother, hearing the familiar glib agreement, released her. Oh, you, you, you, her eyes and twisted mouth said, you fool. Rosie, covering her face, began at last to cry, and the embrace and consoling hand came much later than she expected.

WENDY WILDER LARSEN
TRAN THI NGA

Tran Thi Nga is the coauthor of Shallow Graves: Two Women and Vietnam, *a book of poems about the war in Vietnam. The book is a collaboration by Nga, who emigrated to America from Vietnam in 1975, and Wendy Wilder Larsen, an American who met Nga while in Vietnam in 1970.*

DECIDING

We went to the office every day.
Though the situation was critical,
people at work said nothing.
Province Chiefs were running.
We told the Big Boss our country would be lost.
We told him we would blow ourselves up
if we could not leave.

I sat at my desk doing the financial report.
My thoughts went round and round.

Should I leave?
Should I go alone?
Should I take my mother?
She did not want to go.
She feared they wouldn't let her chew the betel.
Should I leave my children?
How would I make a living?
What would happen when the communists came?

When I made up my mind,
pictures of my childhood floated to the surface
as clear and strong as dreams.

Our old house in Hadong.
The bamboo in the backyard.
We ate the shoots.
The soldiers made a fence from the stalks.
My sister and I painted the fence
first white, then blue, then her favorite yellow.
The small antigonon vine we planted
with its pink blossoms in spring.

Our ponds.
The many steps down
to the small bridge
where we'd sit hour after hour
letting our hands dip into the water
trying to catch the silver-brown fish.

Airplanes bombing
running from our house
people dying, people calling from outside the walls
don't take me. I'm not dead yet.
The family hiding together in our house in Cholon
sunlight coming through the bullet holes.

OUR HOUSE IN HADONG

Our best house, the house where we were happy,
was our brick house on Ha Van Street
with its two hectares of land
lichee and mangosteen and starfruit in the back,
the two Hoa Moc trees white as snow in the front.
We'd put the petals in our tea to sweeten our breath.

From far down the road
I could smell the heavy jackfruit.
Father never allowed us to eat them
said they were too rich for the climate.
He'd give them to the soldiers outside the walls.
When he was away, we ate until we got fevers.
My younger sister climbed the apple trees
and shook the apples down.

We had everything.
There was a flower garden
with dark red roses, orchids and yellow mimosa.
We had our own cauliflower, tomatoes,
the artichokes my father loved,
chickens, pigs, ducks and pigeons.
We needed the market only for beef
and rice kept in giant brown jars in the storeroom.

We even had two ponds.
Each New Year
we'd let the water out of the big pond
to catch the butter fish
we'd fed all year.

On a tiny island in the middle of the smaller pond,
the cook built an imitation mountain
with caves, bamboo, porcelain angels,
and two old matchmakers playing chess.
When the moon came up,
we'd watch the goldfish move in the warm water
and listen to night noises
remembering the sounds of the jungle.

WALTER LEW

Walter Lew is the son of two Korean doctors who emigrated to Baltimore in the 1950s. He grew up on baseball and the Beatles, studied science and thought about medical school, but decided on poetry instead.

LEAVING SEOUL: 1953

We have to bury the urns,
Mother and I. We tried to leave them in a back room,
Decoyed by a gas lamp, and run out

But they landed behind us here, at the front gate.
It is 6th hour, early winter, black cold:
Only, on the other side of the rice-paper doors

The yellow *ondol* stone-heated floors
Are still warm. I look out to the blue
Lanterns along the runway, the bright airplane.

Off the back step, Mother, disorganized
As usual, has devised a clumsy rope and shovel
To bury the urns. I wonder out loud

How she ever became a doctor.
Get out, she says *Go to your father: he too
Does not realize what is happening.* You see,

Father is waiting at the airfield in a discarded U.S. Army
Overcoat. He has lost his hat, lost
His father, and is smoking Lucky's like crazy . . .

We grab through the tall weeds and wind
That begin to shoot under us like river ice.
It is snowing.   We are crying, from the cold

Or what?   It is only decades
Later that, tapping the short glowing jars,
I find they contain all that has made
The father have dominion over hers.

WING TEK LUM

Wing Tek Lum lives in Hawaii. In giving permission to publish this poem he said, "Thank you for liking this poem." We do. When asked to write something about himself for another anthology he said, "Let the poems speak for themselves." They do.

LOCAL SENSIBILITIES

inspired by Frank Chin

When I see a pineapple,
I do not think of an exotic fruit sliced in rings
    to be served with ham,
more the summer jobs at the cannery
    driving a forklift or packing wedges on the line.

When I hear the name "Duke,"
I envision someone other than that movie cowboy,
    gravel-voiced, a true grit idol of the late night set;
instead I see a white-haired surfer by his long board,
    palms so large, flashing smiles along the beach.

When I think of a man-of-war,
it is not the name of a Triple Crown horse
    pacing a stud farm that comes to mind first;
rather I picture the Portuguese kind
    whose stings must be salved by rubbing sand.

When I use the word "packages,"
it is usually not a reference to the parcels
    waiting for me at the post office,
rather the paper sacks I get
    from the supermarket to lug my groceries home.

When I read the term "Jap,"
the image of a kamikaze pilot now turned to Sony exports
    is not what I see;
mainly it is the Sand Island roundup and those old men
    who still wince long after the 442nd has marched back.

When I think of Hawaii,
I do not fancy myself lolling under palm trees,
    a backdrop of verdant cliffs, caressed by a balmy breeze;
instead I give thanks for classmates and our family graves,
    this unique universe that we have called our home.

JANICE MIRIKITANI

Janice Mirikitani lives and works in San Francisco. A third-generation Japanese American, she writes poems and works as a community activist. "Words from the Third World are like food," she says. "Universal, essential, procreative, freeing, connective, satisfying."

BREAKING SILENCE

*For my mother's testimony
before Commission on Wartime Relocation and
Internment of Japanese American Civilians*

There are miracles that happen
she said.
From the silences
in the glass caves of our ears,
from the crippled tongue,
from the mute, wet eyelash,
testimonies waiting like winter.
    We were told
that silence was better
golden like our skin,
    useful like
go quietly,
    easier like
don't make waves,
    expedient like
horsetails and deserts.

        "Mr. Commissioner . . .
        . . . U.S. Army Signal Corps confiscated
        our property . . . it was subjected to vandalism
        and ravage. All improvements we had made

273

before our incarceration was stolen
or destroyed . . .
I was coerced into signing documents
giving you authority to take . . ."
. . . to take
. . . to take.

My mother,
soft like tallow,
words peeling from her
like slivers
of yellow flame,
her testimony
a vat of boiling water
surging through the coldest
bluest vein.
    She, when the land labored
with flowers, their scent
flowing into her pores,
had molded her earth
like a woman
with soft breasted slopes
yielding silent mornings
and purple noisy birthings,
yellow hay
and tomatoes throbbing
like the sea.
    And then
all was hushed for announcements:
    "Take only what you can carry . . ."
We were made to believe
our faces betrayed us.
Our bodies were loud
with yellow
screaming flesh
needing to be silenced
behind barbed wire.

"Mr. Commissioner . . .
 . . . it seems we were singled out
from others who were under suspicion.
Our neighbors were of German and Italian
descent, some of whom were not citizens . . .
It seems we were singled out . . ."

She had worn her sweat
like lemon leaves
shining on the rough edges of work,
removed the mirrors
from her rooms
so she would not be tempted
by vanity.
    Her dreams
honed the blade of her plow.
The land,
the building of food was
noisy as the opening of irises.
The sounds of work
bolted in barracks . . .
silenced.

Mr. Commissioner . . .
So when you tell me I must limit testimony
to 5 minutes, when you tell me my time is up,
I tell you this:
Pride has kept my lips
pinned by nails
my rage coffined.
But I exhume my past
to claim this time.
My youth is buried in Rohwer,
Obachan's ghost visits Amache Gate,
My niece haunts Tule Lake.
Words are better than tears,
so I spill them.
I kill this, the silence . . .

There are miracles that happen,
she said,
and everything is made visible.
     We see the cracks and fissures in our soil:
We speak of suicides and intimacies,
of longings lush like wet furrows,
of oceans bearing us toward imagined riches,
of burning humiliations and
crimes by the government.
Of self hate and of love that breaks
through silences.
     We are lightning and justice.
     Our souls become transparent like glass
revealing tears for war-dead sons
red ashes of Hiroshima
jagged wounds from barbed wire.
     We must recognize ourselves at last
     We are a rainforest of color
and noise.
     We hear everything.
     We are unafraid.

          Our language is beautiful.

(Quoted excerpts from my mother's testimony modified with her permission — J.M.)

DAVID MURA

David Mura is a poet and teacher at St. Olaf College in Northfield, Minnesota. He is a Sansei, a third-generation Japanese American. Both of his parents were children when their families were interned by the United States during World War II. He also contributed the introductory essay to this section.

HUY NGUYEN: BROTHERS, DROWNING CRIES

1

Shaking the snow from your hair, bowl-cut
like an immigrant's, you hand me your assignment—
Compare and Contrast. Though your accent stumbles
like my grandfather's, you talk of Faulkner,
The Sound and the Fury. You mention Bergson,
whom you've read in French. *Durée.* How the moment lasts.
Your paper opens swimming the Mekong Delta.

2

As you lift your face, the sun flashes
down wrinkles of water; blue dragonflies
dart overhead. You hear your brother call.
You go under again, down, down, till you
reach the bottom, a fistful of river clay,
mold a ball in the dark, feel your lungs struggle,
waiting to burst—

Where is your brother?

Against the current's thick drag, stumble
to shore, the huts of fishermen—
My brother, my brother's drowned!

Faces emerge from black doorways,
puzzled, trotting towards you, then
all of them running to the river,
diving and searching the bottom
not for clay but flesh,

and there the man
crawls up on the beach, your brother
slumped over his shoulder, bouncing up
and down as the man runs up and down,
water belching from your brother's mouth
but no air, no air: flings
your brother to the ground, bends,
puts mouth to your brother's lips,
blows in, blows out, until your brother's
chest expands once, once, and once,
and his eyes flutter open, not yet back
in this world, not yet recognizing the blue
of the sky, that your people see as happiness,
even happier than the sun.

3
Five years since you drifted on the South China Sea,
and the night Thai pirates sliced your wife's finger for
a ring, then beat you senseless. You woke to a merchant ship
passing in silence, as if a mirage were shouting for help.
Later, in that camp in Bataan, loudspeakers told
of a boat broken on an island reef, and the survivors
thrashing through the waves, the tide pulling out,
and the girl who reached the shore and watched
the others, one by one, fall from starvation,
as she drank after each rain from shells on the beach.
At last only her brother remained, his eyes staring
upwards at the wind and the sun, calling her name . . .
The camp went silent, then a baby, a woman sobbing.
And you knew someone was saved to tell the story.

4

Now, through Saigon, your mother carries kettles of soup to
　　　　sell at dawn.
While malaria numbs your brother's limbs, he shivers on a
　　　　cot in prison.
You write: "I wait for his death. Safe. Fat. World away." I
　　　　red mark your English.
There was a jungle you fought in. There's a scar above your
　　　　wrist.
A boy dives, splashes and, going down, clutches his stomach
　　　　and twists.
You're at the bus stop by Target. Snow still falling, a fine
　　　　blown mist.

DWIGHT OKITA

Dwight Okita was born on August 26, 1958. When his poems were published in Breaking Ice, *he said, "It is now 1982 and I am still here." In 1991 "here" is Chicago, where he still makes poems, and videos, too.*

IN RESPONSE TO
EXECUTIVE ORDER 9066:
ALL AMERICANS OF JAPANESE
DESCENT MUST REPORT TO
RELOCATION CENTERS

Dear Sirs:
Of course I'll come. I've packed my galoshes
and three packets of tomato seeds. Janet calls them
"love apples." My father says where we're going
they won't grow.

I am a fourteen-year-old girl with bad spelling
and a messy room. If it helps any, I will tell you
I have always felt funny using chopsticks
and my favorite food is pizza.
My best friend is a white girl named Denise—
we look at boys together. She sat in front of me
all through grade school because of our names:
O'Connor, Ozawa. I know the back of Denise's head very well.
I tell her she's going bald. She tells me I copy on tests.
We are best friends.

I saw Denise today in Geography class.
She was sitting on the other side of the room.
"You're trying to start a war," she said, "giving secrets away
to the Enemy, Why can't you keep your big mouth shut?"
I didn't know what to say.
I gave her a packet of tomato seeds
and asked her to plant them for me, told her
when the first tomato ripens
to miss me.

FURTHER READINGS

All references are to most recent editions of works cited.

Aiiieeeee!: An Anthology of Asian-American Writings. Frank Chin, Jeffery Paul Chan, Lawson Fusao Inada, and Shawn Hsu Wong, editors. Washington, D.C.: Howard University Press, 1983. The editors, influenced by the Vietnam war and the civil rights movement, have assembled writings that challenge old stereotypes and "claim America" for Americans of Asian descent. The anthology features selections by Louis Chu, John Okada, Hisaye Yamamoto and others, as well as newer works by the editors and other young writers.

Asian American Authors. Kai-yu Hsu and Helen Palubinskas, editors. Boston: Houghton Mifflin, 1976. An important collection of stories and poems exploring themes of Asian American identity, nationalism, and assimilation. The book also discusses the historical context and chronology of Japanese, Chinese, and Filipino experience in America, and includes biographical sketches of the authors.

Breaking Silence: An Anthology of Contemporary Asian American Poetry. Joseph Bruchac, editor. Greenfield, New York: Greenfield Review Press, 1983. This comprehensive anthology presents works by fifty poets including Marilyn Chin, Jessica Hagedorn, Garrett Hongo, and Nellie Wong. An attractive feature of the book is autobiographical statements and photographs of each of the poets. In his introduction the editor says that Asian American writers "are breaking both silence and stereotypes with the affirmation of new songs."

Frank Chin. *The Chinaman Pacific & Frisco R.R., Co.*. Minneapolis: Coffee House Press, 1988. This collection of eight short stories explores Chinese American history and contemporary experiences: a Chinatown where kids dream of being Susie Wong or Charlie Chan's Number One Son; a movie theater where old men meet to learn English by watching cartoons; and a storefront Buddhist church going electronic and getting rich.

The Forbidden Stitch: An Asian-American Women's Anthology. Shirley Geok-lin Lim, Mayumi Tsutakawa, and M. Donnelly, editors. Corvallis, Oregon: Calyx Books, 1989. A beautifully illustrated book of poetry, prose, art, and reviews that conveys the diversity of Asian American women's writings. Many of the writers are young or being published for the first time, and others are established writers such as Anjana Appachana who contributes the short story, "To Rise Above."

Maxine Hong Kingston. *The Woman Warrior: Memoirs of a Girlhood Among Ghosts*. New York: Vintage, 1977. The first chapter of this novel appears on page 225 of this volume.

Wendy W. Larsen and Tran Thi Nga. *Shallow Graves: Two Women and Vietnam*. New York: Harper & Row, 1986. Two poems from this collection are found on page 266 of this volume.

Making Waves: An Anthology of Writings by and about Asian American Women. Asian Women United of California, editors. San Francisco: Beacon Press, 1989. The anthology presents a woman-centered perspective on the Asian American experience through poems, memoirs, essays, and fiction. The writings are organized around a series of themes that include immigration, war, work, generations, and injustice. The writers trace their roots to China, Japan, Korea, India, the Philippines, Vietnam, Cambodia, Burma, and Thailand.

David Moore. *Dark Sky, Dark Land: Stories of the Hmong Boy Scouts of Troop 100*. Eden Prairie, Minnesota: Tessera Publishing, 1989. Scoutmaster David Moore narrates these stories told by members of the St. Paul troop. The stories cover Hmong life in Laos, escape to Thailand, and adjustment to life in America, including a particularly vivid story of a son's struggle to prepare a traditional Hmong funeral for his father.

Bharati Mukherjee. *The Middleman and Other Stories*. New York: Fawcett, 1989. One of the eleven stories in this collection, "Orbiting," is found on page 237 of this volume.

David Mura. *After We Lost Our Way*. New York: E.P. Dutton, 1989. This collection of poems by St. Paul writer David Mura looks back to the experiences of his grandparents, uprooted by the Japanese American internment, and forward to the contemporary experiences of Asian Americans. Mura's new work, *Turning Japanese*, is a memoir of a year living and writing in Japan. A poem by Mura appears on page 277 of this volume.

John Okada. *No-No Boy*. Seattle: University of Washington Press, 1980. Set in Seattle just after the end of World War II, the novel investigates the effects of racism on the Japanese American community. Although the majority of Japanese Americans eagerly volunteered for the military at the outbreak of World War II, a minority of young men—"no-no boys"—refused to serve in the army of a country that denied them their full rights as American citizens. The community is torn apart by the almost hysterical desire of its members to be accepted as genuine Americans, no matter what the cost.

Jessika K. Saiki. *From the Lanai and Other Hawaii Stories*. Minneapolis, Minnesota: New Rivers Press, 1990. These seventeen short stories center upon the world of Japanese Americans living in Hawaii before and during World War II. Saiki's previous collection, *Once a Lotus Garden*, was named one of the nine best paperbacks of 1987 and praised for its attention to the complexities of ethnic identity.

Amy Tan. *The Joy Luck Club*. New York: Ivy Books, 1989. These sixteen stories alternate back and forth between the lives of four Chinese women in pre-1949 China and the lives of their American-born daughters in modern day California. The four mothers tell their stories through flashbacks, as their daughters describe the problems of growing up in two cultures. The stories weave together fantasy and reality, history and fable.

Hisaye Yamamoto. *Seventeen Syllables and Other Stories*. Latham, New York: Kitchen Table/Women of Color Press, 1988. The title story from this collection is found on page 253 of this volume.

CONTRIBUTORS

I will excuse my son Mike from